COMMUNITY BUILDING

ON THE WEB

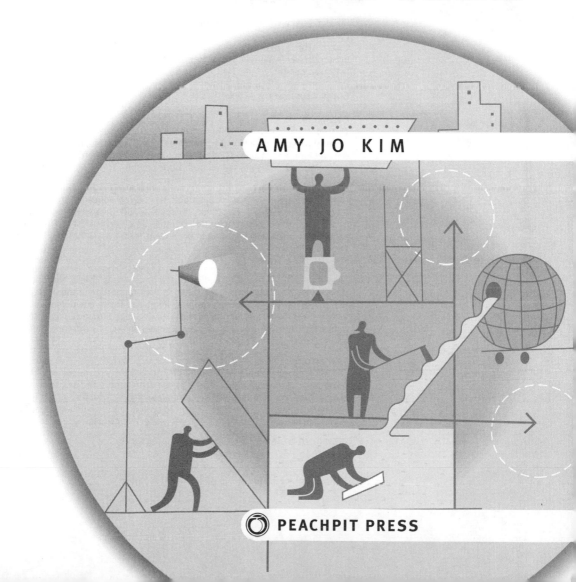

AMY JO KIM

PEACHPIT PRESS

Community Building On the Web

Amy Jo Kim

PEACHPIT PRESS

1249 Eighth Street ○ Berkeley, CA 94710
510/524-2178 ○ 800/283-9444 ○ 510/524-2111 (fax)

FIND US ON THE WORLD WIDE WEB AT:
http://www.peachpit.com

Peachpit Press is a division of Addison Wesley Longman
Copyright © 2000 by Amy Jo Kim

EDITOR ○ Jake Widman, Becky Morgan
PRODUCTION COORDINATOR ○ Kate Reber
COPYEDITOR ○ Becky Morgan
COMPOSITOR ○ Maureen Forys, Happenstance Type-O-Rama
INTERIOR DESIGN ○ Mimi Heft
COVER DESIGN ○ Earl Gee Design
COVER ILLUSTRATION ○ Doug Ross

COLOPHON

This book was created with Quark XPress 4.1 on a Power Computing Power Tower Pro 250. The fonts used were Meta Plus (FontShop), NIMX Quirks (ImageClub), and Missive (T-26). Final output was at Edwards Brothers, Ann Arbor, MI, and it was printed on 50# Arbor Smooth.

ISBN 0-201-87484-9

9 8 7 6 5 4 3 2 1

Printed and bound in the United States of America

This book is dedicated to
Scott and Gabriel Kim,
AKA "The Championship Sleep Team."

Without their undying love, ongoing patience and
(most importantly) long and frequent naps, I never could have
completed this project. Through it all, their devotion to their
craft has been nothing short of inspiring. I salute you, boys!

Acknowledgments

This book was brought to life with the help and support of many people. David Rogelberg and Nancy Ruenzel recognized the potential early on, and Nancy Davis, Marjorie Baer, Jake Widman and Becky Morgan provided clarifying vision, tireless wordsmithing, and ongoing emotional support. Hannah Latham guided the promotion and marketing, and Kate Reber, Mimi Heft, and Maureen Forys created a beautiful book, while Doug Ross created a cover illustration that made me yelp with delight. It was a pleasure to work with so many smart, creative and talented people.

While writing this book, I relied heavily on a network of "thinking buddies"—most especially Richard Garriott, Amy Bruckman, Mike Sellers, and Randy Farmer, who logged countless hours helping me sort the wheat from the chaff, and stretching my thinking about community design. To these folks I'll be forever grateful—and also to Eric Bergener, who helped me navigate the ever-changing landscape of legal issues that are associated with online communities.

I'm also indebted to the many incredible people that I interviewed during the course of researching and writing this book, who shared their stories and insights with me. There are too many to name here (see www.naima.com/community for a complete list) but I'd like to say a special thank you to Christina Allen, Teri Anderson, Jonathan Baron, Reva Basch, Larry Betterton, Jen Beckman, David Bohnett, Marissa Bowe, Matthew Callaway, Melissa Callaway, Candace Carpenter, Jerry Colonna, Joe Cothrel, Jill Davidson, Mike Dixon, Judith Donath, Abbe Don, Elonka Dunkin, Rebecca Eisenberg, Myra Ettenborough, Nancy Evans, Tom Evans, Cliff Figallo, Tod Foley, David Forrest, Michelle Fox, Mary Furlong, Russell Ginns, James Gosling, Doug Hirsch, Katherine Isbister, Mimi Ho, Brian Jamison, Daryl-Lynn Johnson,

Erika Kerakas, Peter Kollack, Laurie Kretchmar, Tori Kropp, Steve Larsen, Rick Levenson, Elizabeth Lewis, Macdara Maccoll, Rob Malda, Miko Matsumura, Teri Meyers, Brad McQuaid, Jerry Michaelski, Rebecca Newton, Jakob Nielsen, Yu-Shen Ng, Mollee Olenick, Rory O'Neill, Bo Peabody, Rich Pearson, Teri Piedrahita, Chip Pedersen, Derek Powazek, Toby Ragnini, Mike Ragsdale, Howard Rheingold, Rich Rhygg, David Rosenthal, Dan Shafer, Ted Silverman, Marc Smith, Jonathan Steuer, Margaret Gould Stewart, Joe Szuecs, John Tang, Bud Tribble, Cynthia Typaldos, Janine Vercoe, John Wampler, Meg Whitman, Gail Williams, Gary Woo, and Amy Yoffreid. Each of you contributed something special and tangible to this book—and without your time and input, these ideas would never have reached fruition.

Any consultant is only as good as her network of clients and colleagues—and I've learned so much from the people I've worked with over the years, most especially Kristin Asleson, Bernie Bernstein, Malcolm Casselle, Pavel Curtis, Allie Eberhard, Scott Fisher, Laura Frasier, Peter Friedman, Tom Gooden, Bing Gordon, Wendy Govier, Gano Haine, Kevin Kelly, Marylou Korba, Dan Leeds, Starr Long, Keith McCurdy, Tom McIntire, Brian Moriarty, Buffy Poon, Suneel Rashad, David Rosenthal, Harriet Rubin, Damion Schubert, Carly Staehlin, Robert Tercek, David Vogler, Kathy Wilson, Mike Wilson, Jenna Woodul, and Neil Young.

A special thanks to the students in my Stanford "Community Design" class—Eric Cheng, Patrick Doyle, Andy Hsieh, Mustafa Jamil, David Jordan, Michael LaHood, Eun-Ju Lee, Xia Li, Gordon McNaughton, Rajat Paharia, Yael Pasternak, Chris Quartetti, Ashley Ring, Isaac Roth, Mark Thompson, and Teresa Torres—who called me on my bullshit, kept me honest, and helped me shape the structure of this book.

And lastly, a heartfelt thanks to the iconoclasts and independent thinkers who have inspired me over the years with their talent and conviction, and by example have given me the courage to pursue my own idiosyncratic vision—most especially Laurie Anderson, Chuck Clanton, Brian Eno, Bill Joy, and Brenda Laurel.

Table of Contents

Introduction

It is not the strongest of the species that survive, nor the most intelligent, but the one most responsive to change

—*Charles Darwin*

Calling all Community Builders

We're living in fluid and dynamic times. It's easier than ever to travel the world and stay in touch electronically with people who live far away. As a society we're working harder, juggling more roles, and spending more of our free time at home — exhausted from our multifaceted lives, fearful of the violence that we see in movies, TV and video games, and physically removed from our family, friends and neighbors. So we go online — to shop, play games, trade collectibles, argue politics, or just shoot the breeze. The Web is becoming our collective town square — more and more, people are turning to Web communities to get their personal, social and profesional needs met. This translates into a tremendous opportunity for Web community builders.

I first felt the power of online communications while working at Sun Microsystems in the mid-1980s. Soon after joining the company, my boss asked me to name my computer, and I impulsively chose "Naima" — the title of a beautiful, haunting jazz ballad by John Coltrane that I'd learned the night before. My public identity on the Sun intranet became "amyjo@naima"; and within a few weeks, I started to get email from Coltrane fanatics all around the company. They invited me to join a private mailing list, and jam with them after hours. Because of my online identity, I'd found people who shared my passion, and that changed my life for the better.

How is a Web community different than one in the real world? In terms of their social dynamics, physical and virtual communities are much the same. Both involve developing a web of relationships among people who have something meaningful in common, such as a beloved hobby, a life-altering illness, a political cause, a religious conviction, a professional relationship, or even simply a neighborhood or town. So in one sense, a Web community is simply a community that happens to exist online, rather than in the physical world.

But being online offers special opportunities and challenges that give Web communities a unique flavor. The Net erases boundaries created by time and distance, and makes it dramatically easier for people to maintain connections, deepen relationships, and meet like-minded souls that they would otherwise never have met. It also offers a strange and compelling combination of anonymity and intimacy that brings out the best and worst in people's behavior. It can be near impossible to impose lasting consequences on troublemakers, and yet relatively easy to track an individual's behavior and purchase patterns—which makes Web communities notoriously difficult to manage. To complicate matters further, the legal issues involving privacy, liability and intellectual property on the Web are just beginning to be addressed, and will evolve rapidly over the next few years.

Although the focus is on Web communities, this book also illuminates deeper and more fundamental aspects of community building—the social and cultural dynamics, the power of a shared purpose, and the roles, rituals and events that bind people together into a group.

Why I Wrote This Book

I've been building online communities for ten years; I've worked on AOL sites, Web zines, technical-support message boards, Java chat room interfaces, online trading posts, and a variety of high-end gaming environments. Again and again, regardless of technology, I've found myself bumping up against the same basic issues in my work—issues like persistent identity, new-comer confusion, etiquette standards, leadership roles, and group dynamics.

So about five years ago, I summarized these issues into a set of design guidelines, and started using them in my consulting practice. Through conversations with community leaders, both on and off the Web, I learned that the patterns I was seeing in virtual communities were echoed in physical communities, and that all communities are ultimately based on timeless social dynamics that transcend the medium of connection. In other words, people are people, even in cyberspace.

This is the book that I wish I'd had when I was first starting out. I've found it incredibly useful to have a framework to help me address the basic design, technical and policy issues that arise in community building. This framework has helped me become a more effective and creative community designer; my hope is that it will do the same for you.

How to Use This Book

If you're engaged in producing, designing, programming, or maintaining communities that are based on the Web, you've come to the right place. This book is a strategic handbook for community builders; it summarizes the "best practices" of suc-cessful Web communities, and brings them to life with behind-the-scenes stories from some dynamic and influential sites. Here, you'll learn about the key issues that every Web commu-nity designer faces, along with guidelines for addressing these issues within the context of your own community. You'll also learn which communications tools are most appropriate for your community, and which technologies are necessary for a large-scale Web community to truly thrive.

What you *won't* find here is an in-depth account of how to program a Web community, configure specific community-building tools, create a business plan, obtain financing, or develop an advertising or subscription strategy. The focus is on teaching you how to grow a thriving community that will attract and sustain members, and on how to adress the design, technical and policy issues that will inevitably arise if your community becomes a success.

All you need to enjoy and make use of this book is familiarity with Internet basics and a desire to create or improve your own online community. You don't need to be an expert programmer, a sophisticated Web designer, or a savvy businessperson—although if you are, you'll get even more out of the ideas presented here.

If you're preparing to launch (or redesign) your Web community, you can use this book as a planning tool to help you formulate your vision, identify your audience, prioritize your feature set, and plan your staffing needs. Community building is a team effort; and accordingly, this book is written to be useful to people in management, marketing, production, programming, and design—all of whom will have input during the strategic planning phase.

If you're running an existing community, you can use this book as a general source of ideas and inspiration to help you meet your goals, improve and develop your community, and better serve the needs of your members.

If you're involved in teaching or lecturing on community design, you can use this book as a teaching tool. On the companion Web site you'll find some examples of class outlines, exercises and projects to complement the book.

Nine Design Strategies

The book is organized around nine timeless design strategies that characterize successful, sustainable communities. Taken together, these strategies summarize an architectural, systems-oriented approach to community building that I call "Social Scaffolding:"

○ **DEFINE AND ARTICULATE YOUR PURPOSE**

Communities come to life when they fulfill an ongoing need in people's lives. To create a successful community, you'll need to first understand why you're building it and who you're building it for; and then express your vision in the design, technology and policies of your community.

○ **BUILD FLEXIBLE, EXTENSIBLE GATHERING PLACES**

A community can begin take root wherever people gather for a shared purpose and start talking among themselves. Once you've defined your purpose, you'll want to build a flexible, small-scale infrastructure of gathering places, which you and your members will work together to evolve.

○ **CREATE MEANINGFUL AND EVOLVING MEMBER PROFILES**

You can get to know your members—and help them get to know each other— by developing robust, evolving and up-to-date member profiles. If handled with integrity, these profiles can help you build trust, foster relationships, and deliver personalized services, while infusing your community with a sense of history and context.

○ **DESIGN FOR A RANGE OF ROLES**

Addressing the needs of newcomers without alienating the regulars is an ongoing balancing act. As your community grows, it will become increasingly important to provide guidance to newcomers while offering leadership, ownership and commerce opportunities to more experienced members.

○ **DEVELOP A STRONG LEADERSHIP PROGRAM**

Community leaders are the fuel in your engine: they greet visitors,
encourage newbies, teach classes, answer questions, and deal with
trouble makerswho might destroy the fun for everyone else. An
effective leadership program requires careful planning and ongoing
management, but the results can be well worth the investment.

○ **ENCOURAGE APPROPRIATE ETIQUETTE**

Every community has its share of internal squabbling; if handled
well, conflict can be invigorating. But disagreements often spin
out of control and tear a community apart. To avoid this, it's crucial to develop some groundrules for participation, and set up
systems that allow you to enforce and evolve your community
standards.

○ **PROMOTE CYCLIC EVENTS**

Communities come together around regular events: sitting down
to dinner, going to church on Sunday, attending a monthly meeting or an annual offsite. To develop a loyal following and foster
deeper relationships among your members, you'll want to establish regular online events, and help your members develop and
run their own events.

○ **INTEGRATE THE RITUALS OF COMMUNITY LIFE**

All communities use rituals to acknowledge their members and
celebrate important social transitions. By celebrating holidays,
marking seasonal changes, and acknowleging personal transitions
and rites of passage, you'll be laying the foundation for a true
online culture.

○ **FACILITATE MEMBER-RUN SUBGROUPS**

If your goal is to grow a large-scale community, you'll want to
provide technologies to help your members create and run subgroups. It's a substantial undertaking, but this powerful feature
can drive lasting member loyalty, and help to distinguish you community from its competition.

Each chapter explores a design strategy in detail, and offers guidelines and tactics for applying that strategy to your Web community. Each strategy builds on the previous ones, and so the chapter order corresponds to a recommended planning process (or teaching order) for community design.

Three Underlying Principles

Before we plunge ahead, I want to introduce to you three basic community design principles that underlie the ideas in this book. The first one is: Design for growth and change (Figure 1). This might sound simple, but watch out, it's harder than it looks. As a community designer, one of the most damaging mistakes you can make is to over-design your community up front and invest too heavily in a design paradigm or technology platform that can't easily be changed and updated. Successful, long-lasting communities almost always start off small, simple and focused, and then grow organically over time—adding breadth, depth and complexity in response to the changing needs of the members, and the changing conditions of the environment.

FIGURE 1
DESIGN FOR GROWTH AND CHANGE

Closely related to this idea is the second principle: Create and maintain feedback loops (Figure 2). Successful community building is a constant balancing act between the efforts of management (that's you) to plan, organize and run the space, and the ideas, suggestions and needs of your members. To manage this co-evolution, you'll need to keep your finger on the community pulse—and you'll do this by creating and maintaining feedback loops between members and management. These loops will keep you in touch with what your members are saying and doing, and give you the information you need to evolve and update your features and platform.

FIGURE 2
CREATE AND MAINTAIN FEEDBACK LOOPS

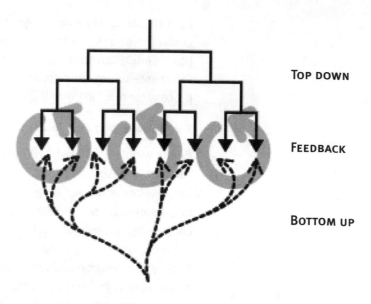

TOP DOWN

FEEDBACK

BOTTOM UP

This brings us to the third principle: Empower your members over time (Figure 3). Initially, it's up to you to define your purpose, choose your feature set, and set a particular tone, but as your community grows and matures, your members can and should play a progressively larger role in building and maintaining the community culture. If you want to grow a large and thriving community, you'll need to develop a progressive strategy for leveraging the ideas and efforts of your members.

FIGURE 3
EMPOWER YOUR MEMBERS OVER TIME

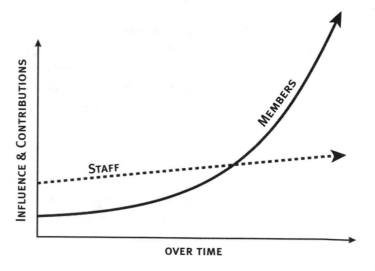

Going Further

Because the Web is ever-changing, keep in mind that the scenes and situations presented in this book may not match what you find. Screenshots were captured during the development of the book; upon publication and thereafter these images may no longer be current, so check the individual Web sites for the most current information. Be aware that practices and policies of the companies mentioned may also have changed.

I've created a companion Web site (**www.naima.com/community**) to accompany this book where you can get up-to-date community building resources, and discuss the issues raised in this book. I invite you to log on and share your stories, ideas, and experiences with other community builders. Good luck with your project—see you online.

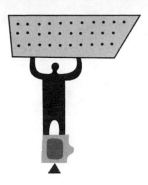

CHAPTER ONE

Purpose

A successful community serves a clear purpose in the lives of its members and meets the fundamental goals of its owners. Whether you're creating a new Web organization or refining an existing one, you'll be more successful if you can define and describe what type of community you're building, why you're building it, and who you're building it for.

Because communities evolve, your purpose will change along with the shifting social and economic landscape of the Web. Nonetheless, articulating your purpose up front will help you focus your thinking and create a coherent, compelling, and successful Web community.

In this Chapter

Building a Successful Community

What is a successful community? Is it a big, bustling city filled with citizens of all ages and backgrounds doing all sorts of inter-esting things? A collection of rabid fans gazing at the object of their admiration? A gathering of true believers holding hands and lifting their voices in song? A group of women seated in a circle, speaking in hushed, sympathetic tones? Subscribers to an email list, sitting alone staring at words on a computer screen?

Any of these communities could be called successful or not, depending on how the people who create, manage, and partici-pate in that group define success. A book club, support group, or mailing list might only have a dozen members, yet be con-sidered a great success by everyone involved because it does everything they need and expect it to. A large church or Web portal, on the other hand, might attract thousands of members and develop a robust social scene but be forced to shut down for not meeting the financial goals of the sponsors.

To attract members and keep them coming back, your commu-nity must serve a clear purpose in their lives. And to get the support and resources to keep it running, your community must deliver a satisfactory return on the investment of those who fund and maintain it.

Define Your Purpose

Communities arise for different reasons. Some form around a vision or cause, such as Earth First, Jews for Jesus, or the anti-war movement. Others form around a charismatic figure such as Elvis, L. Ron Hubbard, or Jesus. Other communities arise organically, such as the folks who gather on Saturday nights at the local pub for a game of darts.

Regardless of how your community gets started, everyone involved will find it more satisfying if its purpose is clear. Ask yourself these questions:

○ What type of community am I building?

○ Why am I building it?

○ Who am I building it for?

Because successful communities must keep pace with the changing needs of their members and owners, you'll need to ask these questions periodically as your community grows and matures. For example, a group of professional women might start getting together monthly for networking and support and evolve into a national organization that focuses on career counseling and continuing education. Or a scientist might create a mailing list to help plan a conference and then see it evolve into a way for far-flung colleagues to stay in touch, gossip about each other, and discuss the latest findings in their field.

Successful communities evolve to keep pace with the changing needs of members and owners

Find a Need and Fill It

Your community's purpose will evolve, but you need to start somewhere. Plant a stake in the ground and define your initial purpose as clearly as you can. To kick-start your thinking, see if you can identify an ongoing, *unmet* need that your members have in common and which your community is uniquely suited to address. Participating in this kind of project takes time and effort, and unless you fulfill a real need, your members won't be motivated to keep coming back. As you ponder this, you may find it useful to refer to Maslow's Hierarchy of Needs (see page 8), which can help you focus on the basics, while keeping up with the evolving needs of your members.

The founder of GeoCities, for example, chose to address the need of inexperienced Net users who wanted to create their own Web pages. Back in 1995, David Bohnett noticed that a growing number of Netizens lacked the technical skills to create a Web page, and provided the tools and infrastructure necessary to offer free home pages in a supportive environment. Geocities soon became one of the largest and fastest-growing communities on the Web (Figure 1.1). Now owned by Yahoo, GeoCities continues to focus on making page building easy and accessible to everyone.

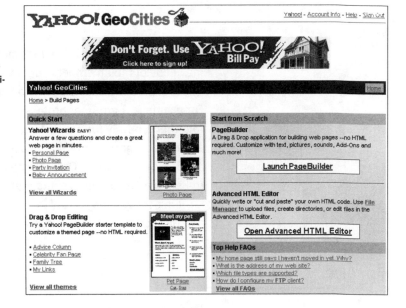

FIGURE 1.1
BUILDING A HOME PAGE AT GEOCITIES
geocities.yahoo.com/members/
build.html
GeoCities pioneered the service of offering free home pages in a supportive environment. Building Web pages is still the core activity at GeoCities.

This story illustrates an important point: people will flock to a place that delivers something they need and can't find elsewhere. This basic truth might seem obvious, but the Internet is littered with ghost towns that fell prey to over-hyped expectations, cutting-edge technologies, and an overall lack of purpose.

The Needs of Your Members

People rely on communities in all areas of their lives (Figure 1.2). As you define your community's purpose, think about which areas of your members' lives it will serve. Is it primarily about work and career, like a professional organization? Or is it for recreation and play, like a weekly card game? Does your community touch on family and civic issues, like the PTA? Are spiritual, political and social concerns part of the community's purpose?

FIGURE 1.2
TYPES OF COMMUNITIES
People participate in communities to fulfill a variety of needs in different areas. Some communities focus on one particular area—for example, a professional organization addresses work issues—while others might function in several. Which type of community are you building? And which needs will your community fulfill?

Area of Life	Type of Community
Family	Extended Family Play group PTA
Work	Workplace Professional Group
Play	Games Hobbies Sports Fan Club
Spirituality	Church or temple Meditation group Bible study group Support Group Drumming Circle
Politics	Political campaign Environmental group

Asking yourself these questions will help you understand the core value your community provides. And while you can't control what your members do, you *can* reward actions that advance your purpose. In a religious community, for example, the leader might publicly praise a member of the congregation for starting a task force to feed the homeless. By contrast, the leaders of an online investing club might post a quarterly top-10 list of the members whose portfolios rose most in value—something that would seem out-of-place on a church message board.

You can further clarify your purpose by categorizing your community according to what the members have in common. In their book *Net Gain,* John Hagel III and Arthur G. Armstrong defined three types of communities, and I've added a fourth:

1. **GEOGRAPHIC,** defined by a physical location like a city or region

2. **DEMOGRAPHIC,** defined by age, gender, race, or nationality

3. **TOPICAL,** defined by shared interest, like a fan club, hobby group, or professional organization

4. **ACTIVITY-BASED,** defined by a shared activity, like shopping, investing, playing games, or making music.

If you look around the Web, you'll find communities whose basic purpose maps to each of these categories (and often encompasses several). At Talk City (www.talkcity.com), a group of local and expatriate Filipinos gets together each week to speak Tagalog (their native tongue), argue about politics, and swap recipes. Over at NetNoir (www.netnoir.com), black singles join Club NetNoir to find that someone special. On eBay (www.ebay.com), doll collectors meet every Monday evening to discuss doll repair with a renowned expert. In Ultima Online (www.owo.com), fantasy game players join medieval guilds, engage in spirited battles, and run their own frontier towns.

Change Happens

You may feel sure of what you're community's about, but you need to be prepared for it to evolve over time, too. Sometimes communities change categories as they find their core audience. For example, NetNoir started out calling itself "The Soul of Cyberspace," a topical community for anyone interested in worldwide African culture. As its membership grew, the community managers discovered that most of their active members were people of African descent. NetNoir gradually evolved into "The Black Network," aimed squarely at the worldwide black community, and developed a more focused business model (Figure 1.3).

iVillage went through a similar evolution after it launched Parent Soup, a support community for parents. Not surprisingly, iVillage found that most of their members were women, and that advertisers and sponsors were used to marketing to a narrower demographic (specifically, women between the ages of 25 and 45) than to parents in general. So iVillage renamed itself "The Woman's Network," and developed topical "channels" aimed at women that include parenting, health, relationships, and money (Figure 1.4).

No matter how you categorize your overall community, one thing that's certain to happen as it grows is that subcommunities will emerge that fall into different categories. The larger

FIGURE 1.3
NETNOIR—THE BLACK NETWORK
www.netnoir.com
NetNoir started out as "The Soul of
Cyberspace," a topical community aimed
at anyone interested in worldwide African
culture. Over time, NetNoir found its audience and became "The Black Network,"
a Web community targeted squarely at
people of African descent. Notice how the
tag line, the club member photo, the May
spotlight issue, the headlines, and other
elements explicitly communicate this
site's identity.

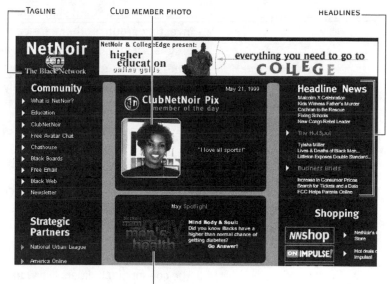

TAGLINE   CLUB MEMBER PHOTO   HEADLINES

SPOTLIGHT ISSUE

FIGURE 1.4
IVILLAGE—THE WOMEN'S NETWORK
www.ivillage.com
IVillage started as a focused support
site for new parents but grew to become
"The Women's Network," a demographi-
cally targeted community with channels
designed to appeal to the different issues,
interests, and concerns that women have.

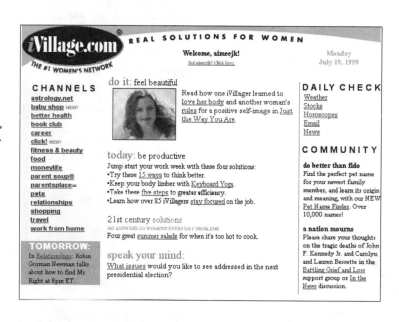

and more general your community, the more likely it is that
such subgroups will arise. At iVillage, for example, the topical
channels function as subcommunities—and smaller subcommunities crop up within each channel (See Figure 1.13). Some

are organized around shared activities, such as book clubs or investing groups; others are based on stages of life, such as pregnancy groups, play groups, and retirement planning; still others are based on shared goals such as losing weight, quitting smoking, or creating a family.

Similarly, some of the 41 Geocities "neighborhoods" (the basic metaphor by which the Geocities community is organized—see **www.geocities.com/neighborhoods**) are based on a topic or activity like cars, games, politics, or investing; others on a geographical location like Tokyo or Paris; and still others on a demographic group such as kids or women.

Maslow's Hierarchy of Needs

The community builders I've worked with have often found it useful to refer to Maslow's Hierarchy of Needs (Figure 1.5) when trying to clarify their goals and prioritize their feature list. The Hierarchy of Needs is the brainchild of Abraham Maslow, one of the founding fathers of humanistic psychology. He believed that people are motivated by the urge to satisfy needs ranging from basic survival to self-fulfillment, and that they don't fill the higher-level needs until the lower-level ones are satisfied.

FIGURE 1.5
MASLOW'S HIERARCHY OF NEEDS
This model for understanding human motivation was developed by Abraham Maslow (www.ship.edu/~cgboeree/ maslow.html), a humanistic psychologist who believed that until lower-level needs are met, people can't pay attention to their higher-level needs. You can use these ideas to help you prioritize the features in your Web community and to make sure you're meeting the most basic needs of your members before offering "higher-level" features.

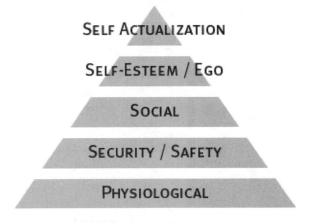

SELF ACTUALIZATION

SELF-ESTEEM / EGO

SOCIAL

SECURITY / SAFETY

PHYSIOLOGICAL

The following table, arranged from basic to abstract, suggests some of the forms these needs take in both offline and online environments.

Need	Offline	Online
physiological	Food, clothing, shelter, health	System access; the ability to maintain one's identity, and participate in a Web community
security and safety	Protection from crimes and war; the sense of living in a fair and just society	Protection from hacking and personal attacks; the sense of having a "level playing field"
social	The ability to give and receive love; the feeling of belonging to a group	Belonging to the community as a whole, and to subgroups within the community
self-esteem	Self-respect; the ability to earn the respect of others, and contribute to society	The ability to contribute to the community, and be recognized for those contributions
self-actualization	The ability to develop skills and fulfill one's potential	The ability to take on a community role that develops skills and opens up new opportunities

Clarify Your Goals

Now that you have a good idea of why you're building a community, and what kind of community it should be, it's time to focus on what specific benefits you and your members will get out of it. A successful community must attract and keep enough members to make it worthwhile. It must also deliver a satisfactory return on investment to whoever is funding and/or maintaining it. If either one of these standards is not met, the community will eventually fail. As a community builder, therefore, you have to pay attention to both the needs of the members and the goals of the owners.

The phrase "return on investment" can obviously mean a financial investment and return, but the principle also applies to a mailing list being run out of a private passion. In general, the form of the investment indicates the kind of return expected. For example, someone running a not-for-profit Web message board is investing time and good will and wants appreciation in return. It's important to be clear about what's being invested, and what is the expected return.

Needs and Goals: A Three-Step Planning Exercise

The following exercise will help you identify the standards of success for your community and come up with a list of goals that will help you focus your efforts, coordinate your team, and prioritize your features. You can use the exercise before launching a new community, when preparing to make changes to an existing community, or simply to update your thinking and refine your goals.

STEP 1: MEMBERS' NEEDS

- **UNDERSTAND YOUR MEMBERS.** Set aside all thoughts of business models, technology, and brand identity, and think about your (current and potential) members. Who are they? Are they homogeneous or varied? Are there distinct subgroups? What are their interests, habits, and affiliations? What other communities do they belong to? Don't worry if you can't answer these questions completely; you can collect more information later (see "Understanding Your Audience") and refine your thinking. What's important at this stage is to start seeing your community through the eyes of your members.

- **MAKE A LIST OF THEIR NEEDS.** Next, consider members' needs and desires. Why are they coming to your community? Are they searching for something specific? What can your community do for them? This is a brainstorming phase, so don't censor your thoughts; the purpose is to write down everything you can think of that your members might look for and possibly find in your community.

- **PRIORITIZE YOUR LIST.** Now it's time to sort your list. Which of the items on your list are most central in your members' lives? Which would they value most highly? During this process, consider what you can actually deliver to your members: do you have access to unique resources? Can you provide them with something that's not offered elsewhere? Try to select the top five or six needs that your community can meet.

STEP 2: OWNERS' GOALS

- **UNDERSTAND YOUR OWNERS.** Now, turn your attention to the people who will be funding and/or running your community (which, of course, might be you). Who are they? Are they developing this community as a business venture? A labor of love? A PR stunt? A research experiment? Understanding the motivations of your funding source will help you get the support and resources you need to succeed.

○ **MAKE A LIST OF THEIR GOALS.** Next, think about what your community's owners are hoping to get out it. What kinds of results will they be expecting, and how soon? How will success be measured? If you don't know the answers to these questions, ask people. Bear in mind that you may not get complete answers, and the motivation and measurements of success may very well change over time.

○ **PRIORITIZE YOUR LIST.** As before, it's now time to sort through your list, select the top five or six goals, and prioritize them from the owners' point of view. Which are most highly valued? Which are fundamental to success? Do some goals depend on other? Are some critical for the continued support of the community? Be prepared to update this list periodically, as your community goals come into sharper focus. What's most important at this stage is to raise these issues with whoever is funding the community.

STEP 3: CREATE A "MASTER LIST" OF YOUR COMMUNITY GOALS

○ **COMPARE AND CONSOLIDATE THE TWO LISTS.** Now that you've identified what's most important to both your members and owners, it's time to combine them into a master list of community goals. Do any issues appear on both lists? If so, consolidate them into a single goal. Are there contradictions? If so, take it as a signal to reconsider your plan and make some adjustments in either your audience profile or your business model.

○ **CREATE AND DISTRIBUTE THE MASTER LIST.** Finally, distribute the list of community goals to everyone on the team and ask for feedback. You'll continue to refine this list as you learn more about who your members are and what value your community provides to them. You'll also want to adjust this list whenever your business model or community ownership changes (a common occurrence in the Web community biz).

The Planning Exercise in Action

Let's go behind the scenes at a successful online gaming company, Origin Systems, and see how they used this exercise to kick-start a major redesign effort.

Origin's Web site, **www.owo.com**, had been designed to support their popular multiplayer fantasy game, Ultima Online. While that site had been appropriate for marketing and launching the game, Origin felt that a more community-focused site would better serve their players (Figure 1.6). So they put together a community design team (which consisted of myself as an outside consultant, and several in-house staff members), to see what it would take to set up such a community.

Step 1: Their Members' Needs

Because the community's purpose was to both support and promote an existing product, it had to offer something to both current and potential subscribers. Some, but not all, of the latter group might already have played UO.

From both email and surveys, Origin knew that better customer support was high on players' wish lists, along with a desire to have more contact with the UO design team. Less was known about potential subscribers, but it was clear that they would need information about the game, and to be shown why it was worth a subscription fee.

Using Maslow's Pyramid for inspiration, the community design team decided that providing game-specific support and information to the existing players was the most basic community need they had to meet. A player who can't access the game because the servers are down, or who logs in to find that his settings have been corrupted, won't care about anything else until that issue is resolved.

Step 2: Their Owner's Goals

As Community Manager, Carly Staehlin was responsible for running the Origin Web community. Since she had to justify her budget and staffing needs to the Origin executives, it was crucial that she understand their goals for the project.

Carly met with the executives and asked them to describe their vision for the UO Web community, paying particular attention to timelines and performance expectations. She also met with the "UO Live" team, who would be maintaining the multiplayer game, and with representatives from Origin customer support and public relations. From these meetings, she compiled a list of goals, including some of her own based on her past experience with Web communities.

Carly also met with David Koslowski, the head of Origin's in-house Web development team, to find out what kinds of tools were available for building the community, and for measuring success. Armed with this information, Carly and her team created a prioritized list of the top five goals for the Web community. They gave this list to the Origin executives, and revised it based on their feedback.

Step 3: Their Community Goals

Finally, the community design team sat down and compared the two lists. They noticed that both members and owners wanted to hear stories about what was happening inside the game. They noticed that the owners wanted to develop a large community, while the members wanted "small community" features such as personal attention from customer support and direct contact with the UO design team.

With input from the team, Carly made a master list of community goals and distributed it to everyone they'd interviewed. As expected, every department wanted its issues to have top priority, but generally, everybody was happy to see their needs addressed as part of the community plan. Carly and David now had a document that would help them choose which features and programs to implement in the Origin Web community.

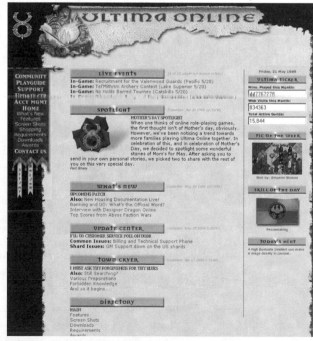

FIGURE 1.6 ULTIMA ONLINE WEB SITE (www.uo.com)
The original owo.com site was developed to support a multiplayer game (Ultima Online) before, during, and after its launch. After the game had been running for awhile, the needs of the subscribers—and the company—were different, so Origin redesigned the site (shown here) to include more of a community focus.

Understand Your Audience

Knowing who you want to reach is not the same as understanding your audience. To create a community that engages your intended audience, you need to understand what makes them tick. That's something professional market researchers do, employing a variety of tools to get inside people's heads.

Among the most common and useful market research tools are surveys and focus groups. I strongly recommend working with a professional firm, if your budget allows. However, don't let a tight budget stop you from doing research yourself. A little testing is better than none, and going through the process of conducting surveys, interviews and focus groups can really help you hone your efforts.

Take a Survey

A survey that's professionally created and run can give you reliable information about the opinions and makeup of your target audience. Depending on the type of product or services you intend to offer, you might ask potential members about some or all of the following:

○ **DEMOGRAPHICS,** such as their age, race, income, and education

○ **PROFESSIONAL INTERESTS,** such as their livelihood, the professional groups they belong to, and the conferences they attend

○ **PERSONAL INTERESTS,** such as the books, magazines, and TV shows they enjoy and the hobbies they pursue

○ **COMPUTER USAGE,** such as the type of computer equipment and software applications they use and the Web sites they frequent

The key issues when conducting surveys are sampling (who is invited to take the survey), self-selection bias (of those invited, who actually responds), question construction (what form the questions take and what order they are presented in), and length (how much time the survey takes to complete).

The results you get from running your own survey might not be as statistically valid as those from a professional one, but you'll certainly get some useful information and ideas. Here are a few survey guidelines to get you started (see the companion Web site for further resources):

- **KEEP IT SHORT.** Respondents will be more likely to complete your survey and give you accurate answers if they're not exhausted by the process. This is especially true for online surveys, given Web surfers' notoriously short attention spans.

- **PROVIDE INCENTIVES.** Your goal is to get a broad range of people to respond to your survey. Offer something like a discount coupon, a gift or payment, or even a chance to win a prize for participating (Figure 1.7). Otherwise, you're likely to get answers from avid devotees and people with a bone to pick, but you won't hear from the "silent majority."

FIGURE 1.7
ENTICING MEMBERS TO FILL OUT A SURVEY
iVillage used two different opening screens to entice its members to fill out an online survey. One approach offered the chance to win a prize; the other simply offered the opportunity to contribute one's opinion. In this case, iVillage discovered that both approaches were equally effective in motivating people to participate. If you decide to run your own surveys, you may want to experiment with different approaches as well.

- **ASK SIMPLE QUESTIONS FIRST.** Surveys usually start with simple, multiple-choice questions to get the ball rolling. Save the longer, more open-ended questions for the end.

Surveys can take place on the telephone, in a mall, through email, or via interactive forms-based Web pages (Figure 1.8). In general, email and forms-based surveys are most appropriate for Web communities, because you know you're reaching people who are already online. If you were trying to bring new people online and into your community, however, phone and mall surveys would work better.

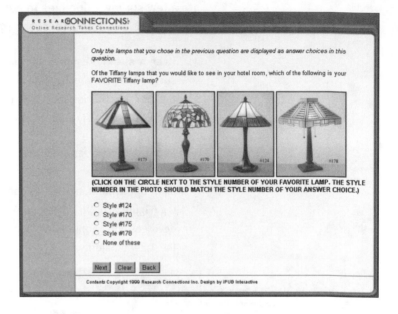

So how do you choose the target audience for your survey? It depends on your goals and the state of your community. If you're looking for a better understanding of an existing community, you'll want to survey your current members. You can do this either by sending out an email survey or by enticing visitors to your site to fill out a form.

If you're trying to expand your membership or haven't yet launched your community, then you'll have to find nonmembers, which can require some ingenuity. First, you'll need to specify a profile for the survey participants—their age, gender, interests, experience, and so on. Next, you'll need to locate people who fit this profile. Professional market research firms often have access to special resources, such as targeted mailing lists. However, there are many ways to locate survey participants, both on and off the Web. For instance, if your profile specifies teenagers, you might look for survey participants at local schools, in hobby shops, at the mall, or in AOL chat rooms. You could also place an ad in the school newspaper, on the library bulletin board, on the message boards of an existing teen community, on anywhere else that teenagers hang out.

Focus Groups

A focus group is a sort of group interview that generally involves some combination of specific questions, free-form discussion, and reactions to visual material. These group interviews usually involve six to ten people who are led through a discussion by one or two moderators that are trained to keep things moving and stay neutral about the issues being discussed. Often, the client—in this case, you or others responsible for your community—can observe the session and communicate with the moderators without being seen by the participants.

Focus groups are often used at key stages of a project as a "reality check" for visual and conceptual decisions. For example, if you're planning to run a subscription-based Web community, you might run a focus group to see how much people are willing to pay for your service. Or if you're considering several different visual designs for your site, you might show sketches to a focus group and get their reactions before finalizing your approach.

Online chat rooms are an increasingly popular way to run a focus group. Some research firms have created customized tools that allow them to control the proceedings (Figure 1.9). However, you can use any chat software to conduct an online focus group, as long as the software offers private spaces, moderator capabilities, and a private messaging backchannel (see Chapter 2 for more about chat software). The issues with selecting participants for an online focus group are similar to those of surveys—you'll either want to use your current members, find nonmembers who fit a particular profile, or both.

Online focus groups have many advantages for a Web community. The cost tends to be lower than for an offline group, especially if a professional firm is running it. It's easier to get a wide geographic reach. You can show a variety of Web images and change your visual materials with ease. And the anonymity of being online tends to bring out more revealing answers.

FIGURE 1.9
AN ONLINE FOCUS GROUP
www.researchconnections.com/
livedemos/focusconnect.html
This is the instruction screen from Focus
Connect, a customized version of the software that Research Connections uses to
conduct online focus groups. This tool
allows the research firm to customize the
introductory screens and lets the moderator control the proceedings

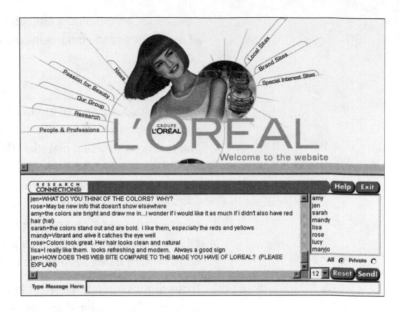

If you decide to run your own online focus groups, try to choose a moderator who's not emotionally invested in your community, to help keep the results unbiased. Also, make sure to prepare all your questions and materials ahead of time. But if the conversation becomes lively, don't feel that you have to stick too closely to your script; you can get a lot of valuable information out of a freeform conversation.

Articulate Your Vision

You know your purpose, you're clear on your goals, and you understand your audience. Now you need to articulate a vision that brings your purpose to life. This vision will be realized through words, images, features, policies, and even the social dynamics that take place within your community.

It's especially important to be clear about your vision if you're trying to attract a particular audience. The makers of L'Eggs pantyhose discovered the importance of this principle in 1995, when they launched an ambitious, expensive Web site for the purpose of fostering brand loyalty and learning more about their market. To develop closer relationships with their customers, they included a discussion area called "The L'Eggs Community." Much to their surprise, the discussions quickly became dominated by men who enjoyed wearing pantyhose and were thrilled to discover an anonymous setting where they could trade tips and not feel so alone in their somewhat unusual habit. The company that financed the Web site, however, was less than enchanted with this turn of events. The women they were trying to attract were put off, and shied away from participating in the discussions.

Since then, the L'Eggs company has learned to market more explicitly to its target demographic. But the point remains: unless you communicate your purpose clearly, people will use your Web community in ways that you never intended.

Craft Your Mission Statement

Your mission statement is the most direct expression of your community vision. It spells out *what* type of community you're building, *why* you're building it, and *who* you're building it for. Not only will developing a mission statement help you crystallize your thinking and focus your efforts, it will also make it easier for you to include other people in the project as your community grows.

The length and formality of your mission statement depends on the requirements of your project and the standards of your organization. If you're starting a mailing list for a few friends, it will probably be short and informal. If, on the other hand, you're launching a multimillion-dollar initiative for a large corporation, you'll almost certainly need to develop a more in-depth document that will undergo an extensive review process.

Inside and Outside

You want to create two different yet related versions of your mission statement, one for internal consumption and one for the outside world. Your internal mission statement will guide the efforts of the community-building team. Creating and running a Web community often involves people with a variety of skills, including marketing, production, programming, design, and management. A clear and concise internal mission statement keeps everyone focused and gives the team a basis for making decisions about design, technology, and policy.

Your external mission statement also articulates your vision, but in a way that's intended for public viewing. Think of it as one of the first things that a potential community member might read; it should clearly communicate what the community is all about and who the intended audience is. A visitor should come away with a strong sense of the site's purpose and whether he or she would feel at home there.

In practice, your internal and external mission statements may not be called that. Your internal mission statement could be a portion of your design spec, and your external mission statement might be distributed among several documents. For instance, on the person-to-person auction site eBay, the "About eBay" page and the "Community Values" page together form a kind of external mission statement.

eBay also provides a good example of the value of having a mission statement. The site was founded on the principles of trust, honesty, and empowering the individual, as summarized in eBay's Community Values statement (http://pages.ebay.com/help/community/values.html). As eBay grew, well-established companies began to approach them, wanting prominent placement on the site in return for payment. The decision-makers at eBay rejected these requests, because their mission was to serve individual buyers and sellers, rather than to becoming an online mall.

But then Rosie O'Donnell approached eBay about creating a program to auction items from her television show, and donate the proceeds to charity. Rosie was already an avid eBay user, and she wanted a permanent link to her charity auctions on eBay's home page. This request caused a heated debate within the company, because it violated the principle of a "level playing field" that eBay had been founded on. After much corporate soul-searching, eBay decided to partner with Rosie, and promote her program—partly for financial reasons, of course, but also because Rosie O'Donnell is an individual promoting a worthy cause, rather than a faceless corporation striving to improve their bottom line, and eBay felt that Rosie's Charity Auctions were consistent with their basic mission and values (members.ebay.com/aboutme/4allkids/).

Tag, You're It

While you're creating your mission statement, give some thought to coming up with a tagline, a sort of quick summary of what your community is all about. A good tagline can really help you attract your intended audience. Here are taglines a variety of Web communities have used:

"Are You With Us" —Ultima Online

"Take Your Place in History" —AncientSites

"Your Personal Trading Community" —eBay

"The Smart Way to Get Things Done" —Women.com

"A Home For Moms in Cyberspace" —Moms Online

"Home Pages and Beyond" —GeoCities

"The Black Network" —NetNoir

"The Web for Grownups" —Third Age

"To educate, amuse and enrich" —The Motley Fool

"Fast, free online gaming" —Heat.Net

"Come for the games, stay for the party" —Mplayer

"Real Solutions for Women " —iVillage

"News for Nerds: Stuff that Matters " —Slashdot

As you can imagine, if the L' Eggs community had used a tagline like iVillage's "Real Solutions for Women," their site would have evolved in a very different way.

If your community is evolving in ways that you hadn't foreseen, you may want to change your tagline to reflect your changing focus. For example, iVillage used to be "Your home on the Web...for the stuff that really matters," and AncientSites's old tagline was "Where History Comes Alive." But you'll want to think very carefully before changing your tagline, because it reflects your community values (which should remain relatively stable throughout the life of your community). If your tagline is working, stick with it, especially if you're running a highly targeted community. For example, Slashdot, aimed at Open Source enthusiasts, has had the same tagline for years (Figure 1.10).

Figure 1.10
www.slashdot.org
Slashot has a clear yet idiosyncratic tagline that accurately reflects the personality of this highly targeted community, and it hasn't changed much since the site's launch.

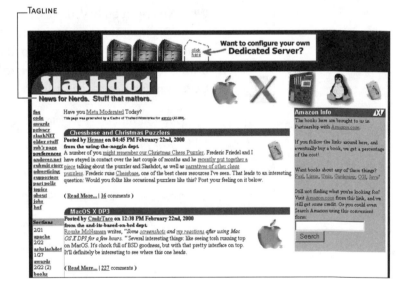

Communicate Your Backstory

The term *backstory* comes from Hollywood; it refers to the part of a movie's story that happened before the first frame. In *Star Wars*, the backstory scrolls up the screen at the beginning ("Long, long ago, in a galaxy far, far away...") and sets the scene for the rest of the movie.

A strong, mythic backstory can help a culture thrive. For example, the story of the Founding Fathers is the creation myth of the USA; it perfectly captures the values of free speech and freedom from tyranny that are so highly valued in American culture. Telling your creation myth can be a great community-building technique, as long as the characters, conflicts, and motivations in the story express your community's purpose and values accurately.

Given the community-building power of a good backstory, make sure there's something to tell. Introduce the community founder(s), communicate their motivation and struggles, and impart a sense of the community's core values. If you read the Moms Online backstory (Figure 1.11), you learn about the struggles of a new mom and the difficulties of a small company, running on a shoestring budget and held aloft by the efforts of passionate volunteers.

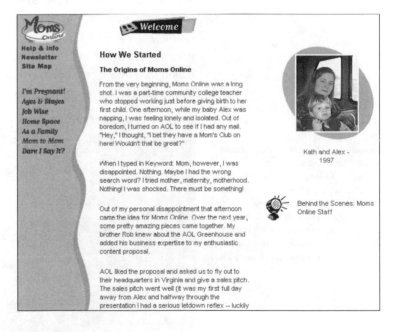

Telling Tales

A backstory gets spread through both written and oral traditions. Written tradition—that is, composed texts—are great for consistency and wide propagation. For example, the Moms Online backstory offers newcomers an easy and engaging starting point for learning about the community. If someone wants to tell the story to friends or link to it from another site, it's easy to do.

Oral tradition complements the written tradition and actively builds social bonds within a community. When an old-timer tells a story to a newcomer, their roles are reinforced, and the newcomer is indoctrinated into the shared knowledge of the culture. Those who were once newcomers will eventually begin to tell this story to the next wave of newcomers, and in this way help your community develop a shared sense of history, depth and soul.

The presence of symbols is a good way to create an opportunity for storytelling. When I first logged on and explored Britannia (the mythical world of Ultima Online), I ran across a structure marked by several large, mysterious symbols (Figure 1.12). I could have gone back to the Web site, clicked over to the Player's Guide, and searched for the backstory; but happily, a passerby volunteered to tell me the Ultima story. In a simple Web-based community interface, symbols that relate to the community backstory could be incorporated into the background art of the site.

FIGURE 1.12

ORAL BACKSTORY: ULTIMA ONLINE
Symbols from the backstory of Britannia (the mythical land where Ultima Online takes place) appear throughout the site and offer opportunities for communicating the complex, arcane history. By using such elements within the visual design of your community, you can stimulate exchanges between newcomers and old-timers and help to keep your history alive.

Develop your Brand Personality

Visitors will form an initial impression of your community within the first few clicks, and you want this impression to be accurate, compelling, and memorable. Part of the way you make sure of that is with words—your tagline, your mission statement, and your backstory. But purpose is also communicated through your "brand personality," which includes how your community looks, how it's laid out, what activities, tools and content are featured, and how it's staffed and managed.

Your mission statement can serve as a useful jumping-off point for developing your brand personality. Don't be afraid to create a vivid visual statement: the stronger your message, the more clearly your purpose will come across and the more likely it is that you'll attract your intended audience. For example, Parent Soup (Figure 1.13) has a distinctive look that immediately tells parents that this is a comfortable place to come for advice, support, and conversation.

FIGURE 1.13
PARENT SOUP
www.parentsoup.com
The look of Parent Soup—warm colors, hand-drawn lines and homespun graphics, images of families and children—communicates a family-oriented, kid-friendly message and gives the site a strong and distinctive brand personality. The message is further reinforced by the site's main categories, which are organized around the key stages of child development.

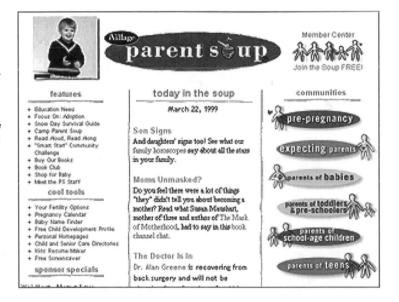

Unlike print or television, the brand personality of a Web community is dynamic and interactive. Defining the look of the site is the first step, but the content generated by members and the hosting style of the community leaders will also contribute to your community's brand personality. We'll be addressing these issues extensively in later chapters—for now, just remember that developing a brand personality for a Web community involves personal interactions as well as static images and content.

Give Them Somewhere to Go

Now that you've made sure that you and your visitors know what your site is about, the next step is to give the visitors somewhere comfortable to hang out. The next chapter explains how you can create such places in your community.

CHAPTER TWO

PLACES:
Bringing People Together

All communities need gathering places. I think of the corner pub, the office lunchroom, the neighborhood bookstore, the local hobby shop, the village church, that hip downtown music club—all places where people can gather into groups.

On the Web, a gathering place can be a mailing list, a discussion topic, a chat room, a multiplayer game, a virtual world, a web site, or some combination of these spaces. To build a successful community, you'll want to set up gathering places that reinforce your purpose and meet the needs of your target audience. To accommodate growth, you'll need to start small and let your members have a hand in the evolution of your community.

In this Chapter

People Are Talking

How do a group of people become a community? Are the people who show up at church every Sunday a community? What about that group of guys shooting pool at the neighborhood bar? Or those moms chatting on the park bench as they watch their kids play? And those Star Trek fans, sitting alone in their living rooms, watching the same TV show week after week— are they a community?

Well, the answer depends on how you define the term. I remember being at a conference in Los Angeles and listening to a parade of Hollywood executives brag about the size of their "communities." I was confused at first, until I realized that they were referring to the people who watched their TV shows and movies. What mattered to these executives was their ability to estimate audience size and demographics—they didn't give a hoot whether their "community members" were talking to each other.

When it was my turn to speak, I began with my definition of community: A community is a group of people with a shared interest, purpose, or goal, who get to know each other better over time. By this definition, I explained, the scattered collection of people who watch Star Trek reruns each week aren't really a community, because they have no way to communicate with each other. The Trekkies who meet up at conventions, fan sites, and mailing lists, however, could be a community, because they can get to know each other better over time.

Afterwards, I was surrounded by Web-savvy conference attendees who thanked me for pointing out that building a community involves more than delivering content to a particular group.
Over lunch, we debated the finer points of what makes a successful community—but we all agreed that, because members
have to have a way to get to know each other, a community
can't really exist without gathering places.

Choose Your Tools

On the Web, communities can form in mailing lists, message
boards, chat rooms, or multiplayer games—wherever a group
of people can come together and talk amongst themselves. You
can bring your community to life by creating such gathering
places, using communications tools and software that ranges
from simple to sophisticated. The first step is understanding:

○ what types of communications software are available

○ what types of applications that software is best suited for

○ what it takes to build and maintain gathering places using that
software

Mailing Lists

Mailing lists are the easiest kinds of online gathering places to
create, maintain, and participate in. Most email programs allow
you to insert a group of email addresses into the "Send to" field
by typing a single word or phrase. That's the simplest example
of a mailing list, but it's more of a convenience than a gathering
place.

An Internet mailing list goes further by allowing a group of people
to share the same list. Using network-based mailing list software
(described below), one person can create a list of email addresses
and give the list its own address. Any message sent to that
address is broadcast to everyone on the list, allowing the kind
of member-to-member interchange that's necessary for a real
community to develop.

WHEN SHOULD YOU USE A MAILING LIST?

Mailing lists can be a powerful community-building tool, used alone or in combination with other communications tools. They're great for Net newbies, because the participants don't have to learn a new interface (assuming that everyone reads email) and don't have to "check in" somewhere to take part in the conversation. And mailing lists are an ideal vehicle for conversations that naturally wax and wane over time, such as a group of people who get together periodically and want to plan their meetings and discuss the aftermath.

You might also want to use a mailing list:

○ **TO SERVE A SMALL COMMUNITY.** A mailing list can be just the thing for building a small, focused community—a group of hobbyists, friends, colleagues, or family members, for example. My step-father Bert, who is an avid collector of used books, belongs to a well-established mailing list of book collectors and sellers. The list has a few hundred subscribers and generates around 15 messages per day. People on this list exchange information, ask and answer questions, and plan occasional get-togethers at book fairs and trade shows.

○ **TO KICK-START YOUR COMMUNITY.** A mailing list is often the best way to get your online community started. If it takes off, you can always add more features and gathering places later. For example, Craig's List (**www.craigslist.org**) began as a mailing list for San Francisco events, and evolved into a robust Web site (with several associated mailing lists) where Bay Area residents can find local jobs, apartment listings, and events of interest.

○ **TO ACKNOWLEDGE YOUR FOUNDING MEMBERS.** If you're in the process of developing a substantial community, you can create a prelaunch mailing list for your founding members—early adopters, enthusiasts, or devotees. You'll get to know some of your most potentially valuable members and let them meet each other, even before your member database is set up and configured (see Chapter 3).

○ **FOR NEWSLETTERS AND ANNOUNCEMENTS.** A regular newsletter can help you stay connected with your members and keep your community on their radar screen. For example, GeoCities sends out a monthly newsletter that's filled with a mix of advertising, announcements, and member highlights. If your community is large enough to have subgroups, you can create newsletters for each one, as iVillage does for each of its channels. And if you're incorporating a "build-your-own-club" service for your members—such as Yahoo Clubs (clubs.yahoo.com) and eCircles (www.ecircles.com)—you can include a broadcast-only or moderated mailing list as part of your offering.

Mailing lists are great for:

○ *small groups with a common purpose*

○ *conversations that wax and wane over time*

○ *communities that are just getting started*

○ *newsletters and announcements*

CHOOSING A MAILING LIST SERVICE

Until recently, running a mailing list involved mastering a rather arcane set of text commands. Now there are a number of easy-to-use services—including Topica (www.topica.com) and eGroups (www.egroups.com)—which offer free mailing lists to individuals and groups. Using these services, anyone can start a mailing list, simply by filling out a Web-based form (Figure 2.1). These services are advertising-supported, which means that advertising banners may appear on Web pages associated with your list or text ads might be inserted into your list messages (check with each service for details).

These services are fine for a small community, but if you're running a large, commercial Web community, you'll probably want to have more control over the contents and appearance of your mailing lists. To do this, you can license mailing list software from a company like L-Soft (www.lsoft.com), or work with a third-party firm like Milo (www.milo.com), or Kara (www.kara.com) who can help you manage your mailing lists.

FIGURE 2.1

www.egroups.com

eGroups makes it easy for anyone to create their own public or private mailing list. Each mailing list has an info page containing a mission statement, posting policy, usage stats, and links to a member roster, a message archive, events calendar, a file upload area, and other features.

MEMBER ROSTER   MESSAGE ARCHIVE   EVENT CALENDAR   FILE UPLOAD AREA

MISSION STATEMENT

USAGE STATISTICS

POSTING POLICY

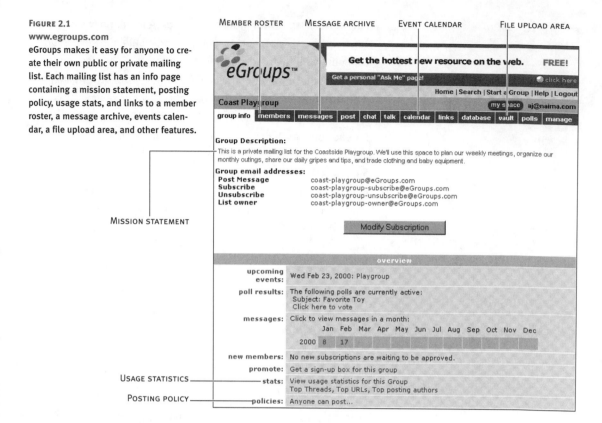

TYPES OF MAILING LISTS

Once you've chosen a list service and decided on a "door policy"—that is, whether to make the list invitation-only or open to everyone—you'll need to decide what kind of mailing list you want and how you'd like to run it. There are three basic types of lists, each with a different purpose.

○ **IN AN UNMODERATED MAILING LIST,** every message goes to every member. Although one person creates and owns the list, no one is officially in charge or filters the messages. Unmoderated lists are good for groups who already know each other—such as college buddies who want to stay in touch—and people who are collaborating on a task, such as family members planning a yearly get-together. The disadvantage of an unmoderated list is that, with no one filtering the messages, it's up to the participants to keep the content appropriate and on topic.

○ **IN A MODERATED MAILING LIST,** the list owner (a.k.a. the moderator) reads each message first and then decides if it should be forwarded to the rest of the list. Often, this person also acts as host—setting a door policy, welcoming newcomers, keeping the conversation going, and dealing with troublemakers. This type of list works well when the members are interested in the moderator's point of view—for example, a book discussion moderated by the author. Moderated lists can also work for busy people who don't want to see every comment or for teams of people that already have a designated leader. The disadvantage is that some members may feel that their comments are being censored or underrepresented.

○ **IN A BROADCAST MAILING LIST,** the moderator is the only one who can send an email to the list. This is similar to how the mailing list in your email program works, except that the recipients don't see each others' addresses. Broadcast mailing lists work well for newsletters, announcements, celebrity-to-fan communications, and any situation in which a group of people need to be kept informed or reminded about events and gatherings. The downside is that broadcast lists don't do much to foster a community among the subscribers, since they have no way to communicate directly with each other. For a community, broadcast lists are best used in conjunction with other methods.

Message Boards

A message board—otherwise known as a newsgroup, bulletin board, conference, discussion, or forum—is one of the most familiar types of online gathering place. Like mailing lists, message boards are *asynchronous*, which means that people don't have to be in the same (virtual) place at the same time to have a conversation. Because of this, message boards can foster conversations that happen over a period of days, weeks, and months. They're also great for asking and answering questions and giving the community a sense of context and history:

Message board software comes in two varieties (Figure 2.2):

○ **THREADED** boards start from one main topic, which branches off into a number of "threads" that are offshoots of the original conversation, like a party that breaks up into small clusters of people. Threaded boards are particularly well suited to Q&A-style conversations, because when someone asks a specific question, it's easy to see if it's been answered. Following all the threads can get confusing, though. Software packages that support threaded boards include eShare (**www.eshare.com**) and RemarQ (**www.remarq.com**).

○ **LINEAR** boards provide a separate topic for each conversation (often grouped together under a general topic, or "conference"), and one message follows another in chronological order—analogous to a group of people having multiple shared conversations. A member (or moderator) creates a new "branch" by starting a new topic, in parallel to the original conversation. Linear boards are great for extended, in-depth conversations, which encourage members to get to know each other better, though newcomers may find it hard to break into the general hubbub. Software packages that support linear boards include Web Crossing (**www.lundeen.com**), Caucus (**www.caucussystems.com**) and the Ultimate Bulletin Board (**www.ultimatebb.com**).

When Should You Use a Message Board?

While mailing lists and message boards have some similarities, message boards offer additional features that give you more community-building power. You can use message boards to:

○ **PROVIDE A SENSE OF PLACE.** Both mailing lists and message boards can foster a conversation across time zones; but unlike a mailing list, whose participants don't have to "go anywhere" to get their messages, a message board can be integrated into a Web site. By adding to its sense of place, a message board can unite geographically distant people and enhance their sense of belonging.

FIGURE 2.2

www.ezboard.com

Choosing between threaded and linear message boards is really a matter of personal preference; tools like ezboard allow members to configure their boards either as threaded (upper image) or linear (lower image).

CREATE   TOUR   LEARN   NEWS   FIND   LOG IN

New Topic

Back to ezboard Forums
Hybrid 2 Example

My Control Center / Logout | Show new only | Mark forum read | Search | Help

Logged in as amyjo

Page 1 2

test-**Buffett** ■-(1)-2/17/00 5:19:52 pm
    Re: test-**Parrothawk** 2/17/00 5:21:29 pm

important notice!!! ALL READ!!!-**askryan** -(0)-9/6/99 2:43:26 pm

geek boy testing -**eventco999** ■-(5)-6/6/99 9:45:44 am
  a-**a** 2/12/00 2:50:54 am
    Re: geek boy testing -**eventco999** ■ 6/6/99 9:47:13 am
      Re: geek boy testing -**inspirationpeak** ■ 2/11/00 3:55:51 pm
        Will this work?-**inspirationpeak** ■ 2/11/00 3:57:17 pm
          und NOCH ein test *g*-**Schnuppelheinzelchen** 2/15/00 1:10:50 am

Testing -**Buster**-(15)-6/15/99 10:15:36 am
    Re: Testing -**An21** ■ 1/4/00 2:19:19 pm
      Re: Testing -**leebok** ■ 2/7/00 9:15:30 am
  I musT say this is the best one..-**Tester** 12/27/99 9:27:44 am
    post placement**-**TidesPride** 1/29/00 9:36:32 am
      placement 2-**TidesPride**-NT 1/29/00 9:33:50 am
  Yz -**Bozo** 6/15/99 10:17:48 am
    tk -**Buffy** 6/15/99 10:19:48 am
      Re: tk -**Ystream** 7/9/00 5:18:11 pm

New Topic

Back to ezboard Forums
Feedback on Our New Site

My Control Center | Register (Optional) | Search | Help

Need help logging in?

Page 1 2

Topic	Replies	Last Comment	Started By
Ezboard - simply the best!	3	2/22/00 1:10:51 pm	Arthur Boe
Information !	3	2/21/00 1:38:08 pm	Pinzoz
my new site.	1	2/20/00 6:03:18 pm	ttyahah
It looks great on my big screen tv!eom	1	2/18/00 12:37:14 am	Tamia
Features coming in 5.1	22	2/15/00 8:12:00 pm	ezboard
Private Forum	1	2/9/00 5:28:37 pm	zeid
Community Showcase ?? How ??	4	2/8/00 9:29:31 am	Cheef
Suggestion for future versions of Ezboard...	5	1/24/00 7:57:40 am	BrianAdmin
I Hate the new Look	24	1/21/00 8:30:31 am	FWDB
EZBoard vs. Ultimate Bulletin Board(UBB)	43	1/21/00 8:22:05 am	Super Charizard
luv 18	80	1/7/00 9:10:10 am	Charon
The Footer Banners and other things...	3	1/6/00 9:02:44 pm	RCTAmerica
New Site, 3/5 Stars...	9	1/6/00 8:17:03 pm	UVDude15
A question...	3	1/6/00 8:10:10 pm	RavensRants
the new site....	4	1/1/00 6:41:17 pm	user
The NEW look as of now....	0	12/31/99 10:31:43 am	SerenityJJ
HELP NEEDED~	10	12/29/99 5:25:33 pm	KILOG
9 ezboards, going for 11	1	12/29/99 4:40:57 pm	gbarrier
WHAT ABOUT THE EZBOARD USERS THAT USE HOMESTEAD? ARE YOU STILL DOING THAT?	3	12/29/99 4:39:52 pm	ryanbilodeau
WE WILL GET TO IT..... SURE...	2	12/29/99 10:42:41 am	ryanbilodeau
Version 5.0 A Disaster!!!	7	12/23/99 9:29:15 am	FWDB
What I meant is	2	12/15/99 12:33:48 pm	JeremyTan

- **OFFER VISIBLE CONTEXT TO THE CONVERSATION.** To provide context in a mailing list, the participants must include snippets of previous emails. A message board shows you the context of each message, which helps to keep the conversation focused and allows newcomers to catch up easily.

- **ENCOURAGE BRANCHING AND SUBGROUPS.** Message boards encourage multiple conversations within a given topic, which allows your community to naturally subdivide into interest groups that are more specific. This feature can help you manage and grow your community and include high-volume conversations, because people can choose to read only those threads that interest them (unlike a mailing list, where a hot topic can quickly lead to an overflowing mailbox).

Message boards are great for:

- *asking and answering questions*
- *encouraging in-depth conversations*
- *managing high-volume conversations*
- *providing context, history, and a sense of place*

- **INTRODUCE IMAGES INTO THE CONVERSATION.** Many message board packages let people compose posts that include images, or at least provide a live link to them. The ability to express emotions graphically or post a photo for discussion (Figure 2.3) helps members feel more personally involved.

- **RECORD YOUR COMMUNITY'S EVOLVING HISTORY.** Some message board software allows you to save all the messages, while others purge old messages. Saved messages can serve as your community's evolving history, and reading through archives can be a great way for new members to get up to speed and learn about the community's culture and background.

FIGURE 2.3

INTERACT '98: USING IMAGES IN A MESSAGE BOARD

The Web is filled with creative uses of simple technology, such as this use of an enhanced message board to host a conference in cyberspace. Here, we see the keynote address from Interact '98, an online conference that uses the Caucus software. Conference participants can read the keynote address (complete with slides), and then start having a conversation with the speaker and each other.

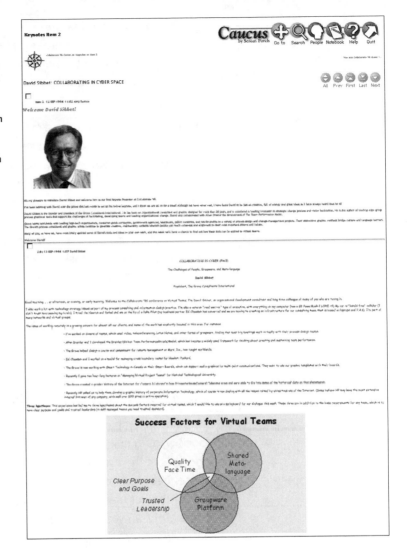

YOUR PLACE OR THEIRS?

If you want to provide a message board for your community, but don't want to install and configure software yourself, you have a couple of options. You can sign up for a free, easy-to-use service such as Delphi Forums (**www.delphi.com**), eCircles (**www.ecircles.com**) or Yahoo Clubs (**clubs.yahoo.com**), which all include some type of message board, along with other community-oriented features. Be aware, however, that your members will be required to register with the service to participate in your community, which means you won't own your member database (see Chapter 3), and your gathering places will come with advertising (so often true with "free" services).

If you want more control over your interface and member database, you can contract with a service—such as Well Engaged (www.wellengaged.com), Caucus (www.caucussystems.com) or RemarQ (www.remarq.com)—to create a board that looks like part of your site but actually runs from the bureau's servers. This approach can help you get started quickly and is especially helpful when you don't have in-house technical expertise or don't want to use it on this task. It can be an expensive approach, however, and you'll be sharing your database with another company.

As for running a message board on your own site, you have several options there as well. If your needs are simple, you can go with any number of free (or very inexpensive) packages, many of which are written in Perl. If you need more features, you could license and customize one of these packages, or even build your own message boards from scratch.

If you need a robust, industrial-strength message board, and you don't want to build one yourself, you'll need to do a more in-depth analysis of the available software packages. Can you customize the appearance of the message area to match the rest of your site? Are your members already used to a particular kind of software? Can you integrate it with the rest of your community infrastructure?

Message board software is a rapidly changing area, and there are over a hundred different packages available at the time I'm writing this. For an up-to-date list—everything from free, low-end packages to industrial-strength systems—I recommend David Wooley's directory of conferencing software (www.thinkofit.com/webconf). This site also contains a number of helpful papers and articles that can help you choose an appropriate package, and understand where message board software is headed.

One particularly interesting trend is combining the features of mailing lists and message boards. In some cases, participants can get an email notification of new postings or replies to specific messages. Or they could receive the full text of a new message and post their reply, all through email. These features would be a big help if your community ever has to make the transition from a mailing list to a message board.

Real-Time Chat

Right this minute, all across the Net, people are logged into chat rooms—working, playing, arguing, gossiping, flirting, and having cybersex. Real-time chat software enables anyone who's connected to the system to correspond instantly with any other participant—it's *synchronous,* as opposed to asynchronous, which means that people in different physical locations are communicating with each other at the same time.

As a community builder, you can use this kind of gathering place for a variety of purposes, from the practical to the playful. In a chat room, you can teach classes, conduct interviews, run support groups, manage meetings, hold office hours, communicate with remote coworkers, and even prepare "backstage" for live events. Chat rooms also offer your members a place to hang out and relax, which is perhaps their most common use.

WHEN SHOULD YOU USE A CHAT ROOM?

Whether they're enhanced with sound and graphics or are simply plain text, all chat rooms serve the same purpose: to let a group of people communicate in real time. Chat rooms are particularly appropriate when you want to:

- **PROVIDE A SENSE OF IMMEDIACY AND PRESENCE.** Mailing lists and message boards are great for Q&A and extended conversations, but a chat room offers a sense of immediacy that, for many people, brings the concept of the "global village" to life. Even when the conversation is inane, making a connection at 3 AM with a like-minded soul from a different part of the world can be a powerful experience.

In fact, finding someone to talk with at any time of the day or night is a big part of chat's appeal.

○ **HOLD SCHEDULED EVENTS.** Chat rooms (and their big brother, auditoriums) work particularly well for real-time scheduled events such as meetings, games, interviews, classes, and topical discussions. Events can help to attract a crowd of compatible people, and ensure that enough of them will show up to bring the gathering to life. Talk City, for example, hosts a wide variety of scheduled events in their chat rooms, including support group meetings, topical discussions, word games, and celebrity interviews (see Chapter 7 for more about events).

○ **OFFER REAL-TIME SUPPORT AND GUIDANCE.** Chat rooms are a great way to let your members get an immediate response from the community staff. On large, proprietary systems, such as AOL, there's often someone staffing an online support room 24 hours a day (although there may be a long line of people waiting to ask a question). Other systems offer live support during established "office hours." A live support option is a good complement to FAQ's (Frequently Asked Questions), message boards (for more in-depth discussions), and email support (for questions that don't need an immediate answer).

Chat rooms are great for:

○ *Holding scheduled events*

○ *Preparing for—and debriefing after—live events*

○ *Discussing offline events as they're happening*

○ *Hanging out—relaxing, flirting, gossiping, visiting*

There are many ways to incorporate chat into your community, from freely available IRC channels to proprietary virtual worlds. As always, the choice of which ones to use will be based on what your needs are and what your members will be comfortable with.

IRC

IRC (Internet Relay Chat) is a free, Internet-wide service that hosts a vast and ever-changing collection of user-created chat rooms called "channels." Anyone with an Internet connection and an IRC client (software for accessing the IRC service) can select a nickname, check out a list of available channels, and jump into the fray. Anybody can create an IRC channel at any time, and it will exist until the last person leaves the room. IRC channels can be either public or private, which means that you can allow only those who are invited to access the channel.

If your members are already familiar with IRC, it can make sense to use an IRC channel as a community gathering place, whether on one of the existing servers or by setting up the software on your own server. For example, members of the Ultima Online support staff hold weekly meetings in a private IRC channel, and many Ultima Online Guilds also meet regularly in IRC channels. But if your members aren't used to installing client software and selecting communications ports, they won't be comfortable using IRC software.

If you do want to integrate IRC into your community or try an IRC channel, there are many free IRC clients available—mIRC for the PC (download from **www.mirc.com**), Ircle for the Mac (**www.ircle.com**), and ircII for UNIX (**www.irchelp.org/irchelp/ircii**), among others. There are also Java-based IRC clients—such as JPilot jIRC (**www.jpilot.com**)—that run inside a Web browser and don't require configuration. For more information about setting up and running IRC clients and servers, the official IRC help site (**www.irchelp.org**) is a good resource, as are the client sites mentioned above.

WEB-BASED TEXT CHAT

Web-based chat solutions don't require a separate download and are easier for participants to configure, although they may run on top of the IRC network. To offer text-based Web chat, you can:

- **MAKE USE OF A FREE CHAT SERVICE.** Services such as Talk City (Figure 2.4) allow individuals and small groups to create and run their own chat rooms. (For a fee, Talk City will also run hosted chats for an organization). Since Talk City chat rooms are built on top of the IRC network, your community members can participate using their favorite IRC client, if they prefer, rather than the Web-based client provided by Talk City. This approach lets you set up and run a chat room for free in a safe, hosted environment with a friendly interface. However, you won't own your member database (see Chapter 3), your chat rooms won't have the look and feel of your community, and your community members will be exposed to random ads while chatting.

FIGURE 2.4
FREE CHAT AT TALK CITY
www.talkcity.com
This conversation is taking place on Talk City, a "chat aggregator" that features EZTalk , a Java-based IRC client. The software makes it easy to create and run a public or private chat room and adds extra functionaltiy like a proprietary buddies list that allows Talk City chatters to locate and communicate with their friends.

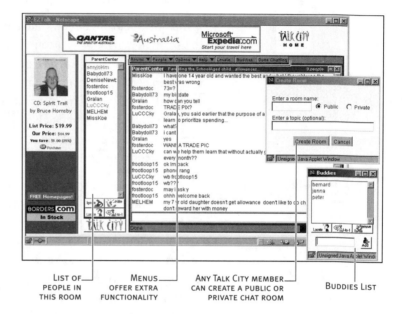

LIST OF PEOPLE IN THIS ROOM   MENUS OFFER EXTRA FUNCTIONALITY   ANY TALK CITY MEMBER CAN CREATE A PUBLIC OR PRIVATE CHAT ROOM   BUDDIES LIST

○ **LICENSE WEB-BASED CHAT.** Alternatively, you can license chat software from a vendor and run it on your own site. This approach will give you control over your member database, and over the appearance of your chat rooms. Choices range from simple, inexpensive packages—such as jIRC—to more robust, industrial-strength solutions like WebMaster (**www.webmaster.com**) (Figure 2.5). You can also license Web-based chat software as part of a larger package (including message boards) from companies such as eShare (**www.eshare.com**) and KOZ (**www.koz.com**).

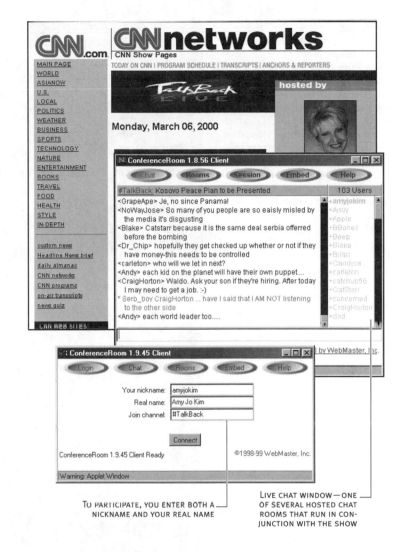

FIGURE 2.5

TALKBACK LIVE AT CNN.COM

www.cnn.com/talkback

CNN uses Webmaster's Java-based chat software to run scheduled chats, including a daily "simu-chat" that runs in conjunction with TalkBack Live, an interactive TV talk show. Chat participants don't have to register with CNN; instead, anyone who wants to "speak" enters both their nickname, and their "real name," and can then participate in these moderated chats. (See Chapter 7 for more about how TalkBack Live integrates the Web and TV).

TO PARTICIPATE, YOU ENTER BOTH A NICKNAME AND YOUR REAL NAME

LIVE CHAT WINDOW—ONE OF SEVERAL HOSTED CHAT ROOMS THAT RUN IN CONJUNCTION WITH THE SHOW

○ **BUILD YOUR OWN SOFTWARE.** If you have the engineering talent, you can make sure your chat software does what you want by building it yourself. For example, Yahoo developed its own chat software (**chat.yahoo.com**) to have control over the interface and integrate chat with other parts of the site. And the gaming networks run by Origin (**www.origin.ea.com**), Blizzard (**www.blizzard.com**), and Mplayer (**www.mplayer.com**) all developed custom chat software because they found that the existing packages didn't do what they needed (Figure 2.6).

FIGURE 2.6
CHATTING IN ULTIMA ONLINE:
BEFORE AND AFTER

FIGURE 2.6
CHATTING IN ULTIMA ONLINE:
BEFORE AND AFTER
When Ultima Online first shipped, it included a gaming-style chat system, in which each character's words appeared over his or her head within the main frame (upper image). Although fine for short sentences and one-liners, this system proved too cumbersome for extended conversations. So Origin developed a proprietary IRC-like system (lower image) that was less "immersive" but made for livelier and more efficient conversations.

OLD-STYLE INTEGRATED CHAT SYSTEM (NOTICE THE DEAD BARTENDER AND THE WALLS OF FLAME—SOMETIMES, ACTIONS SPEAK LOUDER THAN WORDS)

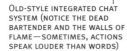

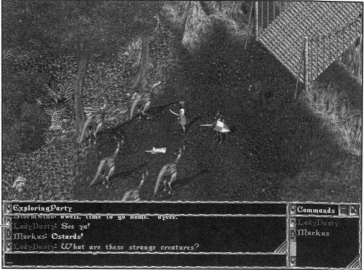

IRC-STYLE CHAT SYSTEM, WHICH INCLUDES A RICHER SET OF COMMANDS

GRAPHIC CHAT

To really put the "place" in your gathering places, you can include characters, art, and sound. This kind of graphically rich environment lets people express themselves in ways that text can't match—by choosing the clothes their character will appear in, for instance—and can be a great way to give your chat rooms visual context and reinforce your brand. Ideally, the enhanced activities will reinforce your community's purpose and match up with the skills of your members.

For your own site, you can use a multimedia toolkit like the Palace (Figure 2.7), which is relatively easy to configure and run. The graphic environment encourages playfulness and role-playing, and your members can add their own art, sounds, and rooms. Until recently, anyone who created a Palace needed to design custom art, and the participants needed to download a client and learn a new interface. The newest version of the Palace includes templates to help you get started and a Web-based "lite" client that requires no configuration.

FIGURE 2.7
www.comedycentral.com/southpark/
noflash/cmp/palace.shtml
The Palace was created to extend the experience of the hit television show *South Park*. Its snide, irreverent attitude and crude animation style translated beautifully to the Web.

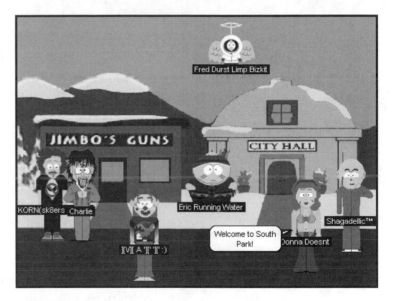

VOICE CHAT

For most people, talking is the most natural way to communicate, and voice chat is fast becoming a viable way to talk online. Many consumer-level computers now come with built-in audio ports and a headset microphone, and fast Net access—via DSL and cable modems—is finally becoming accessible and affordable. Given these developments, voice chat may soon become much more pervasive.

Voice chat makes the Web less anonymous. Hearing someone's voice is more revealing than seeing words typed on a screen. If your members like being themselves online (and are comfortable using a microphone headset), then voice can add a powerful dimension to their community experience.

The lack of anonymity, however, can be a drawback. If people are drawn to your community to live out a fantasy, hearing actual voices could get in the way—there's nothing more disappointing than hearing a powerful warrior speak in the high, thin voice of a 12-year-old boy. Voice chat also doesn't work as well as text for large events: individual voices can get lost in the crowd, and it's much harder to provide a transcript afterwards.

The simplest way to get started with voice chat is to create a voice-enabled chat room at a service like HearMe.com (Figure 2.8), which has similar advantages and disadvantages to creating a text chat room at Talk City. On your own site, you could use or license communications software such as Roger Wilco (www.resounding .com) that allows participants to create and run their own audio chat "channels." This system is currently marketed as an add-on for multiplayer games, but could also be used for other voice chat applications. A higher-end option—if you're planning on running a high-traffic community—would be to license HearMe's voice chat technology (www.hearme.com), which would also give you access to their nationwide network of high-performance servers.

Virtual Worlds

The most elaborate choice in online gathering places are virtual worlds, which create an interactive, navigable environment using graphics, sound, and animation and include customizable characters (or *avatars*) that represent the members. A virtual world can be two-dimensional, such as now-defunct Worlds Away (www.worldsaway.com), or three-dimensional, such as blaxxun (www.blaxxun.com) or Active Worlds (www.activeworlds.com). The inhabitants of a virtual world talk with each other using text or audio (depending on the platform) and can partake in a variety of activities, depending on the environment. Virtual worlds are immersive and compelling, but they require a lot of effort from you and your members to create, use, and maintain.

FIGURE 2.8
ON STAGE AT HEARME.COM
www.hearme.com
HearMe.com is a voice chat "aggregator" where anyone can create and run an audio-enabled chat room. Here we see the "On Stage" lobby, which currently has eight rooms running. A public karaoke contest is taking place in the "Sing anything" room, and a prayer meeting for a sick friend is unfolding in the "Prayers For Sage Aurthor" room.

The most familiar virtual worlds are combat-oriented multi-player games like Quake (www.idsoftware.com) and StarCraft (www.blizzard.com). Partly because of the popularity and visual appeal of these games, people have tried to give a similar look and feel to nongaming Web communities. But appealing as these virtual worlds are, not every Web community can or should look like a game.

If you're developing a multiplayer game, you'll probably build your own virtual world software platform (because you'll need to squeeze every last bit of performance out of the hardware). If you want to use an existing virtual world software package to build a non-gaming online community, you could work with a company such as blaxxun to help you develop a customized environment. You could also "homestead" a community within an existing environment, such as Active Worlds or blaxxun's Cybertown (cybertown.com).

If you're building a community that has a real need to interact within a three-dimensional world, or one that's based around sharing and discussing 3D data, then you might want to create your community gathering place within a virtual world. For example, a high school math teacher created a "geometry museum" in Active Worlds, where she meets with her students to explore larger-than-life geometric shapes. But for most Web community-builders, virtual worlds—fun and compelling though they are—would not be the best choice at this time.

Virtual worlds are great for:

○ *Creating an immersive fantasy environment*

○ *Building multiplayer games*

○ *Real-world simulations*

○ *Viewing 3D data—architecture, geometry, and the like*

Up to now, we've been looking at the characteristics of various types of gathering places. But once you decide on the kind of places you want to have, how do you set them up? How do thriving Web communities use the communication tools I just described? Do they buy, build, or do both?

To answer these questions, let's look under the hood at some well-established Web communities and see what approaches they've taken. We'll be focusing on message boards and chat rooms, because (along with mailing lists) they're the most popular and widespread tools for creating community gathering places.

Community of Aggregators

We've already mentioned that you can set up a mailing list at eGroups, create a message board on Delphi, open a chat room on Talk City, or create a club at Yahoo Clubs. These companies are *community aggregators*; they develop a set of tools and features, build a critical mass of members, and offer their environment to others as a place to build their community. These companies aren't really running a community themselves; instead, they're a place where collections of smaller communities exist. Some of these aggregators, such as Yahoo Clubs, offer their platform for free, in exchange for displaying targeted advertising. Others, such as AOL, charge for their services and strike deals with the companies that use their platform, based on a community's popularity and audience draw.

Nascent online community efforts often start by using the services of an aggregator and then migrate to their own site once they've become better established. For example, many Web communities—including Hecklers Online, MTV Online, iVillage, NetNoir, and Moms Online—got started on AOL, and later developed their own Web sites.

Basically, if you have limited time or resources, or are just testing the waters for your community, it makes good sense to use an aggregator. On the other hand, if you want to maintain control over your community's appearance and message, or if your business model demands it (a subscription-based site, for example), you won't want to use someone else's platform.

Use Off-the-Shelf Tools

If you're ready to run your own Web-based community, but don't want to develop your own custom software, you can license an existing software package. This way, you can concentrate on content, navigation, and design rather than technology (although you may still need to have technical people on staff to install, configure, and maintain whatever you license).

CNN Interactive (www.cnn.com) is one company that's chosen to license both chat and message board software, from WebMaster (www.webmaster.com) and Web Crossing (www.lundeen.com) respectively. Because these tools are from different vendors, they don't integrate easily without some back-end work by CNN's technical staff—for instance, to make sure that someone posting to the message boards has the same identity in the chat rooms. At this time, consistent member identity isn't a priority for CNN, so they live with the possible conflict. Many sites demand consistent identity, however, and the limitations of most current third-party community tools make it difficult to provide a "log in once, access everything" environment. That's one reason so many Web communities build their own tools and platforms.

Roll Your Own

Whether driven by frustration with existing tools, or a need for special features, you might decide to develop your own software. This approach gives you maximum control over the development process, which means that you can fix bugs, add new features, and integrate the various elements according to your own schedule. It also means that you'll be the one responsible for these activities, which can be expensive and time consuming.

Many large Web communities, especially those that have been in operation for many years, rely on custom-built software. For example, AOL's message boards, chat rooms, auditoriums, and instant messaging tools were created internally and used exclusively by that service. The WELL also runs on a custom platform called Picospan, created in 1985 and still in use. In the mid 1990s, a Web-based tool was built to run on top of Picospan and provide a more visual and easy-to-use interface. This tool, Well Engaged, was developed into a stand-alone message board solution and is now the centerpiece of a non-WELL business (www.wellengaged.com).

Both the WELL and America Online were formed at a time when commercial online-community software was virtually nonexistent. That's no longer the case; but some Web communities find that, even today, the available tools still don't meet their needs. For example, AncientSites is built on a custom communications platform that was developed by CyberSites (www.cybersites.com), their parent company. This platform includes email, message boards, chat rooms, instant messaging, and buddy lists, all tightly integrated with a membership database (Figure 2.9).

CyberSites developed this platform because they found that the available software solutions were not flexible or powerful enough to create the environment they wanted. Although it required substantial engineering resources, this approach allowed AncientSites to achieve a high level of integration. Once logged in, a member has access to all the communications features—something that is difficult to do with third-party software solutions.

FIGURE 2.9
CUSTOM COMMUNICATIONS
SOFTWARE AT ANCIENTSITES
AncientSites runs on a custom suite
of communications tools that includes
email, message boards, chat, and instant
messaging. Here, we see the main page
of Machu Picchu, a city within Ancient-
Sites devoted to Native American culture.
This page includes links to city-specific
bulletin boards and chat, which were
set up by the AncientSites staff. We can
also browse through a city newspaper
and a special-interest magazine, or take
a guided tour of some Machu Picchu
homes—all member-created features
that were enabled by the AncientSites
platform. The People Panel displays
everyone who's currently logged into
the system.

PEOPLE PANEL

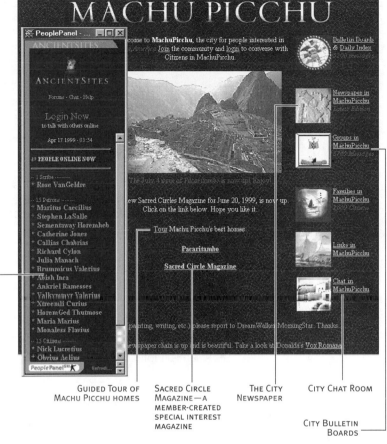

GUIDED TOUR OF
MACHU PICCHU HOMES

SACRED CIRCLE
MAGAZINE—A
MEMBER-CREATED
SPECIAL INTEREST
MAGAZINE

THE CITY
NEWSPAPER

CITY CHAT ROOM

CITY BULLETIN
BOARDS

Mapping the Territory

Just creating gathering places is not enough: you need a plan
for organizing them and integrating them into the rest of your
community. Think of your community as a neighborhood and
your visitors as people who are considering moving in. How
do people pick a neighborhood to live in? They might start by
talking to a real estate agent or reading the paper. But they
almost always check out the streets and houses, the shops

and services, and the other residents before they're really comfortable that this community is a place that they could call home.

As a community builder, your job is to create a visual design and navigational structure that communicates the purpose, content, and features of your community and helps your visitors find their way around. Because communities are dynamic by nature, this structure must be flexible enough to allow your neighborhood to grow beyond its current boundaries without losing its character.

Organize Your Gathering Places

Your visitors (and, ultimately, your members) will rely on a variety of cues—graphics, layout, and naming conventions, for instance—to get a sense of what your community is about (see sidebar on page 61) and to decide which areas to explore. If you're building a small, intimate community—such as a book club, support group, or family Web site—your organizational structure can be minimal and simple, because you'll need only a few gathering places.

If, on the other hand, you're building a growth-oriented community—such as a start-up company or a destination Web site—you'll face a constant demand for new gathering places. That's why your structure needs to be flexible and extensible.

Model Homes

One of your first tasks will be to choose a theme (also called a "model" or "metaphor"). There are three popular types:

- **A CATEGORICAL THEME** is the easiest, most common, and most flexible way to organize a collection of items. You can start with a short, simple list of topics or categories and grow from there, adding depth and breadth as needed. Thus, a categorical theme might show up as a list of issues, a hierarchy of discussion topics, or a collection of product groups (Figure 2.10).

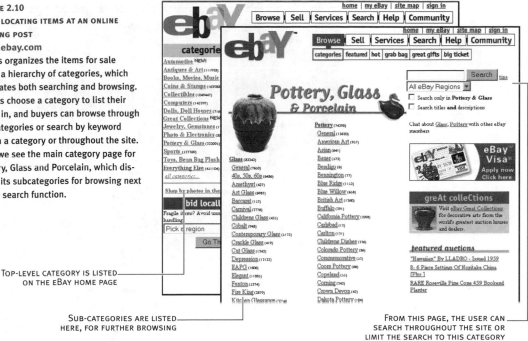

FIGURE 2.10

EBAY: LOCATING ITEMS AT AN ONLINE TRADING POST

www.ebay.com

eBay's organizes the items for sale using a hierarchy of categories, which facilitates both searching and browsing. Sellers choose a category to list their items in, and buyers can browse through the categories or search by keyword within a category or throughout the site. Here we see the main category page for Pottery, Glass and Porcelain, which displays its subcategories for browsing next to the search function.

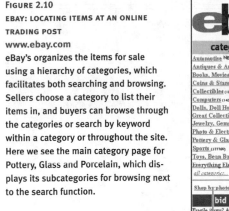

TOP-LEVEL CATEGORY IS LISTED ON THE EBAY HOME PAGE

SUB-CATEGORIES ARE LISTED HERE, FOR FURTHER BROWSING

FROM THIS PAGE, THE USER CAN SEARCH THROUGHOUT THE SITE OR LIMIT THE SEARCH TO THIS CATEGORY

○ **A GEOGRAPHIC THEME** is an appealing and intuitive way to get around within a virtual space. By invoking familiar models like houses, neighborhoods, and cities, you leverage people's associations with the physical world. GeoCities uses a geographic theme for its neighborhoods, as does AncientSites for its cities (Figure 2.11).

○ **A MEDIA THEME,** such as the departments of a magazine or a collection of channels, builds on people's familiarity with existing media and suggests what type of content and activities they can expect. For example, the top-level subdivisions at iVillage are called "channels," suggesting a variety of television-style content.

In practice, Web communities often adopt different organizational themes for different aspects of their community. The main subdivisions at AncientSites, for instance, are organized into cities (a geographic metaphor), while the member-defined groups that exist within each city are organized by topic (a categorical model).

FIGURE 2.11
ANCIENTSITES CITIES

The AncientSites cities are named for historically important places like Babylon, Egypt, and Machu Picchu, which connote a particular set of interests and attitudes.

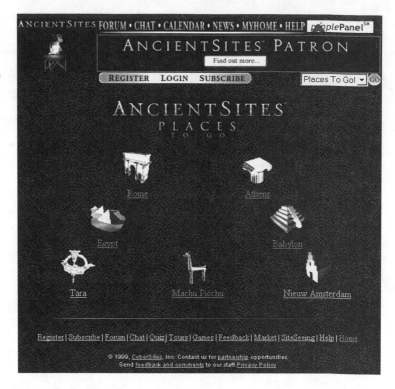

SELECTING A THEME

Your community's theme should be based on *who* your audience is, *what* types of content you will be organizing, and *how* you want people to think about your site. As you're considering which theme(s) to select, ask yourself the following questions:

○ **DOES THE CONTENT SUGGEST A THEME?** This is the most obvious and natural approach. If your community is based around regional content like city guides or local politics, then geographic subdivisions would make sense. If your community is the online extension of an existing magazine, a table of contents model is a natural one for you.

○ **DO I WANT TO SUGGEST A FAMILIAR MODEL?** If you want people to think of your community as a place to find entertainment, then you might choose to call your subdivisions "channels." If you want to encourage your members to take over and run sections of your community, then breaking it down into "towns" or "cities" would create an expectation of mayors, town councils, and representative democracy.

○ **WILL MY THEME HELP OR HINDER NAVIGATION?** What appeals to a Net newbie is often very different than what attracts an experienced Netizen, so it's important to consider the sophistication level of your audience when choosing your organizing theme. For example, the literal and cumbersome graphics of the pre-Yahoo GeoCities neighborhoods were helpful to beginners but sometimes alienated sophisticated Net users (see Figure 2.15).

CATEGORICAL THEMES: CLASSIFYING INFORMATION

Of all the theme types, categories are best suited to browsing, searching, and extending a body of knowledge or information. A well-known example of this is Yahoo, which relies on a hierarchy of categories to provide access to a growing collection of Web sites, chat rooms, message boards, and clubs. Similar content, activities, and discussions are grouped together into categories, which allows Yahoo users to quickly find what they're looking for, as well as to discover similar items by serendipity. This approach also facilitates efficient classification: Yahoo users can classify their submissions themselves, and the internal Yahoo "surfing staff" can reclassify them as needed.

Categories are often the most efficient interface for a task like shopping, too, because similar products can naturally be grouped together. Both Amazon (www.amazon.com) and eBay are examples of category-driven shopping sites. As Web connections grow faster, it make sense to provide a more immersive and entertaining shopping experience; but for efficiency and ease of use, the category interface is currently the clear winner.

Categories also offer a natural way to classify and access something in more than one way. For example, Yahoo lets visitors find their way to the New York Museum of Modern Art by starting with Art or with Region; similarly, the WELL's Popular Culture conference can be found listed under Media and also under Fun.

GEOGRAPHICAL THEMES: CITIES, NEIGHBORHOODS AND BUILDINGS

GeoCities pioneered the influential and widely copied neighborhood model, which gives people a concrete sense of where they "live" within the community. Similarly, the AncientSites community is subdivided into cities of the ancient world, which attract people who are interested in a particular time and place—a scheme that reflects the natural subdivisions that occur among history enthusiasts.

If multiple associations (such as those described above) aren't an issue, a geographical theme can be a good choice. You can implement such a theme by encouraging your members to declare a primary affiliation (to a city or neighborhood, for example), and create a home base (such as a home page or a virtual house).

A geographic theme is also appropriate when your community will be a virtual world. Since virtual worlds give members the illusion of moving around in space, a geographic theme is the obvious extension of that metaphor.

MEDIA THEMES: NEWSPAPERS, NEWSLETTERS, AND CHANNELS

Emulating an existing media format, such as a newsletter, magazine, or television network, can work well for a community that's an extension of an offline media property, especially when the emulation isn't carried out too literally or rigidly. For example, the *New York Times* on the Web (www.nytimes.com) includes discussion forums that are organized around major sections of the paper and have newspaper-like elements, but they also include Net-savvy features like discussions and a search box.

You can also use a media-centric metaphor for one particular aspect of your community, to mimic the familiar role of media in offline communities. For example, the Ultima Online Town Cryer (town.uo.com) is a weekly publication that covers the news in Britannia, the fantasy world in which Ultima Online takes place. By modeling the Town Cryer on a small-town newspaper and inviting players to submit news and events for publication, the designers at Origin are using a familiar media form to strengthen their community the same way a local paper does.

What Goes Where

A *taxonomy* is a classification scheme, a way to organize a collection of individual elements into groups. Just as botanists have a taxonomy for plants that lets them classify new discoveries, you need a taxonomy to organize the elements of your community. Taxonomies can both to lend a structure to what's already there and help you decide where to put new additions.

Your taxonomy also lets your visitors know what you have to offer and how to find what they're looking for. For example, eBay's taxonomy organizes items for sale on the site by category. Within each category, there are subcategories—sometimes three or four levels deep. Anyone who visits eBay can find the product they're looking for by browsing the categories, just as in a department store you might look for cosmetics, then men's cosmetics, and then shaving supplies.

The most obvious taxonomy is a categorical one like eBay's. Similarly, Yahoo uses a hierarchy of topics to classify web sites, message boards, and clubs (Figure 2.12). But a taxonomy can be developed for other models as well—Talk City's Teen community, for instance, features Boombox Blvd., Drivers Ed Drive, and Homie Page Way. And we've already seen how a media model might be broken down into channels, à la iVillage, or into the sections of a newspaper, like the *New York Times* site.

FIGURE 2.12
YAHOO
www.yahoo.com
Yahoo has developed an internal expertise in taxonomies, as reflected in its flexible and extensible hierarchy of topics that allows the staff to quickly classify new Web sites and helps Yahoo users find Web sites that match their interests. Here, we see the main Yahoo site, which is one of the best-known and most influential taxonomies on the Web.

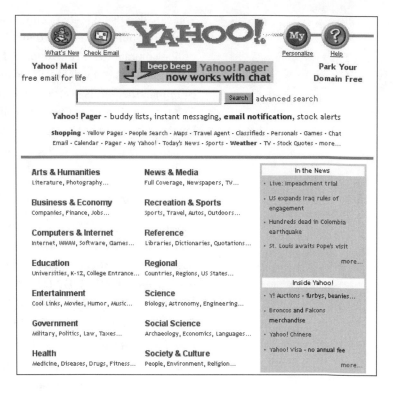

WHAT MAKES A GOOD TAXONOMY?

One of the most common mistakes Web designers make is to structure a site according to how the owners think about the content rather than what the users are looking for. No matter what model your community is based on, your first task is to make sure its subdivisions are meaningful to your audience.

For example, the AncientSites designers chose to build their taxonomy around cities of the ancient world. At first, this choice might not seem obvious or useful. But the designers knew that history buffs are more fascinated by a particular time and place than by generic themes, and the organization they chose allows their members to connect more easily with others who share their particular passions.

One of the biggest advantages of meaningful subdivisions is that your members can take over much of the categorization tasks themselves. You can see this dynamic at work within the GeoCities neighborhoods (www.geocities.com/neighborhoods), which contain collections of self-published Web pages. Someone who wants to create a Web site at GeoCities must first decide which neighborhood the pages will "live in." For example, someone just back from Nepal might create a page to display photos of the trek in the Yosemite neighborhood (www.geocities.com/Yosemite), which is for outdoor enthusiasts.. This approach can be a problem when a content could easily be categorized in several ways or isn't covered by existing categories, but it's allowed GeoCities to group thousands of Web pages around similar themes and to introduce like-minded members to each other.

A good taxonomy should also be extensible—that is, flexible enough to be extended without losing its integrity. The Yahoo taxonomy, for example, started as a list of topics thrown together by two graduate students and has ended up a well-thought-out classification scheme that can handle everything from soup (Business and Economy > Companies > Food > Brand Names > Campbell Soup Company) to nuts (Entertainment > Music > Artists > By Genre > Lounge > Squirrel Nut Zippers)

A text-based list like Yahoo's is a good all-round approach, because it's easy to update and extend. A graphical approach, however, while visually pleasing, can be difficult to change. For example, the navigation scheme of Electric Minds was based on a beautiful image that created a strong visual identity but left little room for the basic structure of the site to evolve (Figure 2.13).

FIGURE 2.13

ELECTRIC MINDS HOME PAGE
Electric Minds launched in the Spring of 1996, when the Internet was younger and more naive. The visual design of Eminds was striking, and—along with a strong presence from the founder—gave the nascent Web community a vivid site personality. But the beautiful integrated graphic on the Eminds home page was labor- and design-intensive to update, which made it more difficult for the Eminds taxonomy to evolve as the site grew.

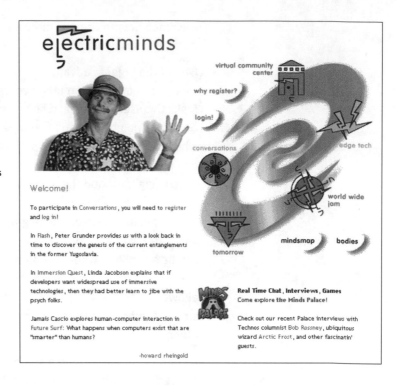

What Kind of Place is This?

As I mentioned in Chapter 1, one way to express your community's purpose is to create a distinct visual personality for your site through your graphical style, navigational layout, and naming conventions. You also want to use those same elements to give a distinct personality to each of your community's subdivisions. Your navigational structure will lead people to the various gathering places on your site, but once they get there, how will they know if they want to stay?

The look of your gathering places should express, as much as possible, what's special and different about each area, even if the functional and navigational designs are similar throughout. You can use whatever visual cues are available within your platform—color, shapes, font style, naming conventions, icons, or images. Compare the Romance lobby on Mplayer (Figure 2.14), for instance, with the "On Stage" lobby (see Figure 2.8). These areas are identical in layout and function, but the room icons let people know what the rooms are for. Similarly, the different neighborhoods at GeoCities use different icons to represent the member Web sites (Figure 2.15).

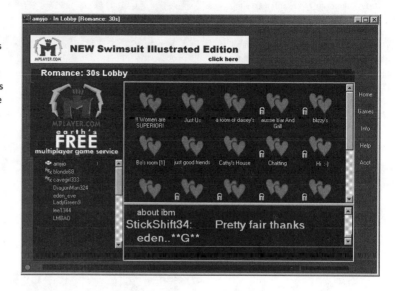

FIGURE 2.14

ROMANCE CHAT AT HEARME.COM

There are many ways to offer visual clues about the purpose of a gathering place. Here, we see the Romance Chat lobby on Mplayer, which uses hearts as room icons to reinforce the romance theme. Compare this with the On Stage lobby (Figure 2.8), which uses microphones to reinforce the performance theme.

Designing Your Community Personality: Graphics vs. Navigation

There are two interlocking aspects of design that go into creating a successful community:

○   **INFORMATION DESIGN** deals with the organizational structure of the site

○   **GRAPHIC DESIGN** creates the visual cues that identify a community

The information design of a Web community is like the layout of a town or the architecture of a house: it deals with the underlying structure of the content and activities on the site and helps visitors find their way around. (See www.publish.com/features/9902/id/idmain.html for an excellent introduction to information design). A site devoted to providing technical support, for example, might be organized around product and platform, while a site for job hunters might be organized by skill and region.

The graphic design of a Web community is like the "look" of a neighborhood or the interior design of a house; it uses imagery and layout to communicate the essence of the place in an immediate way. An adults-only Web site, for example, will probably have a different look than a Disney-sponsored game — and if the designers did their job well, a visitor will notice the difference right away.

As you're building your Web community, use both information and graphic design to make sure your site:

○   communicates your community's purpose up front

○   shows what's available inside in a way that's meaningful to your audience

○   allows someone to quickly find what they're looking for

○   lets someone know where they are within the community at all times

FIGURE 2.15

GEOCITIES NEIGHBORHOODS

Each neighborhood in GeoCities is composed of suburbs, whose streets and "homesteads" are represented graphically. Until recently, a visitor could browse through these streets and view people's Web sites by clicking on the homestead icons. Although the basic page layout was identical, GeoCities reinforced the particular theme of each neighborhood by using different homestead icons. Here, we see how different the homesteads are on the streets of Paris, Heartland, and Area 51.

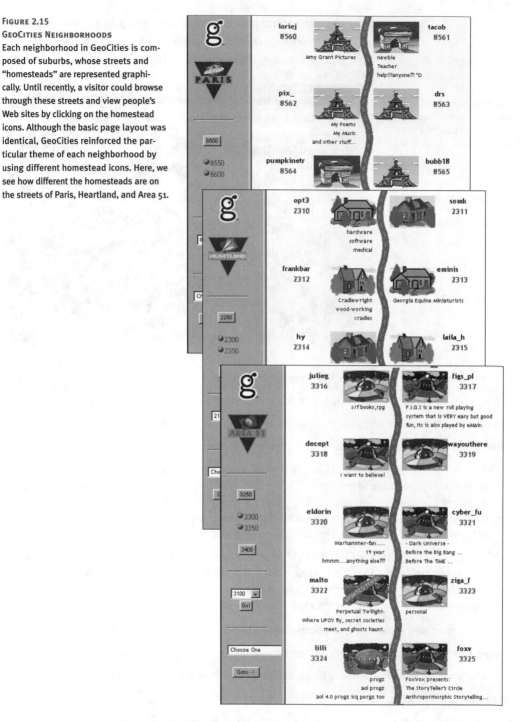

In addition to setting a tone, these types of visual cues can serve as navigation aids, to let people know at a glance where they are. iVillage, for example, uses color and font style to differentiate the major channels. Visual cues are especially important for a rapidly growing Web community or one in which members are adding new subdivisions themselves. You can help avoid a mess by giving members a graphic with which to tag their content, for instance, the way GeoCities used to do with its GeoGuide (Figure 2.16).

FIGURE 2.16
GEOGUIDE: TAGGING
MEMBER-CREATED CONTENT
Before building a Web page, a GeoCities member had to select a neighborhood to "live" in (such as the ones above). Each member could then "self-categorize" their pages by including a GeoGuide on each page, to tag their site as belonging to a particular neighborhood. Here, we see a Heartland page that includes a Geoguide, and also shows off some GeoCities awards and merit badges.

—HEARTLAND GEOGUIDE

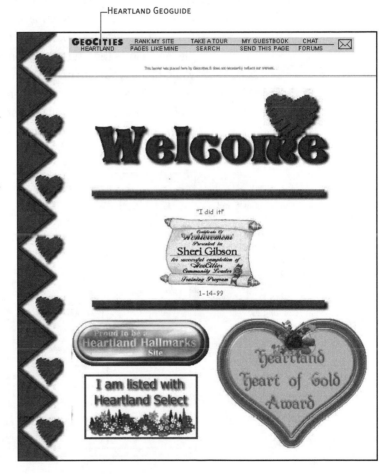

You are Here

Another visual aid your community needs is a map (or directory or table of contents). Derived from your taxonomy, your community map provides a bird's-eye view of the content, activities, and gathering places. It gives visitors a sense of how large the community is and how it's organized. Because a Web community is constantly changing, it's especially important to keep your map up to date.

For a small or medium-size community, one of the best types of maps is an interactive site map, such as the one at SeniorNet (Figure 2.17), which shows all the major areas within the community and allows the user to click on an area to go there directly. If you find that your site map is becoming overwhelming as your community grows, you might want to create a map for each major area of the site. iVillage lists the community's major area on the home page and then offers a separate overview of each smaller area.

FIGURE 2.17
SENIORNET SITE MAP
www.seniornet.com/help_map.shtml
One kind of community map is an interactive site map—such as this one from SeniorNet—which shows the various areas within a community and allows you to click on any area to go directly there. This kind of map works well for small to medium sized communities, or within the sub-areas of larger communities.

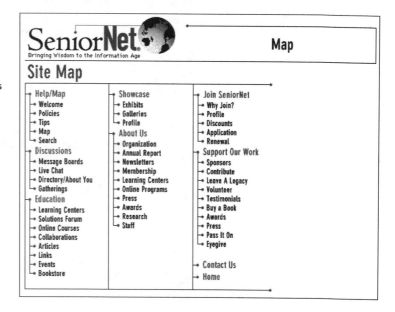

Where Do I Find...?

You also need to offer your users a comprehensive search function. While your site map encourages browsing and exploring, a search function lets members quickly find specific content and activities. As your community grows and browsing becomes more cumbersome, they will come to rely more and more on the search function. This will be especially true for power users who know what your community has to offer and just want an efficient way to get what they need. But a powerful search engine is useful for everyone, not only because it's more efficient than browsing but because it can uncover content or places that are difficult to classify or have been misclassified.

A search engine that works well for a small, focused Web community may need to be upgraded or replaced as the community grows. For example, GeoCities replaced its own homegrown search technology with the Inktomi search engine (www.inktomi.com), and eBay switched from its own search technology to a commercially available engine powered by ThunderStone (www.thunderstone.com).

These communities (as well as many others) also offer the ability to search within a specific subdivision. For example, GeoCities users can limit their search to a specific neighborhood, and eBay does the same for categories. You can use this feature to help reinforce the separate identities of each major subdivision within your community.

Zoned For Growth

When people first sit down to play the city planning computer game SimCity (www.simcity.com), they usually assume that they'll be able to control what happens in a predictable way. Think again! Experienced SimCity players know that, to build a long-lasting city, you have to choose your initial conditions carefully, adapt quickly to unexpected changes, and give up on trying to please everyone. Building a Web community teaches the same lessons, and a key part of your job is to create the structures, policies, and feedback loops that will allow you to manage growth flexibly.

Start Small and Focused

After all we've said about subdivisions and taxonomies, you might be tempted to create a wide variety of different gathering places, with the hopes of attracting a large and diverse audience. Maybe the people who are financing your community are eager to see a quick return on their investment and are pressuring you to make a big splash right away. It's best to resist the temptation: successful, long-lasting Web communities usually start with relatively few gathering places and a minimal feature set. This bare-bones approach to community building may be born out of necessity—such as a small staff or a restricted budget—but like so many things in life, it's likely to be a blessing in disguise. Consider these examples:

○ GeoCities launched with only six neighborhoods, a crude home page building tool, and a simple mission: to make it easy and cheap for anyone to create a home page on the Web. It now has forty-one neighborhoods and a large and growing collection of tools, templates, and features for building home pages, many of which were contributed by the members.

○ The WELL launched with ten public discussion topics and bare-bones conferencing software. It now has over two hundred public discussions, countless private discussions, and a substantial collection of hosting and administration tools.

○ iVillage got started by running a single community, Parent Soup, for new and expecting parents. iVillage now has fourteen channels with multiple subcommunities in each, and new features and content are added daily.

○ AncientSites grew out of a core community of history buffs that formed in a Pathfinder message board. This collection of "founding members" is now just one group among the hundreds of interest groups that now reside at AncientSites.

Starting small allows you to find your core audience, develop a coherent identity, and learn as you go. Running a community takes time, energy, and expertise, and the larger and more complex your community is, the more that you'll have to learn in order to manage it effectively (see Chapter 5 for more about community management).

Put a "There" There

It's never appealing to enter a chat room or click on a message board topic and find it lifeless and empty. It can make a community *appear* to be underpopulated and poorly managed even if it's not. Coming upon a small number of lively, active areas, on the other hand, makes it seem as though the community is well managed and thriving

This is one of the key reasons to start with a few focused gathering places (or even just one). That way, even when your community is small, these places can still be lively and active. As your community grows, you can always add new places as needed.

For example, those ten initial conferences on the WELL revolved around general topics like cars, books, music, telecommunications, and politics. Eventually, participants discovered other members who shared a more focused interest, so they asked the staff to create new conferences and volunteered to host them. In this fashion, the Books conference spawned Science Fiction and Noir; the Music conference spawned Jazz and Classical; and the Grateful Dead conference spawned Grateful Dead Tapes and Literature.

It's also during the early days, when the community members can be in direct contact with the staff and/or founders, that the community will find its core audience and develop a coherent identity. During the first year of the WELL's existence, it amassed a few hundred subscribers, and around forty conferences. People ran into each other in multiple conferences and could have direct email contact with the support staff. And Well members could—and did—comment vociferously on the policies, rules and guidelines that were emerging out of necessity.

Listen to Your Members

As we discussed in Chapter 1, running a Web community is an ongoing balancing act between the vision of the leaders and the needs of the members. It's crucial to integrate the ideas, desires and opinions of your members into your site as it grows. If your members can see how their input is shaping the site, they'll develop a sense of ownership and be more likely to take an active role in the community.

To understand what your members *truly* want and need, however, you must pay attention to what they do, as well as what they say. As anyone who has ever done market research or user testing knows, people are notoriously inaccurate at self-reporting. That's why it's important to collect, and pay attention to, two different kinds of member feedback:

○ **CONVERSATIONAL FEEDBACK,** including email, message boards, chat sessions, surveys, and interviews

○ **BEHAVIORAL FEEDBACK,** including page hits, time spent on site, message board and chat statistics, and responses to direct marketing

What They Say

Email is the simplest way to get conversational feedback. You can provide email links on your site, in your community newsletter, and in any other messages that go out regularly to your members. Make sure that it's clear to members that you welcome their comments, and let them know where to send different kinds of messages (such as complaints about technical problems, a wish list for new features, and requests for new gathering places or topics).

Message Boards are another way to solicit member feedback. You can set up specific topics for discussing new features or suggesting changes and additions to the site. If possible, encourage the community staff to post to these topics regularly, so that the members know the topic is hosted and the community staff is listening to their opinions. (It's frustrating for a community member than to express an opinion and then be ignored by the people who run the community.)

Surveys, polls, interviews and focus groups can be particularly useful during the planning phase for a major site expansion. For example, when eBay was preparing to revamp their interface and add several new areas to their site, the staff ran focus groups in three different cities to make sure they understood what their members were looking for and what kept them coming back to the site.

When you're setting up your feedback loops, be sure to let your members know what kind of response they can expect from the community staff. Maybe you can't answer every email message, but do intend to read them all—that's fine, just make sure that you say so up front. The same goes for message boards: let the participants know what kind of response and staff participation they can expect. When you conduct surveys or polls, post a summary of responses where members can read them. Completing the loop in this way will encourage your members to keep sending you their opinions and let them know that someone is listening.

What They Do

The kinds of member behavior you keep track of will depend on the capabilities of your platform, the goals of your community, and the needs of your advertisers, sponsors, or owners. Standard things to measure include:

- **IMPRESSIONS:** the number of unique visitors who viewed a particular page or graphic

- **TIME SPENT ON SITE:** the average amount of time that visitors spent logged into particular areas of your community

- **TRAFFIC:** the number of posts to various topics within a message board

- **ATTENDANCE:** the number of attendees at a chat event

Some message board software automatically generates posting statistics for all the active topics, and some chat software can do the same. Some software packages allow you to write scripts to obtain this information from the database, while others may not provide these capabilities at all. The ability to get this kind of information is definitely something to consider when you're choosing your communications tools.

Web communities that are advertising-based often need to keep track of impressions (and other related statistics) for their advertisers. But you can use these kinds of statistics to shape your community as well. For example, if you're experimenting with different ways of running your chat events, as CNN has done, you may want to know how many people attended them and how long they stayed. Statistics about your traffic can also help you identify your community's hot topics, which you may want to highlight on your front page.

Plan for Controlled Growth

An important part of your job as a community builder is to encourage members to add their creativity and input to the community setting. This is a key strategy for developing loyalty: when a member creates something that others can see and interact with, whether a personal home page or a post to a message board, his or her connection to the community is strengthened and desire to return increases.

But you need to decide how much freedom to give members to create new content and gathering places. Unrestricted contributions often lead to a site overwhelmed by low-quality material—while setting up a gathering place, for instance, can be easy and fun, keeping it lively and interesting is another matter entirely. Similarly, new members will often want create their own gathering places before they've gotten a clear sense of the community and before they've looked to see if a similar place already exists. On the other hand, you don't want to make your restrictions too tight, because then they'll make it harder for your members to develop a sense of ownership.

Building Codes

What you want to do is create appropriate hurdles for member contributions, particularly those that extend the public space within your community. What's appropriate, of course, depends on the community. For example, both AncientSites and Yahoo Clubs offer members the ability to create and run their own "clubs" (gathering places that include a message board and a chat room), but each sets different hurdles for club creation. At Yahoo Clubs, the purpose is simply to let people start their own gathering places, so the barrier is set very low: any member can create a club, public or private, at any time. In contrast, AncientSites is a themed community with a very specific purpose (creating an immersive and entertaining environment for history buffs). Here, the barrier is set higher: it requires five individuals to start a club, and their application must be reviewed and approved by AncientSites management.

These club creation policies lead to very different results. There are fewer clubs at AncientSites, but the ones that exist tend to be focused and well-managed. Yahoo Clubs, on the other hand, is growing rapidly, with clubs that run the gamut from large to small and orderly to chaotic, and many that appear to have been abandoned altogether.

It's up to you to figure out the restrictions that best meet the needs of your members and support the kind of community you're trying to create. There are several different ways to approach the issue.

SOLICIT SUGGESTIONS, BUT MAKE THE DECISION YOURSELF.

Like all aspects of community building, adding new subdivisions involves balancing the judgement of your staff with the desires of your members. If your goal is to create an orderly and focused environment, you'll want to keep your members from creating their own gathering places, but you can ask them what new areas they'd like to see, through a message board topic or a specific email address. The community staff can then respond to these suggestions at their discretion by creating and managing new areas, possibly with volunteer support.

For example, AncientSites launched with five cities: Rome, Athens, Babylon, Machu Picchu, and New York. As their population grew, the founders actively solicited member input through message boards, chats, and email about which cities to add. After many debates, they decided to launch two new cities, Egypt and Tara, based largely on member requests. They also considered adding Jerusalem (it received even more requests), but decided against it because of the administrative headaches that such an inherently controversial City would likely entail.

You can also get help from your members when creating subdivisions of existing areas. When eBay began to grow rapidly, for instance, the designers found that they needed to create subcategories within the top-level categories they'd initially defined. They quickly realized that their members knew much more about how to subdivide topics like Dolls, Stamps, and Pottery than they did, so they enlisted a group of avid collectors from each area to help them define appropriate subcategories.

LET YOUR MEMBERS EARN BUILDING RIGHTS

This can mean different things in different communities, but the basic idea is to use some measure of community participation (e.g., weeks since signup, hours spent in the community, pages or objects created, willingness to undergo host training) as a prerequisite for creating new gathering places. For example, to build a house in Ultima Online, a user must first earn money in the game, purchase land and a deed, and only then build a house. This policy prevents newbies from creating houses willy-nilly, before they've figured out if they really want to be part of the Ultima Online community.

The Clubs policy at AncientSites is another example of this idea. Brand-new members can create their own "domus," which is similar to a home page, and include a private message board for visitors to leave messages. But it takes a month's membership to earn the right to create a club—and even then, there are the restrictions described earlier.

Most chat communities, including IRC (described above), offer the option of opening a chat room that only lasts as long as it's occupied, along with the ability to create rooms that are public or private. This policy is intended to avoid clutter while still allowing members to freely create and host their own gathering places. You could even combine this approach with allowing members to earn the right to create persistent gathering places through their efforts and devotion. For example, at HearMe, any member can create an ephemeral chat room quickly and easily, but only community leaders can reserve a room name permanently.

You may find that different policies evolve as your community grows: many communities start off with restrictive policies on member-created gathering places and over time develop programs that allow members to create and host their own areas. No matter which policy you adopt, though, be sure to create a process for pruning topics and areas that have fallen into disuse.

How Your Members Get to Know Each Other

Now you've created gathering places and made sure people can find them, but you can't abandon them to their own devices. Like the host of a party making introductions, you need to find out something about your guests and communicate it to the group. The next chapter outlines the roles that people play in an online community and how you can keep track of and acknowledge them.

CHAPTER THREE

PROFILES:
Getting to Know Your Members

Whether you belong to a club, a clique, or a company, you need some way to establish your identity and develop your reputation within the group. In the physical world, people meet and interact in person; on the Web, sensory information is limited, so each community member's identity must be explicitly constructed, maintained, and verified.

To recreate this missing social context, you'll want to develop unique, persistent and evolving profiles for your community members. These profiles will help you build trust, foster relationships, and create a rich and meaningful social infrastructure within which your community can flourish.

In this Chapter

Why Profiles?

At a party full of strangers, how do you decide whom to talk to? You might start by checking out what people look like, how they're dressed, and the way they talk, gesture, and move. Perhaps you wander around and eavesdrop on a few conversations. Or maybe the host will introduce you to people with similar interests. At a convention, you can glance at people's badges to learn their names and affiliations. And if you're at a particularly cutting-edge convention, your electronic badge might start to flash when someone with similar interests comes into range.

Entering an new Web community can feel like walking into a party full of strangers: there may be a lot going on, but it's not clear how to jump in. Just as there are different ways to meet people at a party, there are a variety of ways to get to know people in a Web community. Most people start by checking out a community's gathering places (as discussed in Chapter 2).

But once they find a place that interests them, how do they find out more about the community members they encounter? Who do they talk to, and what do they talk about? People may come to your community for the content, but they'll stay for the relationships—and your job is to help your members establish and develop those relationships.

Provide Context

That's where member profiles come in. A profile is a collection of information that says something about who a person is in the context of your community. Profiles can reflect both what your members say about themselves—name, age, gender, mailing address, interests—and also what they do within your community—post messages, play games, make purchases, and customize their interface. (See sidebar, "Three Types of Profiles.")

Three Types of Profiles

Among Web community-builders, the term "member profile" is used in different ways. For someone in business development, a profile often refers to the entire collection of information about each member, while a community manager might use the term to describe what they see when they click on someone's name in a chat room or message board.

To avoid confusion, it's important to differentiate between the data that's tracked and stored about each member, and the different ways that this data can be viewed within your community. There are three common ways to view this data.

- THE SYSTEM PROFILE. This is what you, the community builder, are tracking and storing about your members. It can include information about each member's account, activities, preferences, and participation history. It may also include tracking information, such as a member's viewing habits, and purchase history. (In most cases, this profile includes the information in the other two types of profiles.)

- THE PERSONAL PROFILE. This is what the member can see about him- or herself. This includes member name and password, and personal data, preferences, and account information. Some of the information may be visible to others, some only to that member.

- THE PUBLIC PROFILE. This is what others can see about each member. Depending on the community, the public profile may include some personal data—such as an email address and favorite movies—and also information about that member's participation history, such as awards, accomplishments, contributions, affiliations, reputation, and length of membership.

Depending on the context, the term "member profile" can refer to any of these views. For example, when marketing folks talk about a member's "profile," they're usually referring to the system profile , and when a member refers to someone's "profile," it's usually the public profile. To avoid confusion, I'll be using the more specific terms throughout this book.

Many Web communities feature profiles that are not much more than souped-up name tags—simple, straightforward and static. An AOL profile, for example, displays a few basic facts about a person, including name, location, marital status, and hobbies (Figure 3.1). Even these basic forms-based profiles are useful, though, because they allow AOL members to find out more about the people they meet online and make it easy to search for like-minded members in the member directory (Figure 3.2).

FIGURE 3.1
AOL Member Profile
Clicking on a name in an AOL chat room reveals background information that the member has chosen to share with others. From the profile for Scott Kim, we can see that he's interested in math, calligraphy and puzzles.

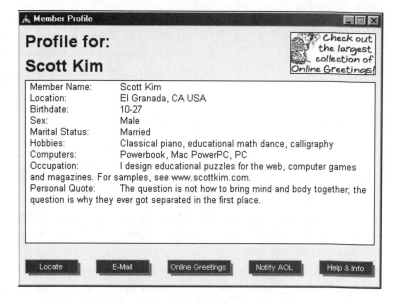

FIGURE 3.2
AOL Member Directory
A searchable member directory lets you look for people with particular characteristics. Here, we're searching for people who are interested in calligraphy and live in California—and many names come up, including Scott Kim's.

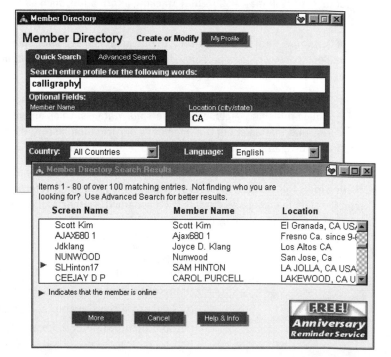

But profiles also have the potential to be much more dynamic and offer an ongoing insight into a member's online identity. For example, a Builder Buzz profile (Figure 3.3) shows a member's last ten posts, which gives a quick overview of how that person participates in the community. An eBay feedback profile (Figure 3.4) shows what other people have to say about doing business with that person. And an Ultima Online profile (Figure 3.5) offers a vivid visual portrait that communicates a member's profession in the game, current level of skill, and history of attacking innocent newcomers—information that can help you decide whether to ask that person for help, or run in the opposite direction. Such dynamic profiles are more than just a badge; they're an evolving record of each member's actions within the system.

FIGURE 3.3
buzz.builder.com
Each profile at Builder Buzz, a site dedicated to sharing information about building Web sites, contains a member's name, tag line, and favorite URLs, which offer a glimpse into the member's interests. Recent posts show the level of participation.

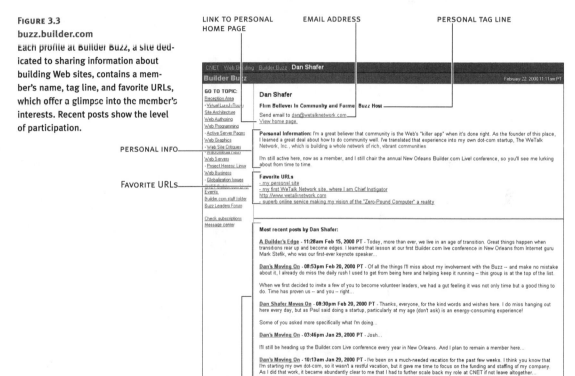

LINK TO PERSONAL HOME PAGE

EMAIL ADDRESS

PERSONAL TAG LINE

PERSONAL INFO

FAVORITE URLs

RECENT POSTS

FIGURE 3.4
eBay: Building Trust Between Members
eBay allows its members to rate each other's trustworthiness (see sidebar for details). Here, we see the seller's "About Me" page, which is her public profile. This kind of "hybrid" profile integrates free-form HTML with system-specific information like the member's feedback scores and current auctions

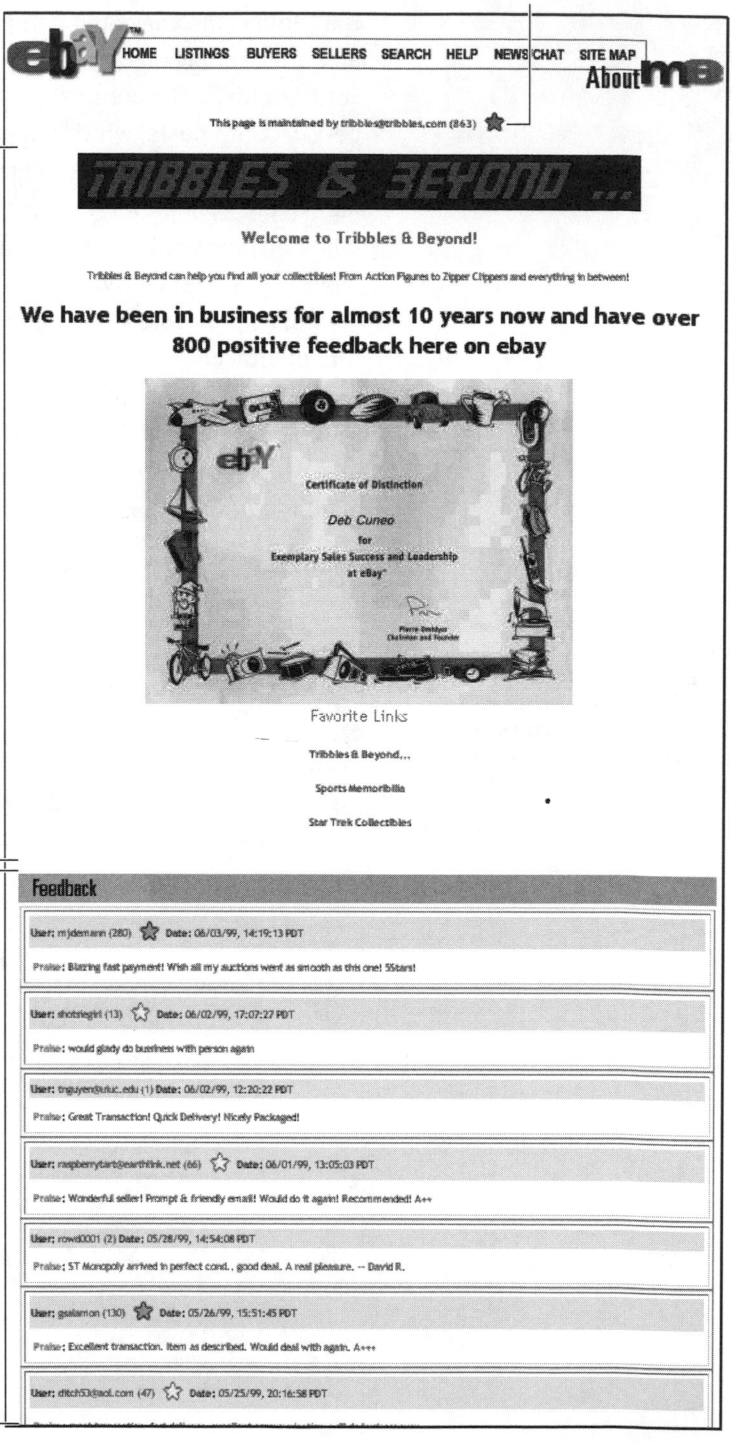

MEMBER'S NAME AND FEEDBACK SCORE

FREE-FORM HTML

RECENT FEEDBACK

Figure 3.5
Member Profiles at Ultima Online
In Ultima Online, each member's profile
is a multi-faceted and ever-evolving view
into their online persona. Here, we see a
closeup of Sosostris, whose clothes, skill
levels, and knapsack contents tell us that
this character is a sophisticated player in
the game.

Showcase Your Members

One of the first things a visitor to your community will want to
know is what kind of people hang out there. They can get a sense
of this by looking at the profiles of members they encounter in a
message board or chat room, or by browsing through the profiles
in your member directory.

But you can use profiles to showcase your members without
waiting for visitors to find them. For example, NetNoir highlights
a different member every day on its home page, which makes it
clear that NetNoir is a place for African Americans (particularly
black singles) to meet (Figure 3.6). And AncientSites devotes
much of its home page to members who have recently won a contest, updated their personal information, or posted to the message boards (Figure 3.7). Along with the People Panel (which
lists all the members currently logged on), this approach lets
everyone (including the members) know that the Citizens of

AncientSites are one of the major attractions. It also provides a snapshot of what the community considers valuable—which helps attract people who share those values.

FIGURE 3.6
MEMBER PROFILES AT NETNOIR
Here, we see an image and quote from a NetNoir profile featured on the home page. Clicking on the image brings up the member's entire profile, along with a form that lets you search the member database for other people to meet.

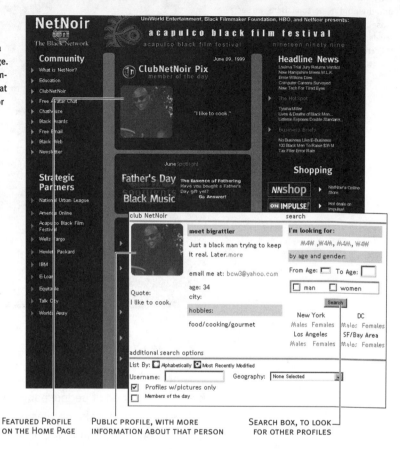

FEATURED PROFILE   PUBLIC PROFILE, WITH MORE   SEARCH BOX, TO LOOK
ON THE HOME PAGE   INFORMATION ABOUT THAT PERSON   FOR OTHER PROFILES

Build Trust

Because online identity is fluid and changeable, you can never be absolutely sure who you're dealing with—this makes it tough to hold someone accountable for their actions. Without accountability, you can't build trust, which is the foundation of any robust and healthy community. You don't need to trust someone to enjoy chatting with them at a party or challenging them to a Quake game, but if you're going to become a member of a support group or an online investment club, you'll want to know something about the people that you're dealing with. It's one thing to find out you just lost a game to an eleven-year-old kid, and quite another to discover that the self-professed psychiatrist who's been leading your online support group for incest survivors is actually a convicted child molester.

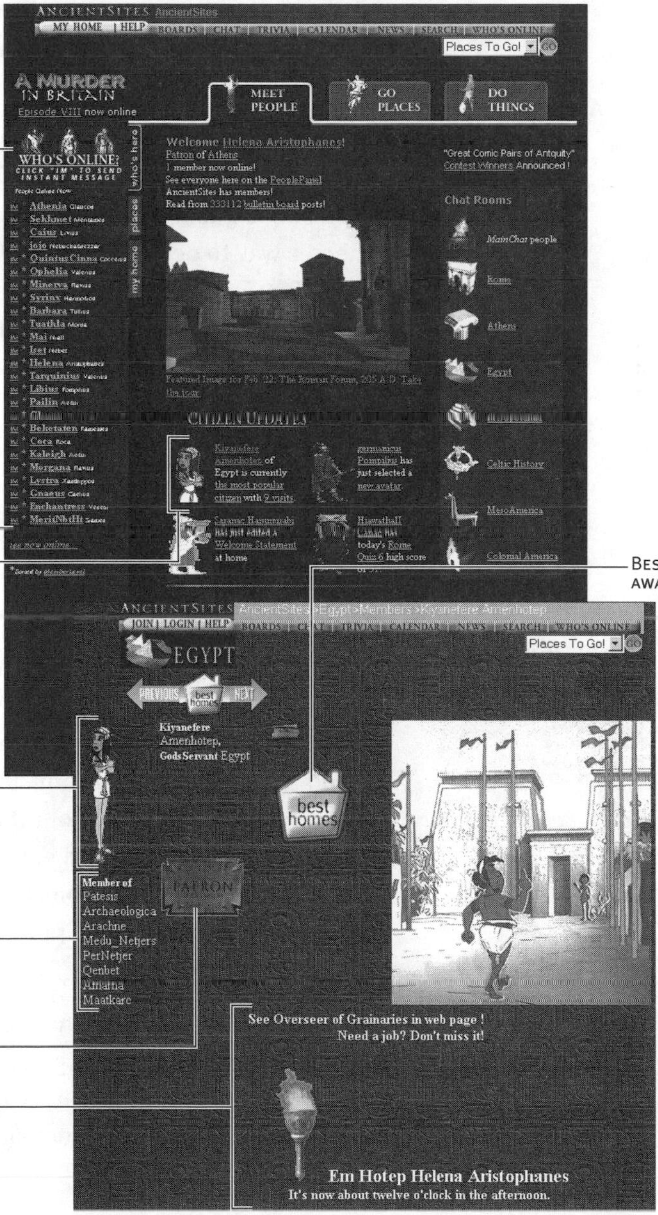

Figure 3.7
www.ancientsites.com
The home page of AncientSites (upper image) shows who's currently online, and highlights recently active members using statistical tracking. Here, we see the personal profile of Kiyanefere Amenhotep (lower image), whose "domicile" was visited most frequently that day.

WHO'S ONLINE

TODAY'S MOST VISITED HOME SITE

BEST HOMES AWARD

2D AVATAR

LIST OF GROUPS MEMBER BELONGS TO

MEMBERSHIP LEVEL

FREEFORM HTML

They Trust Each Other

Whether you're building a permanent fantasy world or a community that's more closely tied in with "real life," profiles will help foster trusting relationships between your members by providing context and promoting accountability. People need to know that the John Smith they meet one day in your community will be the same John Smith that they encounter on a subsequent visit. And in some communities, people will also want to know something about the reputation of the person they're dealing with.

In a public trading community like eBay, for example, people need a way to decide who's trustworthy enough to trade with. The eBay Feedback Forum allows members to rate their experiences with particular buyers and sellers (see Figure 3.4). As part of their public profile, members accumulate a feedback history, or reputation, that's visible to everyone within the community. Although not every Web community needs (or should have) a reputation system like eBay's, the trust it engenders is vital to a site that involves money changing hands.

They Trust You

Don't overlook the value of trust in the relationship between you and your members, either. As your members become more involved in your community, they'll naturally be revealing more about themselves. To feel comfortable with this process, they need to believe that the community owners won't exploit their personal information without their consent. This applies to something as simple as an email address and becomes even more important when a community is handling sensitive personal data like credit card numbers, medical records, and sexual preference data.

In response to growing concerns about privacy, most Web communities now post their privacy policies, (see Chapter 6) which reveal what information will be collected and how it will be used and shared. A privacy statement is a good start, but it means nothing without actions to back it up. To build trusting relationships with your members, you'll need to earn their trust by keeping the promises you make. For example, Amazon.com built one of the most trusted brands in cyberspace by not only delivering books on time, but also by communicating its privacy policy in clear language and allowing members to view and control their account information easily (Figure 3.8). This kind of reliability will help you earn the trust of your members, no matter what kind of information is stored in your profiles.

FIGURE 3.8
ACCOUNT MAINTENANCE AT AMAZON.COM
www.amazon.com
Amazon.Com has build a trusted brand in part by having a straightforward and well-organized account maintenance area (upper image that makes it easy for members to view and edit the information in their accounts. Amazon also supplements its Privacy Policy with a Bill of Rights (lower image), which hlets Amazon members know what they can expect from the service.

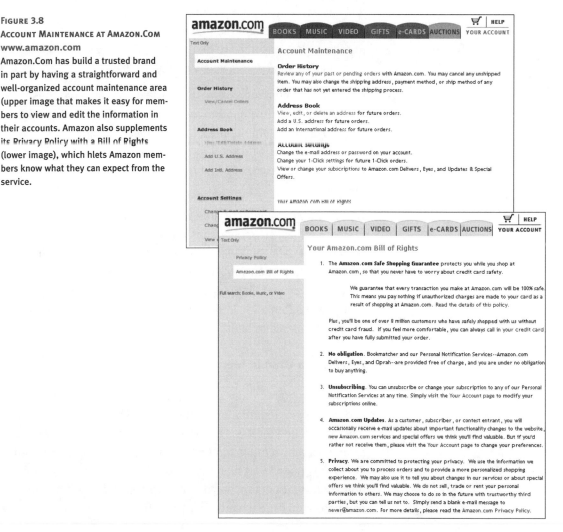

Your Member Database

To accomplish the goals we've outlined so far—providing context, showcasing your members, and building trust—you'll need to set up and maintain a member database. This is where you'll store the data that you collect and track for each of your members—the system profile described earlier (see sidebar).

What goes into your system profiles? For starters, everything that you ask your members to tell you about themselves, such as their real names, contact information, gender, birth date, and interests (if they choose to share them). This kind of data is basically static, although it may need to be updated when someone moves, gets married, or acquires a new hobby.

Because communities evolve, it's crucial to set up a database system that's flexible enough to grow along with your changing needs. For most communities, this will mean using a relational database, such as Oracle (www.oracle.com), Microsoft SQL server (www.microsoft.com/SQL), or MySQL (www.mysql.com)on the low end.

Try to figure out ahead of time what you'll want to store in your system profiles, so you can design your database accordingly. Decide what data you'll want to collect from each member directly, and what information you'll want to track. You won't have all the answers when you first launch your community, but it's always easier to fit information into a flexible database structure than to change the structure later.

Establish a Unique Identity

The starting point of any system profile is to establish a unique and permanent identity for each member. That means that each member's name (or ID) is associated with only that person, for as long as they remain a member of the community. This identifier is the "hook" that allows you to collect and store information about that person, so you need to record at least a name and password for each member when they join.

Beyond that, the information you ask for when setting up an account depends on the nature of your community. The most common piece of information required is a valid email address, which can be tested by sending a temporary password to that address. The member must log in using this temporary password in order to gain access to the system, and then the password can be customized (Figure 3.9).

```
From: slashdot@slashdot.org
To: amyjo@naima.com
Cc:
X-Mailer: Perl Mail::Sender Version 0.6.7 Jan Krynicky
<Jenda@Krynicky.cz> Czech Republic
Subject: Slashdot user password for amyjo
Date: Thu, 24 Jun 1999 23:48:08 -0700 (PDT)
X-Rcpt-To: amyjo@naima.com

The user account 'amyjo' on http://slashdot.org has this email
associated with it.  A web user from 205.149.176.32 has
just requested that  password be sent.  It is 'H3SbgxTX'.
You can change it after you login at http://slashdot.org/users.pl

If you didn't ask for this, don't get your panties all in a knot.
You are seeing this message, not "them".  So if you can't be
trusted with your own password, we might have an issue, otherwise,
you can just disregard this message.


--Rob "CmdrTaco" Malda
  malda@slashdot.org
```

Tell Me Everything

Be careful not to require too much information at the time of registration. Not only does make your community more difficult to enter, but it can cause the potential member to wonder what the community will be doing with all the information. Even if you explain why you need the information, someone who's about to join a Web community has no way of knowing (other than word of mouth) that the privacy policies will be honored. In short, your community may become more forbidding than inviting.

On the other hand, if you make it too easy to join a community, people are more likely to join casually and then fail to participate, although many Web communities are more interested in increasing their membership numbers than in attracting a focused group of participants. You'll have to look at what you really want from potential members. For most Web communities, though, the advantages of minimizing the amount of required information from new members outweigh the disadvantages.

Universal Recognition

Ideally, each member's ID will be recognized by all your communications tools, such as message boards, chat rooms, and buddy lists, so your members can log in once and then move freely about the system. For example, when a person first joins AOL, he or she chooses a unique member name and password (Figure 3.10). From then on, whenever that person enters a chat room, posts to a message board, builds a home page, or sends an instant message to a friend, it's with that member name.

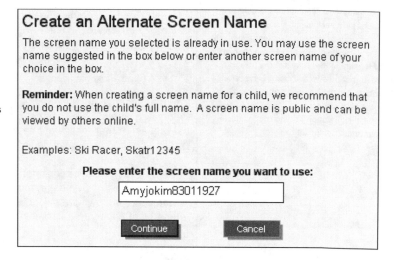

For this kind of universal recognition to work, your communication tools need to be integrated with your member database. This will be relatively straightforward if you're building your own communications tools, or using third-party tools that can talk to a relational database. Although database integration is becoming increasingly common, many communications tools still use a proprietary record-keeping scheme, which makes it more difficult (and sometimes impossible) for members to "log in once, participate everywhere" as your community grows. Make sure you consider this issue carefully while you're choosing your communications tools (as discussed in Chapter 2).

Design Evolving Profiles

Your system profiles will be even more valuable—to both you and your members—if they also contain an evolving record of each member's accomplishments, contributions, and interests. You may not know ahead of time exactly what information you want, because you'll probably introduce new features and programs as your community grows. For example, you may not need a volunteer hosting program (described in Chapter 5) when you launch, but if you introduce one later, you'll need to know which members are participating in that program. Or you may create a "Member of the Week" award, and then want to keep track of which members received that honor.

What Do You Want to Know?

When you're deciding what information to track, start with some basic elements that are common to most communities:

○ Length of membership (such as the date joined, elapsed time since joining, or the number of hours logged on the system)

○ Official role(s) within the community (such as host, leader, sysop, mentor, elected official)

○ Membership in community subgroups (guilds, clubs, task forces, interest groups)

○ Contest and awards won (such as page of the week, leader of the month, tournament champion)

Beyond that, you should track information that reflects the purpose of your community and offers your members relevant context about each other. In a competitive gaming community like Heat, for instance, where bragging rights are the primary social currency, it's useful to track and display information about skill level, game ratings, and tournament results (Figure 3.11). In a conversation and investment community like Motley Fool, where the quality of someone's opinions is important, it's useful to know who is respected and admired within the community (Figure 3.12).

FIGURE 3.11
HEAT MEMBER PROFILES
www.heat.net
The public profiles on Heat offer lots of social context, including a member's favorite games, current rankings, and any awards and trophies won. By looking at his "trophy case," we can see that he's been a member of Heat for at least a year and that he plays a variety of roles on the system. We can also see that he's rated on the Quake ladder and has hot links to many different games. Obviously, this is a longtime member who has been very active.

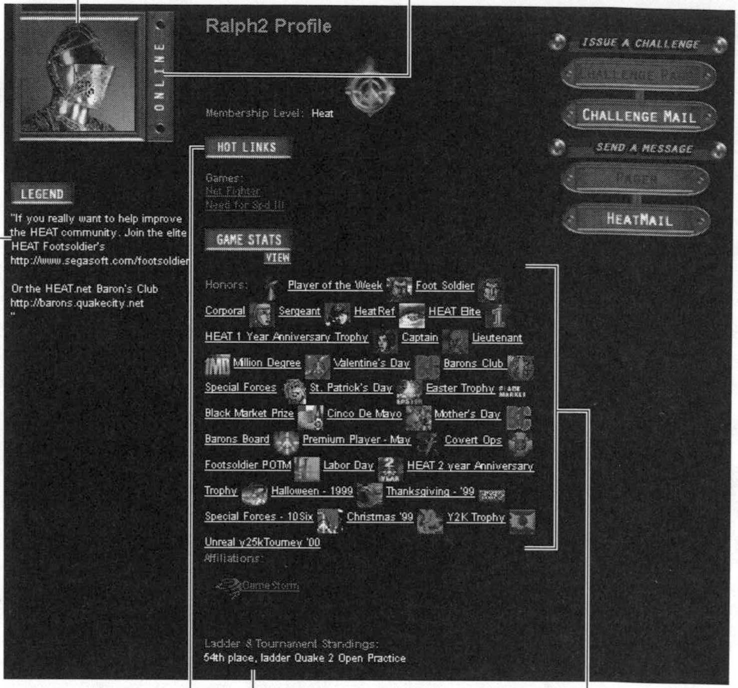

IMAGE SELECTED FROM A PRE-CREATED SET

CURRENTLY ONLINE

PERSONAL QUOTE

LINKS TO THIS PLAYER'S FAVORITE GAMES

CURRENT STANDING IN AN ONGOING QUAKE TOURNAMENT

THE TROPHY CASE

So you have system profiles that contain everything you know about your members—what they told you when they joined, and what you've learned by tracking their participation. But remember, there are two other versions of these profiles to consider: personal (the information your members can see about themselves) and public (what they can see about each other). And information added to those profiles can be fed back into your system profiles, making them more useful to you. The rest of this chapter describes how personal and public profiles function in a community, from the point of view of both the members and the managers.

FIGURE 3.12
THE MOTLEY FOOL:
MEMBER PROFILES IN CONTEXT
www.fool.com

Public profiles at The Motley Fool include a rich collection of information, including the member's posting activity , investing style , favorite stocks and outside interests . From his profile, we can see that TMPBogey Is a longtime member who's deeply involved in the community. He works for the Fool (you can tell because of the TMF prefix, and the email address), he's been around since 1997, and he's posted quite a few messages. He's also "loved" by 183 other fools,which is a good indicator of his involvement and status within the community.

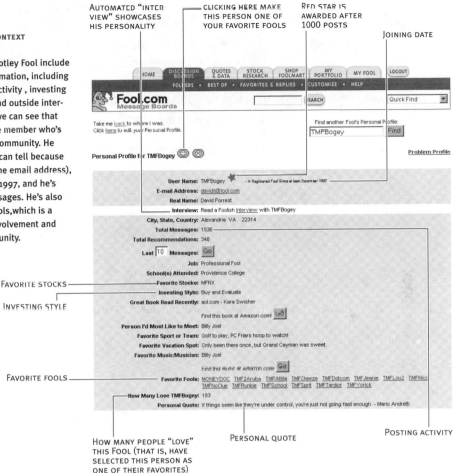

AUTOMATED "INTERVIEW" SHOWCASES HIS PERSONALITY

CLICKING HERE MAKE THIS PERSON ONE OF YOUR FAVORITE FOOLS

RED STAR IS AWARDED AFTER 1000 POSTS

JOINING DATE

FAVORITE STOCKS

INVESTING STYLE

FAVORITE FOOLS

HOW MANY PEOPLE "LOVE" THIS FOOL (THAT IS, HAVE SELECTED THIS PERSON AS ONE OF THEIR FAVORITES)

PERSONAL QUOTE

POSTING ACTIVITY

Getting Personal

Using system profiles, you can personalize each member's community experience, by offering only the content and activities they've expressed an interest in. Although this can reInforce a member's sense of belonging, and create a feeling of being "known," it's a *very* tricky line to walk: you want your members to feel welcomed without feeling like Big Brother is watching their every move. And although your members may enjoy seeing a limited portion of the site, this reduces the number of common experiences that are shared by all your members and removes the sense of serendipitous discovery that browsing through a site can offer. Nonetheless, when used with discretion, there is much to be gained from delivering personalized or customized services to your members.

Targeted Ads and Opportunities

Web communities often depend on advertising and/or sponsorship for some portion of their revenue stream, and there are many ways to use profile information to improve your advertising strategy. For starters, you can compile aggregate information about your members to attract advertisers and sponsors whose products might appeal to your members. At the Motley Fool web site, for example, there's a section for potential advertisers that includes demographic and interest data about the Fool's audience (Figure 3.13).

Targeting ads to a large group is something that most media companies already do. But your system profiles can also allow you to move beyond this familiar model to reach particular subgroups of your community. For example, one of iVillage's advertising partners offered a service that would only be of interest to parents who live in California. So iVillage inserted a small text ad into only the California edition of their parent-oriented newsletters.

Personal Start Pages

An increasingly common feature in Web communities is the "personal start page." To create this page, the member fills out a form, checking off items that they're interested in. From these choices, a page is generated that provides a customized view of the content and activities offered within the community. For example, the Motley Fool offers "My Fool," (my.fool.com) which allows members to track stocks, read articles of interest, and see at a glance whether there's anything new to read on their favorite message boards.

FIGURE 3.13
DEMOGRAPHIC DATA AT THE MOTLEY FOOL
www.fool.com/Media/
FoolishInterests.htm
This graph shows the demographic makeup of Motley Fool members. The data was obtained through registration and member surveys and is used to lure specific advertisers to the site. This stategy is good for both advertisers and members; ads that match the members' interests are less annoying and more likely to generate results.

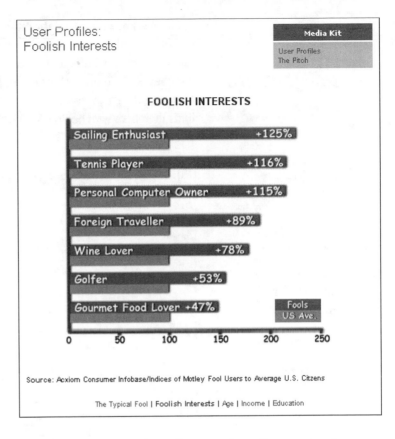

In a large community that offers a variety of content and services, a personalized interface can help members use services more efficiently (as explained in detail in Chapter 4). It can also promote loyalty, because a member that has gone to the trouble of customizing the interface is more likely to stick around. The choices members make in creating their pages tell you still more about their interests, which you can use to alert them to content or activities they'd probably enjoy. For example, because I follow Amazon's message board and stock price, I'd probably welcome an invitation to an online interview with Jeff Bezos, the founder and CEO of Amazon.

Suggestions and Recommendations

Someone who knows you is often able to recommend things you might enjoy. You can do this in your community by using a technique known as "collaborative filtering," which is makes use of the collective knowledge in your member database. Amazon.com uses this technique to recommend books to their members, based on each person's purchase history (Figure 3.14). As you purchase more books, the collaborative filtering algorithm finds members with buying habits similar to yours and calls your attention to other books they've purchased.

FIGURE 3.14
INSTANT RECOMMENDATIONS AT AMAZON.COM
Once particularly nice feature of Amazon's account management system is the ability for members to view their complete order histories (upper image). This information also reveals which data Amazon uses to generate its Instant Recommendations (lower image), suggestions of books, movies and music based on a member's previous purchases. Amazon doesn't make this connection explicitly, but the fact that you can easily see your purchase history and check on or change the status of your current orders adds to members' overall feeling of control over their data.

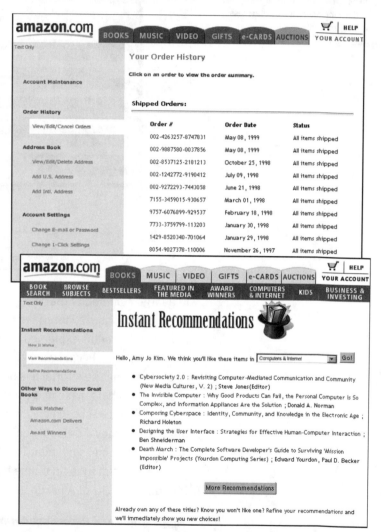

Creating a Persona

On the Web, you usually can't see what people look like or what cars they drive; everyone has the opportunity to create an online identity from scratch. When someone joins a Web community, chooses a member name, and fills out a registration form, they've just taken the first steps in constructing a fresh new personal identity. From that point onward, their identity will be shaped by these choices, along with their words, deeds, and creations.

Building Blocks of Personal Identity

An online identity can be built of many different pieces: someone's name, lifestyle, appearance, and group affiliation all help determine who that person chooses to be on the Web. Your members will control their identity by viewing and editing their personal profiles, and their ability to construct personae will depend on the power and flexibility of the tools you provide and the choices you make in setting up those tools.

What's in a Name?

The most basic aspect of online identity is a member's name, which shapes the initial impression that he or she will make. Some people are most comfortable being themselves and prefer to use their real names (or some variation). Others choose names that express a role, profession, or hobby—JorysMom, for example, or InvestorGuy. Some people are looking for attention and choose provocative names like SexyChick or HardBody. Others express their fantasies by adopting the names of fictional characters, such as CaptainPicard, BigBird, or Hercules.

In a large, general-purpose community like AOL, GeoCities, or Talk City, it's important to allow members to choose all different kinds of names, because they're engaging in different kinds of activities. In a smaller, more focused community, it makes sense to introduce some suggestions or restrictions about names, to reinforce the community's overall purpose and tone. For example, the signup process for AncientSites sets a playful and escapist tone by asking potential members to choose a fantasy name that's *not* their own (Figure 3.15). Applicants are also asked to choose a city to "live" in, and a family name that's associated with that city. Thus, even if I disregard their suggestion and call myself "Amy" during the signup process, my family name will still reinforce the theme of the community.

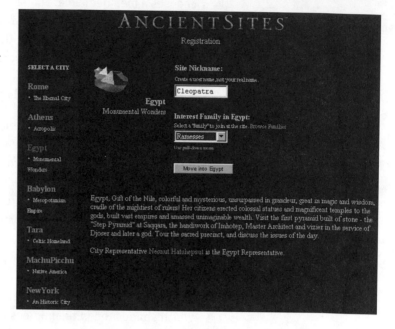

This is also one possible way to deal with a vexing problem that plagues any large, successful Web community: how to implement unique member names when there are thousands or even millions of members. The larger the community, the more likely it will be that desirable names will already be taken, and no one really wants to be known as FoxyLady30583 or ModemMan22581. A first-name, last-name scheme like AncientSites' makes it less likely a name will be taken, and obliges each member to affiliate with a community subgroup from the moment of registration.

You may want to reserve certain letter sequences to designate specific roles. On Talk City, for instance, members cannot create names that include the letters "CCC" or "TCC," because these sequences are used to identity Talk City community leaders. We'll delve more deeply into this issue in the next section, and also in Chapters 4 and 5.

Whatever kinds of names you let your members choose, you'll need to make sure that their choices don't violate your content standards (if you have them—see Chapter 6). Some Web communities, such as AOL, automatically pre-screen member names against a list of prohibited words, and simply inform the applicant that the requested name is not available. Other communities rely on member complaints to tell them when a name is offensive, or even screen the names individually if the community is small enough.

Multiple Identities

Some Web communities permit their members to develop multiple identities—known as aliases—for each account. Aliases can be used by a single individual or by several different people. On AOL, for example, each account can have up to five aliases, each of which is associated with a distinct member name, password, and database profile. An AOL member might use these aliases to "role play" several different personas, or a family could use these aliases to share a single account.

Alternate personae are also common in MUDs and online gaming environments, where pretending to be someone else is an integral part of the experience. For example, in the fantasy environment of Ultima Online, each member can create and develop to five characters at a time within a given virtual world.

Other online communities, such as the WELL, do not permit multiple aliases per account, and require that members reveal their real names. Both approaches are valid; you just need to adopt a policy that's appropriate for the style of your community.

Just the Facts

An important part of creating a persona is having the opportunity to tell other people something about yourself. To facilitate this, many Web communities let their members create or edit their public profiles and thereby control how they are perceived by others within the community.

Ideally, the public profiles in your community will provide enough information to help people decide who they want to communicate with. Your first hurdle, though, is to get your members to fill out their profiles. Some communities—including Yahoo, the WELL, and AncientSites—automatically create a public profile for each registered member with the information that's collected when they first establish their account. This means that every member has a profile, but if you didn't ask for much information at signup, the profiles will be sketchy.

On the Web, full disclosure is good business

A different approach—used by AOL, Talk City, and the Motley Fool—is to give each member the option to create a public profile once they've established their account. So even though some members won't have a profile, the profiles that exist will tend to be higher quality and more complete, because the member consciously created it.

Structuring a Profile

If you're using the services of a community aggregator (see Chapter 2), or relying on communications software that doesn't provide profiles, you won't have much control over the form and content of your members' personal profiles. But if your system is flexible enough to allow you to structure the profiles yourself, you can tailor them to fit the purpose of your community and the needs of your audience.

Some basic guidelines to keep in mind:

○ **ASK QUESTIONS THAT REINFORCE YOUR COMMUNITY'S PURPOSE.**
Your member profiles are expressions of your community's identity, so make sure that the questions you ask are consistent with your purpose. Some of the information in your profiles, such as name, location, and hobbies, may be straightforward and common to many communities. But if you have the freedom to craft your

own profiles, you can differentiate yourself by asking questions that reflect your members' interests. For example, in addition to investment-oriented questions, the Motley Fool personal profile includes an optional "interview" that reinforces the irreverent and humorous personality of the Fool, while offering a deeper glimpse into a member's attitudes and interests.

o **EXPLAIN WHY YOU'RE COLLECTING INFORMATION.** On the Web, full disclosure is good business. Your members should always know why you're asking for personal information and what you're planning to do with it. It's best to address this issue briefly and clearly whenever you're asking your members for information, even if it's covered in your privacy policy and/or your terms of service. Also, be sure to let your members know which information they provide will be private and which will be public.

o **ENCOURAGE MEMBERS TO SPECIFY A PERSONAL TAG LINE.** A simple yet effective element to include in a member profile is the personal quote or tag line. This feature can be a quick way to get a feeling for someone's point of view and outlook on life, like reading the slogan on someone's T-shirt. At Builder Buzz, for example, each member's profile contains a quote, which is appended to their name whenever they post (see Figure 3.3). This is a built-in feature of Web Crossing (a message board tool discussed in Chapter 2). The WELL also allows members to attach a personal quote or phrase whenever they post and to change it at will, which results in a more dynamic use of this feature.

o **ALLOW PART OF THE PROFILE TO CONTAIN FREE-FORM INPUT.** The best profiles are a mix of structured information and free-form expressiveness. In addition to your forms-based information, you can include a text box where members can type in their bio, their welcome message, or whatever is appropriate for your community. You'll usually get better results if you label this box and give members a suggestion for what to type in.

Picture This

Text-based personal profiles are good—and necessary for a searchable member directory—but you may also want to include images to help your members express their identity in a more immediate way. There are a number of different ways to incorporate images into personal profiles. The right approach for your community will depends on the needs and sophistication of your members and the technical constraints of your system.

Leverage the flexibility of HTML

If you allow your members to include free-form HTML in their profiles, they'll be able to link to any image they want. Although this approach gives your members lots of flexibility, it also means that you don't have control over the images they include, and you may have to expend extra energy to make sure the images don't violate your content standards.

Another approach is to include a link to a member's personal Web page, as Yahoo and Talk City do. If the Web pages aren't stored on your site, you're not responsible for their content—although you'll still want to post a disclaimer to this effect.

The most extreme version of this approach is to eschew personal profiles altogether and let your members display their identity by creating Web pages, which is essentially what GeoCities does. Although this approach gives members maximum flexibility, it loses the advantage of structured personal profiles, including the ability to generate information about that member's participation in the community (something we'll discuss further in the next section).

An intriguing "hybrid" approach is to start members off with a template, and then allow them to switch to free-form HTML, which can optionally include custom tags that incorporate system-generated data. The "About Me" pages at eBay (see Figure 3.4) are one example of this approach.

OFFER A PRE-CREATED PORTRAIT

Another option is to provide a collection of portraits for your members to choose from. Because you control which portraits are allowed, you can introduce thematic consistency and prevent violations of your content standards. For example, the personal profiles at Heat.Net use this scheme (see Figure 3.11), as do the profiles at Mplayer.com (www.mplayer.com).

The downside to this approach is that the portraits will not be unique—that is, two or more members can easily have the same portrait (unless you provide enough for everybody). In this situation, the portraits are acting as more of an expression of interest and attitude than a unique identifier.

If you choose this route, you should definitely plan on increasing the number of portraits available over time—perhaps by holding contests for members to add their own portraits, a strategy both Heat and Mplayer have used with great success. You can also start people off with a pre-created portrait, but then allow your more experienced members to upload their own portraits, which is how AncientSites handles the issue.

PROVIDE AN AVATAR CONSTRUCTION KIT

If you're building a gaming or fantasy-oriented Web community, you may want to include an avatar construction kit as part of your personal profile system. For example, Ultima Online allows each member to choose the sex, skin color, hair color, and hairstyle of his or her character (Figure 3.16). Although this feature is highly engaging and fun, it requires a considerable amount of development effort. (An in-depth discussion of these issues is beyond the scope of this book.)

One thing to note is that an avatar construction kit doesn't have to be limited to a virtual world. It's entirely possible for a Web-based community—such as AncientSites—to include an avatar construction kit as part of its personal profile system, if that kind of expressiveness is a priority for the members.

FIGURE 3.16

FIGURE 3.16
CREATING A CHARACTER ON ULTIMA ONLINE
Before a new member can enter the fantasy world of Ultima Online, they must design the physical appearence of their character by choosing gender, skin color, hair color and style, and facial hair (upper image). The character can then start to participate in the bustling virtual world of Britannia, the fictional universe in which Ultima Online take place (lower image).

There's No Place Like Home

Besides choosing a name, listing their interests, and designing their visual identity, you can also let your members select a place to "live" within your community. If your community uses a geographic metaphor, this is a natural way to organize your profiles, and it has the bonus of providing contextual information about each member's interests. For example, AncientSites automatically displays each member's home city in their profiles (see Figure 3.7).

Even if your community is organized topically, it may be useful to encourage your members to affiliate themselves with one or more subcommunities, and to display these affiliations in their profiles. This turns your profiles into browseable, searchable categories, which make it easier for someone to locate people who share their interests. For example, a trading community like eBay could let members announce their favorite collecting categories in their personal profiles, and then create a member directory that included this information. This scheme would help people with shared interests find each other—for example, someone could search for all the doll enthusiasts who live in Chicago. It would also help eBay highlight members within an appropriate context—for example, to showcase a "Beanie Baby Collector of the Month" in the Toys area.

Just as someone can have multiple homes in the physical world, it's certainly possible for someone to have more than one "home" within a Web community. For example, a number of GeoCities members have multiple accounts because they want to create Web pages that address a variety of topics. Although this can sometimes be appropriate, it's usually best to start with a simple scheme and then consider opening up the multiple-home option at a later time—perhaps as an advanced feature for your most devoted members.

Keep Identity Current

The profiles that your members create can be one of your greatest assets—but only if they're accurate and up-to-date. If someone visits your community and comes across a number of incomplete member profiles, they'll be left with a negative impression. Another problem is that some of the contents of a profile (such as the last book read or last movie seen) may be out of date and not reflect an accurate current picture. While this doesn't pose a threat to the basic functioning of the community, outdated personal information decreases the value of the profiles and gives the community a stale air.

Fresh Profiles

Some rare individuals regularly update their profiles (or their personal home pages) to reflect their changing circumstances and interests. But most people need incentives and/or reminders to keep their profiles fresh and interesting. Here are some ideas for how to encourage members to create great profiles and keep them up-to-date:

- **SHOWCASE RECENTLY UPDATED PROFILES.** Everyone loves attention, and you can encourage your members to keep their profiles current by highlighting profiles that have been recently created or updated. For example, AncientSites uses part of the site's main pages (as shown in Figure 3.7) to highlight members who have recently edited some aspect of their profile. You could also simply feature a list of the names of people who recently created and edited their pages.

- **HIGHLIGHT THE HIGHEST-QUALITY PROFILES.** You can let your members know that profiles are important, and remind them to update their own, by highlighting the best profiles—by mentioning them in a monthly newsletter, for instance, as eBay does (Figure 3.17). You could also hold a "profile of the week" contest and solicit nominations from the members themselves. This strategy will reward members who put in the effort to create a high-quality profile, and will also inspire others by showing them great examples.

- **REMIND MEMBERS TO UPDATE THEIR PROFILES.** To help keep the profiles fresh, you could include an occasional reminder to update profiles in your regular email newsletter. If appropriate, you could also include an incentive (such as a discount coupon for your online store, if you have one).

FIGURE 3.17

eBay Life: Showcasing "About Me" pages
pages.ebay/com/community/life
One way to encourage members to create high-quality personal profiles is to showcase the best ones. eBay accomplishes this by devoting a section of its monthly newsletter, eBay Life, to outstanding profiles nominated by the members themselves.

June 1999

Here Are Some Of Your Favorite "About Me" Pages!

We asked you to nominate your favorite About Me pages, and we received some outstanding ones! Click on the links below to see some terrific, very unique About Me pages that your fellow eBay users created. We know you'll be amazed — we were!

http://cgi-new.ebay.com/aboutme/mrs.linda/

http://cgi-new.ebay.com/aboutme/milleneum/

http://cgi-new.ebay.com/aboutme/anna1770/

http://cgi-new.ebay.com/aboutme/yorkielove/

http://cgi-new.ebay.com/aboutme/charmar/

http://cgi-new.ebay.com/aboutme/gonejunkin/

http://cgi-new.ebay.com/aboutme/trynket/

http://cgi-new.ebay.com/aboutme/cottagecathy/

http://cgi-new.ebay.com/aboutme/schnobbly/

http://cgi-new.ebay.com/aboutme/lilnorm/

- Articles -

It's a Tie! A-1
Letter From the Editor A-3
New Paging Service B-1
Greatest eBay Find B-2
Has eBay Changed Your Life? B-3
Getting to Know Us B-4
About Me Showcase B-5
And The Winner Is... eBay! B-6
It's Happening in June C-1
Uncle Griff and Aunt Flossie C-2
We Need Your Help!!! C-3

Have you created your own About Me page yet? About Me pages are one of the best ways to show people who you are and what you're like. They're fun and easy to create. For more information on creating an About Me page, click here.

Do you know of a superb, interesting, fun About Me page that we could highlight in eBay Life? Email ebaylife@ebay.com and please be sure to include the address to the page (URL).

Updating the Account

Even if your system doesn't include personal profiles—or if your members choose not to fill them out—they'll still need to gain access to their accounts. Someone who moves, for example, will need to update their mailing address and phone number. If a member gets a new job, they may need to associate a different credit card with the account. And as their interests change, they'll want to alter their personalization settings.

To let your members view and update their accounts, you'll need to create Web pages that display information retrieved from the member database, and then save any changes back into that database. This is one of the most sensitive tasks that your members will perform, and one that's potentially subject to abuse—especially if you're storing information like credit card numbers. For this reason, you may want to take extra security measures when allowing members to update their accounts. For example, anyone who lets Amazon.com leave a cookie on their system can immediately see their personal recommendations when they visit the site, and even order a book with a single click—but to view or edit their account information, they'll have to log into the system.

Once particularly nice feature of Amazon's account management system is that it lets members see their complete order history with Amazon. Not only can they review their buying habits and check on the status of current orders, but they can see what data Amazon is using to calculate their Instant Recommendations (as shown in Figure 3.15).

Evolving a Social Identity

Now that we've looked at how a community member creates a personal identity, let's explore how you can strengthen your community by integrating your members' participation history— what they say, do, and contribute—into their public profiles. When you spot someone across the room at a crowded party, you can guess his age, see how she's dressed, watch his facial expressions, or notice how she's greeted by the host. In Web communities, these signals are largely unavailable, but you can compensate by offering features that allow your members to create an online persona, as described in the previous section.

Actions Speak Louder Than Words

That's a great start, but to really add contextual power to your profiles, it's important to track and display something about each member's participation history. After all, it's by actively participating— by talking, playing, building, shopping, selling, teaching, and competing—that your members will build their reputations, and bring their online identities to life.

How Long has This Been Going on?

In a community setting, perhaps the most basic contextual cue is how long someone's been a member. If someone posts an inflammatory comment to your message boards, for example, it helps to know whether it's a clueless newbie in need of guidance, or a cranky old-timer who likes to shake things up.

It's generally a good idea to disclose length of membership, there are a variety of ways to accomplish this. If your community is text-based, you could take a straightforward approach and display the joining date in each member's public profile, as does the Motley Fool (see Figure 3.12). In a skill-based community, such as a gaming system, you might choose instead to display the number of hours logged, or even the number of times someone has logged in.

In a richer graphical environment, you have the opportunity to indicate member longevity in a more implicit and subtle way. In Ultima Online, for instance, longevity is not explicitly displayed—but a character's clothing turns out to be a good indicator of seniority and savvy. All newcomers arrive in the world dressed in drab, simple clothing; over time, they meet people, earn money, and purchase a wide range of clothing, accessories, weapons, and tools. Thus, a participant can identify the more experienced players by the sophistication of their outfits and the quality of their paraphernalia (see Figure 4.17).

I Post, Therefore I Am

In addition to knowing how long someone's been around, it's helpful to know how active that person is in the community. This is especially important in text-based communities, where people's presence goes unnoticed until they participate in an active way—that is, someone who's reading a mailing list or a message board is essentially invisible until he or she posts something to the group. And even when a member is visible—such as when they enter a chat room, or show up on someone's buddy list—their impact and reputation is directly tied to their actions.

So how do you communicate a member's activity level? Focus on the central activities within the community, and then choose some aspect of them that's useful for other members to know about (and that your system lets you implement). In a community built around conversations, information about each member's posting contributions would be relevant, as in the Builder Buzz public profiles (see Figure 3.3). The Motley Fool profiles include a link to each member's last ten posts (see Figure 3.12). They also show the member's total number of posts, a list of "Favorite Fools", and how many other members have selected that person as one of their favorites. Though quite simple, these features (made possible by the Fool's own message board software) allow the public profiles at The Motley Fool to grow deeper and more interesting over time.

The Trophy Case

Everyone likes to have their contributions acknowledged, so you should establish programs that shine a spotlight on your members' outstanding contributions and accomplishments and give them lasting awards that they can display. For example, the Best Homes program at AncientSites acknowledges member-created Web sites that add substantial value to the community. The recipients of this award are listed in a special section of AncientSites and they can display a special icon on their pages or have them linked to the Best Homes Web ring. Such recognition brings more exposure for the sites, which is how AncientSites measures member success.

Awards and badges can be even more effective when they're inserted directly into a member's public profile by the system. For example, the profiles at Heat.Net (see Figure 3.11) include a "Trophy Case" section, where any awards the member has won are put on display. Heat uses trophies to acknowledge all kinds of accomplishments, including winning a tournament, earning a certain number of degrees (the currency at Heat, similar to frequent flyer miles), and helping out new members. Each member's actions are tracked by the system, and whenever they do certain things—such as joining the Heat Newbie Helper program, or wining a tournament—the member database is updated, and a new trophy appears in that member's profile.

Institutionalized Gossip

Reputation is a fundamental aspect of social identity; it helps people know how to interpret each other's words and actions and make decisions about who to trust. The strength of someone's reputation is tied to participation. A person who frequently voices an opinion will have a stronger reputation (for better or worse) than someone who tends to keep quiet.

In both offline and online communities, people develop reputations primarily through word of mouth. But you'll need a more explicit way to track and display reputation in communities where actions speak louder than words, where those actions are measurable, and where they're meaningful for decision-making. In a financial context, for instance, a borrower's credit rating is an aspect of reputation that's highly meaningful to a lender.

Similarly, in a gaming community, knowing if someone has a history of cheating (or stealing, or killing) can help you decide whether or not to avoid them, as can knowing their level of expertise. In Ultima Online, players acquire a reputation based on their actions. Players' reputations are automatically calculated by the gaming engine and displayed in their public profiles, and they reflect the context and moral implications of actions like fighting, stealing, killing, sharing, and begging. The more deeply the player participates in the game, the stronger their reputation grows, whether it's good or evil.

In a commerce-based community, knowing someone's trading history is an important criterion for a member contemplating a financial transaction. Were the goods delivered as advertised, and in a timely manner? Did the payer's check clear? On eBay, buyers and sellers start off with neutral, blank-slate reputations, which change as other members rate their interactions. Unlike Ultima Online, where the system does most of the calculating (with some input from the members), each person's eBay reputation is a cumulative summary of the positive, negative, or neutral marks that others assign to them. Because each positive or negative opinion adds or deducts one point, a high positive reputation score can only be achieved through great interactions with many different people.

In a conversation-oriented Web community, implementing an explicit reputation system is tricky, because reputation is highly subjective in social interactions. Someone who is annoying to one person could very well be entertaining to another. Unless there are specific, relevant actions to measure, a reputation system is usually not called for—it's better to rely on word of mouth.

One exception to that rule might be a community that's oriented towards providing advice or knowledge, such as the Motley Fool, which is focused on teaching people how to be better investors. The "Favorite Fool" feature mentioned above is a casual type of reputation system; the people who are known for giving the best advice—such as Tom and David Gardner, the cofounders—become the "best loved" members within the community (see Figure 3.12). This system also allows a member to give a "thumbs-up" or "thumbs-down" to particular posts, which could conceivably form the basis of a reputation system.

Clothes Make the Character

When you go see a play, a concert, or a sporting event, you can tell who the performers are by how they're dressed and where they are in relation to the audience. Some of these performers are "on stage"—acting, singing, or playing a game. But there are also "performers" who are not so obvious—the people who are taking tickets, selling concessions, and showing fans to their seats. These performers can be more difficult to spot, so they often wear special uniforms that designate their roles.

Any social situation that requires people to play a specific role is a type of performance, with costumes and uniforms that go along with it. For example, religious leaders wear special clothing while performing their duties, which identifies them as holding particular office—priest, shaman, bishop, or rabbi. And at a catered party, the staff is usually dressed in some kind of uniform that differentiates them from the invited guests. If the waiters are dressed alike, you can see their common affiliation—as you can with the colored bandanas of a street gang, the coordinated uniforms of sports teams, or the company T-shirts at an annual picnic.

Every Web community is a performance space of sorts—and in your community, you can use the virtual equivalent of uniforms to help your visitors and members know how to interact with the people they meet, and figure out whom to turn to for help. Ideally, these visual identifiers should appear in each member's public profile and as an integral part of their name or character. In practice, your ability to implement these markers depends on the capabilities of your community platform. For example, if you're using third-party message board software like Web Crossing or the services of a community aggregator such as AOL or Talk City, you'll be constrained by their capabilities. If, on the other hand, you're developing your own tools, you'll have much more freedom to integrate these ideas into your design plans.

Here are some guidelines for creating markers that express social roles:

○ **ACRONYMS.** A simple way to provide "virtual uniforms" is to use special letter sequences or acronyms in member names. Acronyms can be used to denote someone's role—at Talk City, hosts are identified with the acronym CCC (for City Conference Crew), which is enforced by the system. Acronyms can also be used to show group affiliation—such as at the Microsoft Gaming Zone, where members form close-knit clans, and then include a self-designated guild acronym in their member names.

○ **COLOR.** Another simple way to communicate someone's social role is with colored elements. AncientSites uses a system of colored asterisks, and in Ultima Online, each member's name is colored to correspond to their in-game reputation. Some systems use both acronyms and color; for example, in Talk City's EZTalk Pro interface, the hosts' names appear in red in addition to including the CCC acronym.

- ○ **ICONS.** Another way to designate a social role is by attaching icons to a member's name. For example, in the Mplayer gaming system, symbols that denote each member's gaming rank appear alongside their name in the chat rooms. And on eBay, colored stars appear next to each person's name that denote their "rank" in the reputation system (see Figure 3.18).

- ○ **AVATARS.** The richest form of identity expression can be achieved with avatars, 2D or 3D visual representations of a member's online identity. For example, Ultima Online offers a variety of clothing options, and members can customize their clothing using a wide range of colors. This allows groups of players to dress alike and differentiate themselves from other groups. UO Game Masters, who provide online support, have special clothing that is reserved for them.

If you do adopt special letter sequences, colors, or icons to indicate rank, be sure to post a key that explains these identifiers, so that members know what they stand for (**pages.ebay.com/ help/basics/g-stores.html**). See Figure 3.18.

FIGURE 3.18
EBAY: EVERYBODY IS A STAR
pages.ebay.com/help/myinfo/star-chart.html
These stars represent arbitrary "ranks" in the eBay feedback hierarchy, based on the number of positive and negative comments a member receives from others. Members can earn progressively higher ranks by being honest, reputable, and helpful. Their ranking accompanies their names everywhere on the site.

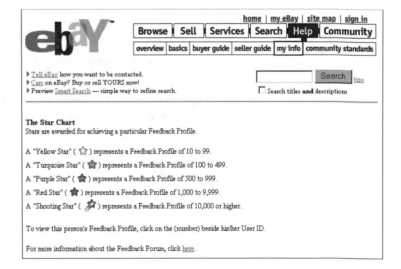

Role Playing

With a robust set of system profiles and an understanding of
the value of private and public profiles—and what elements go
into them—you'll be in good shape for supporting the changes
in your members' roles and identities as they spend time in your
community. The next chapter takes a closer look at the life cycle
of a community member, the different roles one might play over
time, and how you can benefit from them at each stage.

Character as Currency

Sometimes, an online "character" has value that transcends the boundaries of that community. For example,
members who have developed positive reputations on eBay sometimes link their feedback scores with their
own Web sites, or even with auctions on the sites of eBay's competitors. A positive eBay reputation means
something outside the context of eBay, which is quite a testament to the power of their reputation system.

Another example of "character out of context" are the Ultima Online and EverQuest auctions on eBay.
Players who have spent months, and even years, developing their characters and amassing wealth and
property are now selling their well-tended accounts to the highest bidder. Although many of these
accounts are being purchased for the real estate (houses and castles are hard to come by these days in
Britannia), some people are obtaining fully developed characters, and then playing those characters
within the game.

CHAPTER FOUR

ROLES:
From Newcomer to Old-Timer

All around the world, in all kinds of communities, you see the same timeless social roles in action. Newcomers arrive and must prove themselves before being fully accepted. Natural leaders emerge and take charge of running the show. And old-timers sit on the sidelines telling stories, performing rituals, and kvetching about how much things have changed. These familiar and universal roles are being played out right now in churches and bars, playgrounds and workplaces—and also in the mailing lists, newsgroups, chat rooms, and virtual worlds of cyberspace.

Each individual's role, however, changes over time. Shy visitors evolve into confident contributors; eager students become knowledgeable teachers; and novice game players become tournament champions. It's your job as a community builder to create an environment that fosters these basic social roles, while meeting the changing needs of your members as they become progressively more involved in community life.

In this Chapter

THE MEMBERSHIP LIFE CYCLE

WELCOME YOUR VISITORS

INSTRUCT YOUR NOVICES

REWARD YOUR REGULARS

EMPOWER YOUR LEADERS

HONOR YOUR ELDERS

The Membership Life Cycle

Imagine that you have just moved into a neighborhood. You peek into the café and peruse the bulletin board, in the neighborhood bar you eavesdrop on a man complaining about his boss, you visit the park and inquire about classes at the community center. It all feels strange and new, and you're relieved and grateful whenever someone helps you out.

Fast-forward twenty years: you're still living in the same neighborhood, but it certainly doesn't feel strange anymore. In church one Sunday, you strike up a conversation with a woman who's new in town and doesn't know a soul, but who recognized you from the café, where you were laughing with your friends. Almost without noticing it, you've become one of the community elders, someone other people look to for information and a sense of belonging.

These kinds of transitions get played out in every thriving community. Newcomers arrive, filled with curiosity and unanswered questions and eager for acceptance. Established citizens go about their business, attending meetings, exchanging gossip, and hanging out with their friends. Leaders emerge to welcome newcomers, resolve disputes, and keep the various systems running smoothly. And the old-timers kibitz—telling stories, sharing knowledge, and transmitting the local culture.

A Basic Lesson

Over the past decade, as I've helped clients build a wide variety of Web communities, I've noticed something fascinating: even when the platform and the purpose of these communities were radically different, the same basic social roles emerged again and again. And I watched my clients learn the same basic lesson about community roles over and over.

What's the lesson? In a nutshell, it's that communities are held together by a web of social roles, and you can help your community flourish by providing features and programs that support these roles.

Membership Life Cycle—Five Key Stages

These archetypal roles make up the Membership Life Cycle, which outlines the progressive stages of community involvement (Figure 4.1). This conceptual framework can help you design your platform, prioritize your feature set, and create the programs and policies that will shape your emerging culture.

FIGURE 4.1
THE MEMBERSHIP LIFE CYCLE
The five essential stages of community membership

The Membership Life Cycle outlines five successive stages of community involvement.

1. **VISITORS:** people without a persistent identity in the community.

2. **NOVICES:** new members who need to learn the ropes and be introduced into community life.

3. **REGULARS:** established members that are comfortably participating in community life.

4. **LEADERS:** volunteers, contractors, and staff that keep the community running

5. **ELDERS:** long-time regulars and leaders who share their knowledge, and pass along the culture.

To illustrate how the Life Cycle works, let's return to the neighborhood. When someone visits an attractive yet unfamiliar neighborhood, they're eager to explore the place, but not quite sure how things work. *Visitors* will arrive at your doorstep wondering where to go, what to see, and who to trust. Some will only visit once or twice—but others will return again and again and start to get involved in the local scene.

Some of the latter group will become new members, or *novices*. Novices are eager to fit in and make friends with the locals, but first they need to be welcomed properly and instructed about the prevailing customs.

Some novices will keep to themselves, but others will be drawn into community life and become fixtures on the scene. These *regulars* are the mainstays of a community; they keep the taverns and shops in business, and provide local color for everyone's entertainment.

Regulars who have the time and energy to take on more official roles will become community *leaders*. Leaders help newcomers get settled in, operate the shops and taverns, volunteer for charities and committees, and run for mayor—a thriving community has many leadership roles to offer.

Over time, some leaders will tire of their day-to-day activities and step down from their official roles. Because they're familiar with the history and inner workings of the community, they're now *elders*—respected sources of cultural knowledge and insider lore. Along with other long-time residents, they're the teachers and storytellers of the community, the people who give the place a sense of history, depth and soul.

Time Passes Quickly

At this point, you might be wondering: "Do I really need to be thinking about all these roles? I haven't even built my community yet; why should I worry about long-time members and respected elders?"

Time passes quickly on the Net. Social dynamics that take months and years to evolve in the physical world can emerge in a matter of days and weeks on the Web—especially when a community becomes hot. You set up a gathering place, and before you know it, you're faced with a contingent of regulars who think they own the place and are complaining loudly about the clueless newbies bumbling around and ruining their culture.

To make your community friendly for both newcomers and old-timers, think about these roles early on. Initial conditions matter; and the features, policies and programs that you put into in place at the start will profoundly shape how your community develops.

Welcome Your Visitors

Visitors will arrive in your community with different needs and expectations. Some may have heard about your community from a friend or read about it in a magazine, others might have stumbled across it in a search engine or clicked on a banner ad. Some are looking for information; others are looking for someone to talk to. Some will be searching for a particular item; others will want to explore all the depth and breadth that your community offers.

Create a Visitors Center

Although your visitors will find their way to your community by different paths, they'll all be unfamiliar with the local customs and have many unanswered questions. For a first-time visitor, a thriving Web community can seem confusing and overwhelming. To make your visitors feel comfortable, you want to provide a place where they can get their questions answered and learn more about the community.

You can accomplish these goals by creating a "Visitors Center" that helps visitors learn what they need to know and find what they're looking for. Don't get hung up on the name; this area might just as easily be called the "Welcome Wagon," or even "About Us." What's important is that newcomers can find this area easily, get the information they're seeking, and leave with a good sense of your community.

In a National Park, the Visitors Center is right up front, marked with big, obvious signs. Similarly, yours should be clearly visible from the front page of your site (or whatever page visitors are likely to go to). For example, the "New to eBay" link on eBay's home page leads to an area that gives an overview of eBay and answers the most common newbie questions (Figure 4.2).

FIGURE 4.2
pages.ebay.com/help/basics/
n-index.html
eBay provides a prominent button on its home page to lead new users to a page designed especially for them.

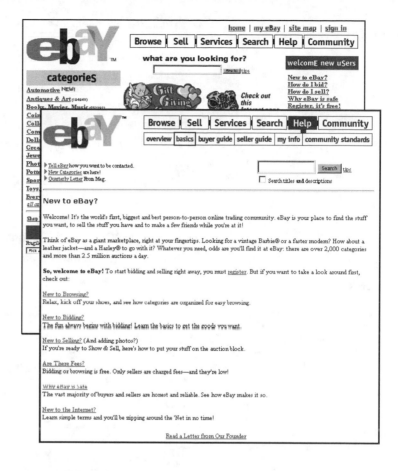

What's in a Visitors Center?

Once you've invited someone into your Visitors Center, what might they find there? Some or all of the following:

○ Frequently asked Questions and Press Releases

○ A guided tour

○ A letter from the founder

○ Membership requirements

○ A site map and a search function

○ Backgrounders and white papers

- Your mission statement and backstory

- An overview of features, with instructions for beginners

- Policies and guidelines for participating in the community

Which elements you include depends on the depth and breadth of your community, and on the types of visitors you're likely to see. If, for example, you're running a narrowly focused community for Open Source enthusiasts like Slashdot, your Visitors Center might consist of a brief welcome message and a single FAQ (Figure 4.3). By contrast, eBay's center includes an extensive collection of FAQs and instructions, appropriate for a community with broad appeal and a variety of features.

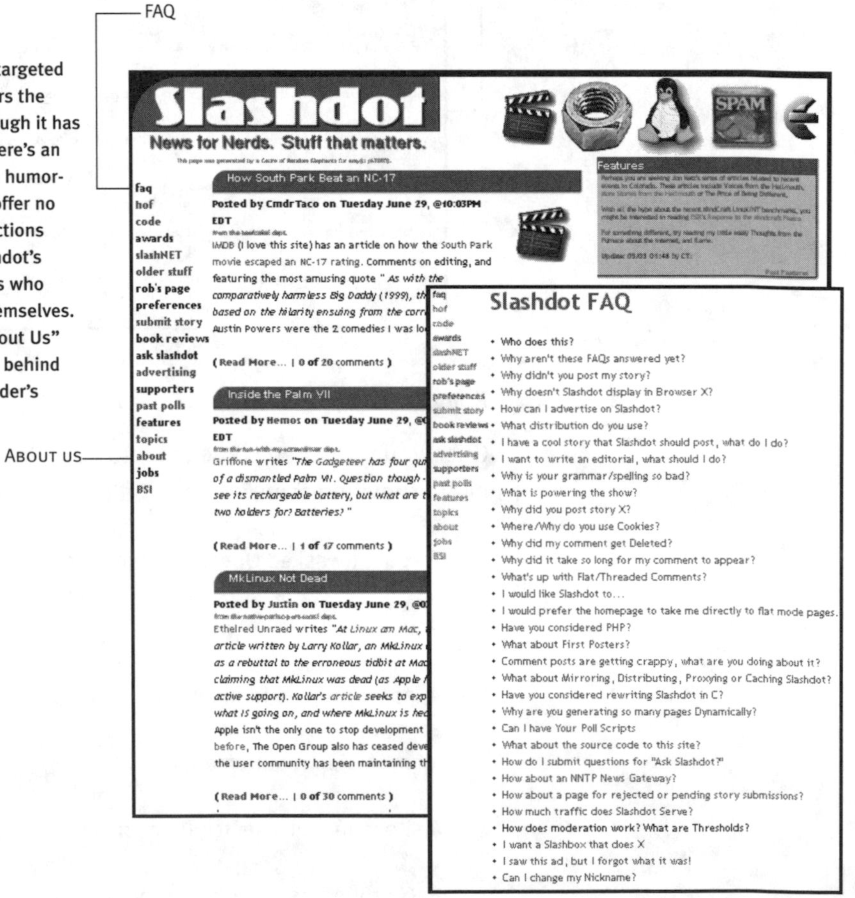

FIGURE 4.3
SLASHDOT FAQ
Slashdot ("News for Nerds"), targeted at Internet sophisticates, covers the Open Source movement. Although it has no "Visitors Center" per se, there's an ever-evolving FAQ, written in a humorous, no-nonsense tone. They offer no welcome message, and instructions are minimal, which suits Slashdot's audience of geeks and hackers who like to figure things out for themselves. Slashdot also includes an "About Us" page, which briefly lists who's behind the site, and a link to the founder's home page.

You've Got Questions? We've Got Answers.

Above all else, you need to make sure that your visitors get their questions answered quickly and effectively. You can initiate this process by creating a FAQ that answers the most common questions a newcomer might have. FAQs are inherently designed to evolve; you start with the most obvious questions and later add others that come up as your community grows.

In addition to FAQs, you may also want to include instructional information if your audience is new to the Net, or your community platform is especially complex. For example, eBay caters to a mainstream audience, and offers step-by-step instructions for using all the various tools and features. By contrast, Slashdot caters to geeks and hackers, who like to figure things out for themselves, so instructions are minimal.

If your visitors fall into distinct categories, you can streamline your Visitors Center by providing a separate area (and FAQ) for each group. For example, the "About Us" area of drkoop.com (www.drkoop.com/aboutus) (Figure 4.4) has special sections for consumers, advertisers, investors, and press. Each section answers questions for that particular type of visitor, so there's less extraneous content for everyone to wade through.

Branded!

Determine the qualities of your community that are most important for newcomers to understand at first glance and then express those qualities through images, language, and page layout. Your Visitors Center is a great place to express your brand; don't be afraid to make a strong statement and show some personality. If everybody likes what you're doing, you're probably not doing it right. For example, eBay has garnered criticism for its simple, almost childish graphics, but they give eBay a distinctive personality and communicate a friendly, down-home attitude.

FIGURE 4.4
DRKOOP.COM VISITORS CENTER
www.drkoop.com/aboutus
The "About Us" section of drkoop.com is divided into areas geared towards investors, consumers, advertisers, and the press. This section also features a picture and quote from Dr. Koop himself, who, as the elder of the site, conveys a sense of comfort and trustworthiness.

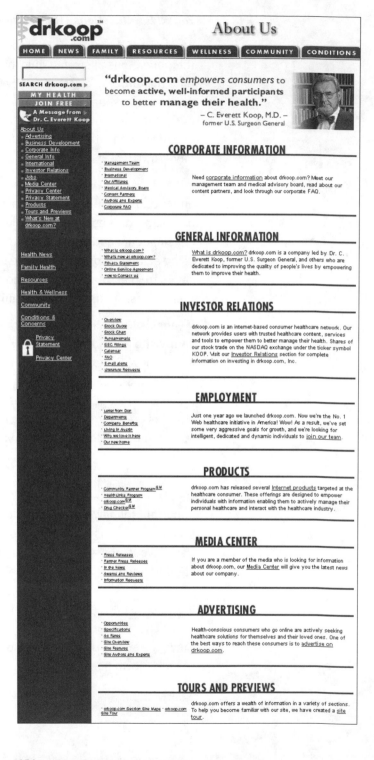

This is also a good place to tell your backstory—the history of how your community got started. (See Chapter 1 for more about backstories.) At iVillage MoneyLife, for example, the community backstory is combined with a welcome letter from the founder (Figure 4.5); the overall effect is personal and welcoming. And at Moms Online, the backstory is part of the "Help and Info" section, which includes links to many kinds of support materials (Figure 4.6).

FIGURE 4.5
iVILLAGE MONEYLIFE WELCOME LETTER
A button at the top of the MoneyLife home page leads visitors to a friendly welcoming letter and backstory from the founder. This page links to more introductory materials and includes a site map and search box.

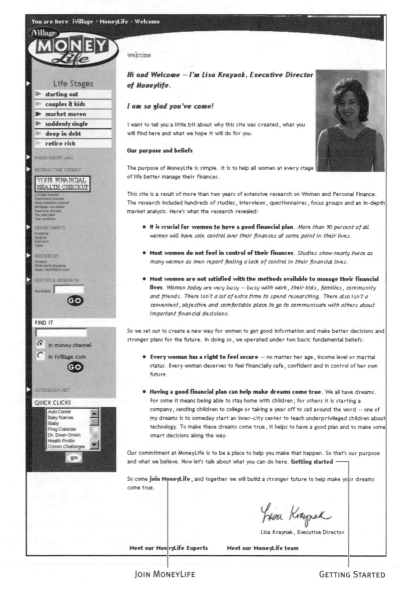

FIGURE 4.6
MOMS ONLINE—HELP & INFO
www.momsonline.com/info/

Moms Online doesn't have a visitors center as such, but it does include introductory information in a section called Help and Info. It would be even better to greet first-time visitors with a well-marked sign right on the home page.

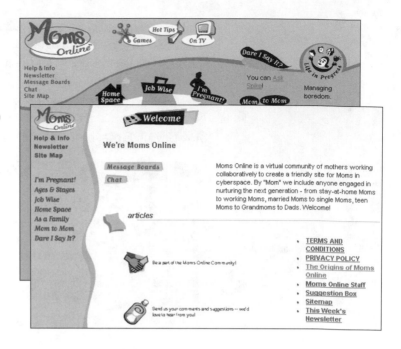

The Grand Tour

Visitors have different ways of exploring a new community (see sidebar, "Player Types"). Some like to jump in feet first and start exploring on their own. You can accommodate these "explorer" types by providing a site map and search box in your Visitors Center (as the eBay and iVillage visitor areas do).

Others will enjoy a guided tour as a quick and easy way to get an overview of the community. A tour is another great branding opportunity, so if you create one, make sure that the contents, organization and look leave a strong impression. Like most tours, the tour at Parent Soup consists of a series of Web pages (Figure 4.7). The graphics are simple and fun; the information is presented in manageable chunks; and it's always clear what to do next. The visitor is left with the impression that Parent Soup is a friendly, accessible, and helpful place.

This approach gives you the widest accessibility, which is important if your visitors might not have the latest and greatest technology. However, if you're addressing a more sophisticated audience—Web professionals, say, or hardcore gamers—you can create a more dynamic tour using a technology like Macromedia Flash (www.macromedia.com/flash). WebMD, for example, offered an animated Flash tour (Figure 4.8) that was fun, engaging, and appropriate for the wired doctors that WebMD is targeting.

FIGURE 4.7
PARENT SOUP GUIDED TOUR
www.parentsoup.com/tour/
Parent Soup's simple HTML-based tour offers a good overview of the site, using simple graphics and casual language to communicate a friendly, down-to-earth feeling that's consistent with the Parent Soup brand.

FIGURE 4.8
WEBMD TOUR
WebMD, geared toward health care professionals, used to offer a Flash-based tour that took visitors through the interface and explained the system.

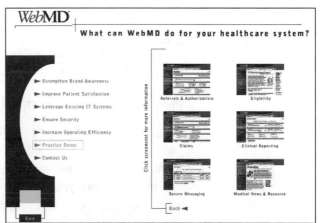

TIP ▶ *If you do create an enhanced tour, it's best to also offer the simpler alternative, so that no one is left out.*

What Can Visitors Do?

Like tourists, your visitors may want to get a taste of community life by hanging out with the locals. But because they don't have a persistent identity and are therefore unaccountable for their words and deeds, visitors clearly need to have different rights than members. Where exactly to draw the line is a tricky issue. What can visitors do? What *should* they be able to do? Can they:

- **PERUSE** the archives of a mailing list?

- **BROWSE** through a member directory?

- **ENGAGE** in (or eavesdrop on) a discussion or chat?

- **CHALLENGE** a local to a game of checkers?

- **START** their own private gathering place?

The larger and more diverse your community, the more you need safe, somewhat controlled places for your visitors to mingle. (We'll delve deeper into this issue in Chapter 6.) Visitors need guidelines: they need to know where they can go, what they can do, and what restrictions will be placed on them. To determine these guidelines, ask yourself the following questions.

WHAT CONTENT AND CONVERSATIONS CAN VISITORS READ?

Many commercial Web communities—including GeoCities, Third Age, eBay, and iVillage—allow visitors to read essentially all content on the site, including message board postings. The idea is to entice visitors by showing them conversations and activities they'd want to be part of. This approach works well for generating interest among a wide selection of people and maximizing the number of hits, which is great for an advertising-based site. However, some of your members won't want to discuss certain topics with visitors around. You can resolve this by offering members-only areas while allowing visitors into the more public spaces.

Other business models argue for limiting visitors' access to content and/or conversations. If your community is subscription-based—like the WELL and the Wall Street Journal Interactive (www.wsj.com)—it makes sense to limit visitors to a few areas designed to tantalize them into becoming members. You might also decide to limit access if you're providing technical support to existing customers and you want to integrate that process into your customer database.

CAN VISITORS PARTICIPATE IN CONVERSATIONS?

Letting a visitor jump into an ongoing conversation is a controversial issue. Many Web communities—including CNN and Salon—adopt a read-only policy for visitors, whereby they can 'listen in' on conversations but not participate themselves. This policy allows visitors to get a sense of the style of discourse and topics of interest but prevents them from disrupting the conversational flow.

Other Web communities—such as GeoCities and Talk City—allow visitors to choose a temporary screen name and immediately start posting in public chat rooms and on message boards without offering any further information. This approach helps visitors get engaged quickly and encourages people to freely try on different personas. Yet because visitors don't have a permanent identity, they can easily disrupt conversations without repercussions. Whether intentional or not, such disruptions can be quite harmful to community life and drive away your most valuable members. You'll probably only want to allow full participation from visitors if you have the resources to moderate the effects of uncontrolled access, and your community culture is strong enough to withstand occasional disruptions.

CAN VISITORS LEAVE THEIR MARK ON THE COMMUNITY?

One of the fundamental pleasures of the Internet is expressing yourself on a global soapbox. People love to see their words appear on a Web page, so it can be smart to let your visitors post a message in a public forum even if you're limiting their access otherwise. For example, your Visitors Center could include a guestbook i n which visitors can read other people's comments and add their own impressions (this has the added advantage of giving your feedback on your Visitors Center). Or you could solicit comments on a particularly provocative topic, as iVillage does in its "Dilemma of the Week" feature, where visitors can voice their opinions alongside the advice of an expert (Figure 4.9).

FIGURE 4.9

www.ivillage.com/relationships/ iVillage features a variety of interactive advice columns, including "Ask Mr. Answer Man" in the Relationships channel. Every week, this resident expert answers a member-submitted question, and visitors and members can post their opinions alongside his answer.

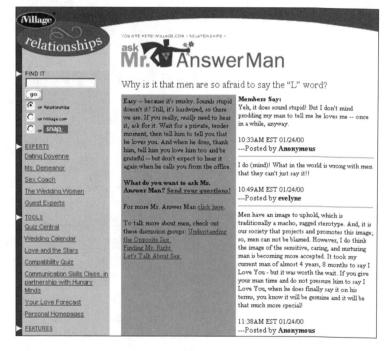

Is This Community For Me?

After they've sampled your community, some visitors will be motivated to become members, while others will depart for good. That's not necessarily a bad thing; after all, many tourists visit wonderful places once or twice and get everything they need.

Many community builders are overly fixated on moving people through the transition from visitor to member; increasing membership base is a key business goal and a common measure of success. But be careful—pushing too hard can backfire. People want to explore a place and understand the benefits of membership before signing up for something. They want to feel welcomed, not trapped with a used-car salesman who's a little too eager to close the deal. Don't waste your visitors' time with hollow sales pitches; it's waaaaay too easy for them to click away to somewhere else.

Membership Has Its Rewards

Information is the currency of the Net—and you'll get off on the right foot with your visitors by offering them clear information about the benefits and requirements of membership, rather than simply waving a big membership flag in their face.

In general, people join Web communities because there's some thing that they want to *do* that requires membership. If your community offers some tangible and valuable activity that people *know* they want, your job will be easier. Someone can wander endlessly through the vast collection of items for sale on eBay, for example—but to make a bid on that long-lost childhood toy, they'll have to become a member. People can browse through genealogy Web pages at GeoCities to their hearts' content—but to build their own, they'll have to become members.

Assuming that there really is some value to membership (which is not always the case), be sure to let your visitors know up front what that value is. You've got a great opportunity to start building trust here, so try to avoid raising expectations that exceed what you can deliver. If you're going to tell your visitors that your community is harassment-free, or that your service is up 24/7, you'd better deliver on that promise or you'll be building a shaky foundation. Amazon.com doesn't just lure visitors with a "100% safe shopping" experience, they also provide the policies, instructions and customer service to back that up. I've experienced this personally while shopping at Amazon, and my comfort level with them has grown because my experiences matched what I read on the site.

Getting off on the right foot with a new member can only make it easier to make them a valuable contributor to your community. Once you've managed to sign up a new member, your real work begins.

Player Types

In 1996, a longtime MUD developer named Richard Bartle wrote a paper called "Hearts, Clubs, Diamonds, Spades: Players Who Suit MUDs" (journal.tunymush.org/v1n1/bartle.html), in which he identified four different types of MUD players. The roles he identified are universal to Web communities and are worth understanding for any community builder:

- **ACHIEVERS** (a.k.a. Champions, Performers) care about being "the best" at something and enjoy showing off the tangible results of their success—whether it's a Heat tournament trophy, an Ultima Online professional title, or an eBay feedback score.

- **EXPLORERS** (a.k.a. Guides, Gurus) take pride in knowing everything there is to know about a system and enjoy being in situations where their expertise is sought after and admired.

- **SOCIALIZERS** (a.k.a. Hosts, Greeters) are interested in people and relationships; they take pride in their circle of contacts and enjoy being at the center of the social scene.

- **KILLERS** (a.k.a. Harassers, Dissidents, or Brats) get their kicks by dominating a situation, imposing themselves on others, or breaking the rules—perhaps by spamming a message board, using racial slurs in a chat room, or taunting and killing newbies in a multiplayer game.

In an online gaming environment, these player types are fairly easy to spot. These archetypal roles also emerge in non-gaming communities; for example, some WELL regulars habitually dominate (and derail) every conversation they're in, while others enjoy showing off their knowledge, and still others like to greet newcomers and make them feel welcome.

Knowing about these types can help you build a more robust and comprehensive Web community. For example, consider the design of your Visitors Center. Socializers will want to know where the conversations are, while explorers will want to explore the breadth of the system, and achievers will want to know how skill development is measured. To satisfy them all, you could include a pointer to the chat rooms or message boards, a site map and search box for the explorers, and a description of any contests or rating systems.

It's also useful to keep these player types in mind when you're designing member appreciation programs and creating leadership roles. For example, you could create special awards to acknowledge members who share their knowledge of the system, which would attract explorers.

A special note about killers, or brats: The Internet is overrun with people who are acting out their aggressions, and if your community is successful (and public), you'll inevitably attract some of these "problem children." You'll need to be prepared to recognize their behavior and not play into their need for attention and dominance. We'll look at some specific strategies for dealing with Brats in Chapter 6.

Instruct Your Novices

New members play a special role in the community, with needs that are fundamentally different from those of more experienced members. Novices need to learn what they can do, whom they can do it with, where they can do it, and how they're expected to behave. Your job is to engage your novices and educate them about community life, while protecting them from getting into too much trouble.

The Membership Ritual

You can do this by creating a "Membership Ritual" (Figure 4.10), which marks the transition from visitor to novice. This ritual will help you to welcome each new member into the "tribe" and teach them what they need to know to start participating.

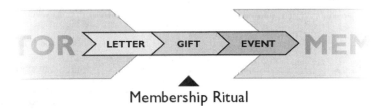

Membership Ritual

Now You're One of Us

Send your novices an email letter confirming their membership and telling them something about how the community works. At minimum, this email needs to confirm some mechanical basics, such as member name and password, and determine that the member has a valid email account. But it's also a great opportunity to reinforce your brand, and help novices get acclimated. For example, the Third Age welcome letter is written in a friendly and accessible tone (which is consistent with the Third Age brand), and it's filled with pointers to resources and activities that are geared to new members (Figure 4.11).

You want the letter to engage and inform your novices without overwhelming them with too much information. It's something your members will scan through and then tuck away for future reference. Be sure to include any links that they're likely to need during those first few weeks, such as gathering places, support areas, and guidelines that members are expected to follow (see Chapter 6).

FIGURE 4.11
THIRD AGE WELCOME LETTER
Third Age sends this friendly and helpful email to all new members. The letter is brief but includes useful links to a welcome page, a message board especially for them, and a class where they can learn the basics of participating in Third Age.

Welcome to the ThirdAge community!! My name is Chas and I'm the Third Age Community Forums Moderator. It's my job to make sure that you get happily settled into our community. Since you're new, you might have a lot of questions. We're here to answer them and to help you get comfortable in your new online neighborhood. Here are four important links for new members:

1) Our "Welcome!" page, especially for new members of Third Age:

<http://www.thirdage.com/community/welcome/index.html>

2) The "Introduce Yourselves, Newcomers" discussion: this is a great place to start. Read about other new members and post something about yourself.
<http://www.thirdage.com/cgi-bin/WebX?14@@.ee6b435>

3) The "Welcome Newcomers" chat room, where you can talk live to other Third Agers. Plus, every Wednesday at 5 PM (PST), we host an "Introduction to Third Age" class to answer any and all questions you might have.
<http://www.thirdage.com/chat>

4) Our Third Age Newsstand, where you can read about and sign up for our free email newsletters: the "Long Life Letter" and "Web Guide for Grown Ups."
<http://www.thirdage.com/newsletters/index.html>

5) Forget your password? Don't worry! We'll send it to you...
<http://www.thirdage.com/join/sendpw.html>

ALSO CHECK OUT THESE AREAS!

Third Age Free Email <http://www.thirdage.com/community/email/benefits.html>
Your own Third Age email, to get to know other Third Agers better!

Personal Portraits <http://www.thirdage.com/portraits>
Third Age's five-minute homepage.

Speak Out Poll <http://www.thirdage.com/polls/>
Vote and share your opinion on current issues.

Daily News <http://www.thirdage.com/news/>
Read about news geared specifically for Third Agers.

Again, welcome to ThirdAge.com. We're glad you've joined us, and we hope you make this your online community. I look forward to seeing you on the site!

-Chas
....

Charles Brown ThirdAge.com
Community Forums Moderator The Web...for GrownUps
chas@thirdage.com <http://www.thirdage.com/>

Whenever possible, your welcome letter should be signed by an established community leader—ideally, someone that can be contacted with follow-up questions. This will feel more personal than a letter signed with something anonymous like "Community Manager" or "All of Us at Community XXX." The Third Age welcome letter, for instance, is signed by Chas, the community forums moderator. You can actually send an email to Chas, and he'll respond.

Welcome to the Neighborhood

My family and I recently moved to a new and unfamiliar neighborhood, where we were greeted with home-baked goodies from the neighbors and a booklet of coupons from the local merchants. As I chatted with my cookie-bearing neighbors and browsed through coupons, I learned more about the community and started to feel like I belonged there.

Similarly, you can welcome your novices with a gift—perhaps a coupon for the community store or a free auction listing. Gift giving is a universal gesture of welcome, and it offers an ideal opportunity to educate your novices about some aspect of your community (such as the types of products offered in your store, or the pricing scheme for auctions). The type of gift you'll want to give depends on what's valued within your community. If your community has an internal economy—such as user points or virtual money—you could start your novices off with an initial stake framed as a gift.

Gifts are most effective when they come from a person rather than a corporation, so whenever possible, a gift should be given by (or at least signed by) a community leader. Ultima Online players begin with one hundred gold coins, which automatically appears in their knapsack when their character first enters the game. To leverage the power of gift giving, the game designers could have created characters to greet each novice and present him or her with one hundred gold coins. Same impact on the virtual economy; different emotional impact on the player.

Learning the Ropes

In addition to welcoming your novices, you want to educate them about community life and help them find their place in the social scene. It's intimidating to join a group of people who already know each other; and newcomers who enthusiastically jump into ongoing conversations may run into suspicion and hostility, especially if they violate social norms that they didn't even know existed.

Meeting and Greeting

You can help your novices become part of the community by creating special events and places where they can meet other members, learn the ropes, and ask questions without fear of ridicule. You can use message boards to host topics especially for newcomers. Some popular ones are:

- A **"TEST" TOPIC,** where newcomers can try out the mechanics of posting without getting in the way of ongoing conversations

- An **"ABOUT THIS CONFERENCE"** or **"CONFERENCE BUSINESS"** TOPIC, where basic conference rules are covered and questions can be asked and answered.

- An **"INTRODUCTIONS"** TOPIC, where new members are encouraged to introduce themselves to the group

These topics should be clearly marked, and the host should make sure that newcomers have a positive experience. On the WELL, for example, hosts usually acknowledge a newcomer's first post in the Introductions topic (Figure 4.12); other posters then follow the host's lead and welcome the newcomer, taking up any interesting thread started in that first post. This gives newcomers a safe and structured way to meet people and start to get involved in the conversation (see Chapter 5 for more about hosting).

```
TOPIC LIST                    everquest.ind
FORGET                  Introduce your characters here...
                 Topic #1, 75 responses, 0 new, Last post on Fri 01 Oct '99 at 05:12 PM
_____

everquest.ind 1: Introduce your characters here...
  [ ] #0 of 74: i'm confusing my heart dying with murderous rage (jet) Thu 08 Jul '99 (06:18 PM)

          What's your name, race, class, level,  server, all that good stuff.


everquest.ind 1: Introduce your characters here...
  [ ] #1 of 74: Jamais Cascio (cascio) Thu 08 Jul '99 (06:30 PM)

          Ookino
          Half-Elf Paladin of Qeynos
          3rd level, on the verge of 4th
          Povar server

          Terror of the Gnoll-Pups!!!


everquest.ind 1: Introduce your characters here...
  [ ] #2 of 74: Ronald Hayden (ron) Thu 08 Jul '99 (06:37 PM)

          Deadron
          Halfling Rogue of Rivervale
          6 1/2 level
          Povar server

          We shall see whether Rogues provide any value in the end!
```

If your community includes chat rooms, you can schedule live
events for your new members. The Third Age welcome letter we
looked at before includes an invitation to the weekly "Introduction to Third Age" chat, where new members can learn how to
use the basic interactive features of the site in a protected
social environment.

Practice Makes Perfect

If your community is a complex environment like a multiplayer
game, you may want to create a special practice space where
newcomers can test out features and practice their skills. For
example, Castle Infinity (the late, lamented multiplayer children's
game) offered a training track where new members could learn

the rules and mechanics of the game before being thrust into the action (Figure 4.13). Even in a more straightforward environment, you may want to offer Internet newcomers a safe place to practice their online skills, as third age does (Figure 4.14).

FIGURE 4.13
WELCOMING NEWCOMERS AT
CASTLE INFINITY
At Castle Infinity, visitors could choose to plunge right in, or go to the Training Track to learn the ropes (top image). The Training Track (middle image) put them through a series of exercises that taught the basics of how to interact within the system. When they were ready, new members could start interacting with other players in real time (bottom image).

FIGURE 4.14
www.thirdage.com/learning/
community/meet_online.html
The Third Age Learning Center offers a
variety of classes for Internet neophytes,
including this six-week course that helps
newbies learn how to socialize online,
and gives them a safe and friendly place
to practice their skills.

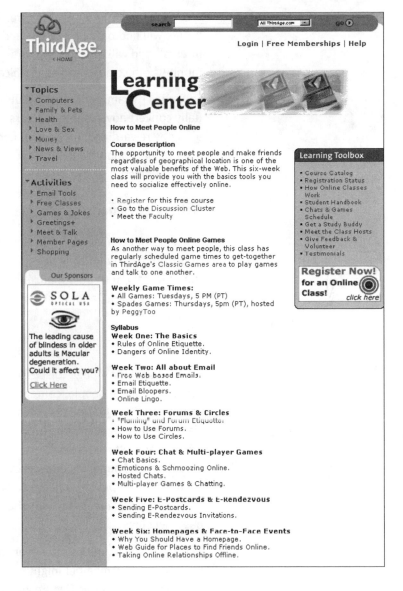

Reward Your Regulars

After mastering the basics, a new member is ready for the next
transition in the Membership Life Cycle: from novice to regular.
Just as some visitors will decline the opportunity to become

members, some new members won't stick around for long. But others will find particular areas and activities that spark their interest, and will become regulars—the lifeblood of your community, both socially and economically.

To grow a dynamic and successful community, you must continually convert novices into regulars. You can help this process along by rewarding members for continued involvement and by offering new opportunities to keep your members challenged and interested.

Getting Personal

Regulars have mastered your environment and explored the opportunities; what they need now are tools and features that allow them to personalize their interface, communicate with their friends, and quickly find who and what they're looking for.

Start Me Up

The personal Start page (discussed in Chapter 3) displays a filtered view of the people, content, and gathering places within a community. This feature becomes more valuable over time, especially for ongoing activities, such as discussion threads, gaming tournaments, stock trading, or auctions. For example, eBay's personal Start page, My eBay, shows an up-to-date snapshot of each member's buying, selling, and feedback ratings (Figure 4.15). The more a member uses the site, the more valuable this page becomes.

Many Web communities offer every member their own Start page; but a new member might not be ready to use it effectively. You should design this feature with your regulars in mind, and encourage them to take advantage of it. You could even offer an enhanced Start page as a reward to regulars who actively participate in your community.

FIGURE 4.15

MY EBAY: AUCTION MANAGEMENT FOR REGULARS

eBay's version of the personal Start page is called My eBay, where eBay members can create links to their favorite eBay areas, view their most recent feedback, and track their buying and selling activities. These features aren't very useful to a new member, but they're great for a serious eBay user— especially someone who's making their living off the site.

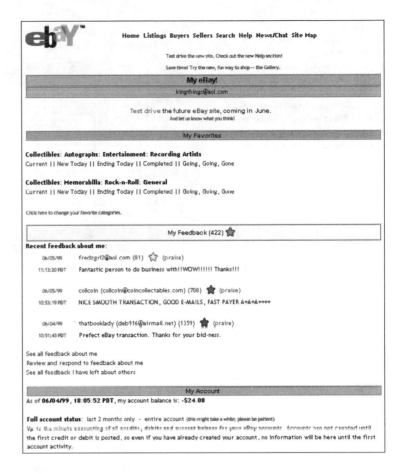

Me and My Buddies

Another feature whose usefulness grows over time is the community-specific buddy list, which allows a member to keep track of and instantly communicate with others who subscribe to the same service. Pioneered by AOL, they have been widely adopted by other online communities, such as Yahoo, Talk City, iVillage, and the Zone.

For a new member of a community, such a list is useless. But as your members become more involved, their buddy lists will grow, and they'll spend more of their online time socializing with their friends (Figure 4.16).

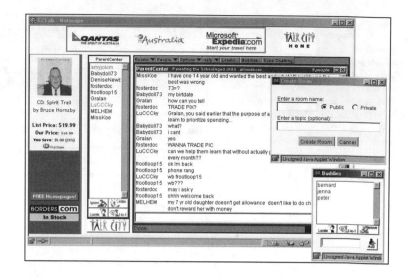

FIGURE 4.16

TALK CITY — BUDDY LIST AND PRIVATE ROOMS

Like many other Web communities, Talk City allows each member to create a community-specific buddy list and a private chat room where friends can hang out. These features become more useful as members develop a web of relationships within the community.

To incorporate this feature, you can license software from a tools company like PeopleLink (**www.peoplelink.com**) that offers buddy lists, or build your own proprietary list. Many community owners are attracted to the idea of a community-specific buddy list, because it reinforces the relationships people make within their community, and offers a unique branding and advertising opportunity. Although this approach can work for a large or highly immersive community, in practice, people often participate in more than one Web community, and want to keep track of their buddies all across the Net. If your members already subscribe to an Internet-wide buddy list such as ICQ (**www.icq.com**) or AOL Instant Messenger (**www.aol.com/aim**), they may find your community-specific buddy list too constraining.

For members, it would be ideal for all Web communities to somehow share the same underlying buddy list protocol, so that they could stay in contact with family, friends, and colleagues no matter what site they're logged into. A standard messaging protocol for buddy lists is a possibility for the future, but until it appears you should think carefully about who your users are and whether building a community-specific buddy list would really enhance their experience within your community. (See Chapter 6 for more on this issue.)

A Room of One's Own

Many Web communities offer private gathering places to all members, regardless of longevity. For example, any Yahoo member can create a private club that includes a chat room, a message board, a member roster, and broadcast mailing list, along with other group-oriented features. And any Talk City member can create a private chat room (see Figure 4.16).

As with the other personalization features, this is one that becomes more valuable as a member becomes more involved. (We'll discuss this in the next chapter.) It's a good idea to restrict novices' use of private spaces, and offer your regulars a more robust version of this feature (such as a permanent and/or customizable private space). This will give your members something to look forward to and help delineate that fuzzy boundary between novice and regular,

Building Character

One of the strongest attractions to being part of a community is a sense of belonging; as we discussed in Chapter 3, evolving member profiles are a good way to make your members feel at home.

The payoff for those profiles comes when your members actually have some history to track—after they've become a regular or leader (Figure 4.17). Letting everyone see who your regulars are will make them feel even more like it's their community.

If you succeed if making your community interesting to your regulars, some of them will want to get more involved and take on leadership positions within your community. The next chapter explores community leadership programs, but first, we'll examine the role of a leader in a Web community and what features you need to support a leadership program.

Empower Your Leaders

Becoming a leader is a major transition point in the Membership Life Cycle—as significant as the transition from visitor to member. Not every regular will want to take on a leadership position, but those who do will relish the status and visibility that comes with an officially sanctioned role.

Although it often requires substantial time and effort, playing a leadership role can be tremendously rewarding. It deepens and extends a member's web of relationships, binding him or her even more tightly into the social fabric of the community. Leaders often learn valuable skills on the job, and they get the satisfaction of helping others and the automatic social status of the insider.

Defining a Leader's Role

To develop effective leaders in your community, you have to define the roles you need them to play. Different communities require different kinds of leadership, and a detailed account of all possible positions and responsibilities is beyond the scope of this book. There are, however, a few roles that emerge spontaneously, over and over again, in communities all across the Web. Keep in mind, though, that this isn't an exhaustive list.

- **SUPPORT PROVIDERS** answer questions, help members solve problems they're having with the system

- **HOSTS** keep the key community activities (games, conversations, shopping, etc.) running smoothly

- **GREETERS** welcome newcomers, show them around, and teach them the ropes.

- **COPS** remove disruptive members and/or inappropriate content

- **EVENT COORDINATORS** plan, coordinate, and run one-time and regular events

- **TEACHERS** train community leaders, offer classes, or provide tutoring

- **MERCHANTS** run shops, provide services, and fuel the community economy

Of course, not every community needs all these functions. If your community centers around conversations, you may need hosts to keep the discussions lively and focused, greeters to welcome and instruct new members, and cops to remove inappropriate comments or disruptive people. For games or contests, you'll need support personnel who can resolve technical issues, and deal with reports of cheating and system hacking. For planned and scheduled events (see Chapter 7), you'll need people to promote, coordinate, manage and follow up those events. These duties aren't always performed by official leaders, nor are there strict divisions between the roles—the responsibilities can be split apart and recombined depending on the scale and style of your community. For example, hosts on the WELL are responsible for greeting newcomers, keeping the conversation going, and removing inappropriate content.

All these roles may seem a little overwhelming at this point; if your community is small, you probably won't be dealing with most of them. But as I've mentioned, things can change: if your community gets some positive press, you could easily experience a rapid influx of new members that throws your community into disarray. If you've thought about leaders in advance, you can respond quickly and effectively if the need arises.

Who's in Charge?

Any member of a Web community with ideas and initiative might end up an unofficial leader, hosting conversations, scheduling events, or mentoring new members. This may be all a small or casual community (like a mailing list) needs. But if that mailing list were to grow into a full-fledged professional organization, with a bustling Web site, you'd need officially sanctioned leaders with the authority and skills to keep the community running smoothly.

Your formal leaders might be volunteers, staff members, or part-time contractors. Whoever they are, they must be properly selected, trained, and then empowered to do their job effectively. This is not a trivial process: to start with, you need to choose people who are genuinely enthusiastic about the community and eager to improve it, rather than those just seeking social status and power. Then you'll need to educate them, with both a written leadership manual and some kind of formal training. You'll need to identify your leaders to the rest of the community, by providing some kind of uniform or identity tag, for example. And you need a way to communicate with your leaders and a way for them to communicate with each other "out of earshot" of the other members.

All these elements go into building an effective leadership program. In the next chapter, we'll examine each of them in detail and show how to implement them successfully.

Honor Your Elders

Elders (that is, respected, knowledgeable old-timers) play an integral role in all successful communities. Churches have elders, as do tribes, villages, universities, corporations, and families. They're the community storytellers—the people who've seen it all before and can't wait to tell you about it. They're the teachers, mentors, advisors, editors, and coaches—people who share their knowledge, pass along community beliefs and traditions, and embody community values through their words and deeds.

Elders are often the people called on to perform important community rituals. Whether the event is a formalized rite of passage like a marriage or funeral or a more casual gathering like a party, it will take on greater significance and weight if an elder is present.

Words of Wisdom

Being an elder isn't always a clearly defined role—it's earned through longevity, dedication, and knowledge sharing. On the WELL, long-time members can function as elders even if they've never played an official leadership role; their posts show that they've seen the community evolve over time. These people are viewed as role models (whether they like it or not), and newer members look to them for guidance about how to behave. And anyone who has played an official leadership role in the past—such as host, mentor, or community manager—could become an elder, if they stick around and continue to share their knowledge with the community.

Although elders will emerge naturally, you can strengthen the social fabric of your community by creating specific ways for them to share their knowledge. For example, an experienced leader who is no longer interested in the day-to-day work of community management could teach new recruits. Or a well-established regular who has grown bored with daily community life could sit on a Member Advisory Board and comment on new community features.

The Founder Speaks

By default, community founders and founding members are considered elders. One of the most powerful actions that a founder can take is to communicate regularly with the community. This gives the members a sense of security—a feeling that someone's home. For example, Steve Case, the founder of AOL, publishes a monthly letter in which he typically addresses current issues and future enhancements (Figure 4.18). It's a particularly effective approach because Steve doesn't wait for a crisis to respond to; he writes the letter every month regardless.

Similarly, Mary Furlong, the founder of Third Age, publishes an interactive weekly column called the Community Insider where she discusses current events, shares her philosophy of life, and articulates what it means to be a Third Ager.

FIGURE 4.18
A LETTER FROM STEVE
AOL keyword: Steve Case
Every month, Steve Case publishes a letter to AOL members in which he addresses current community events. Even though these letters have a strong PR spin, they add a human touch to this massive online service and give members the feeling that someone's home.

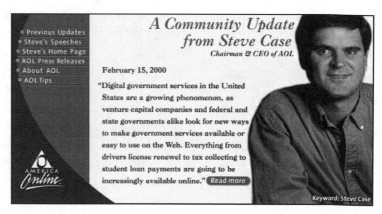

Another way for the founder to maintain an ongoing presence the community is to write a regular column addressing members' questions. For example, Tori Kropp, the founder of Stork Site (now a division of Women.com) writes a weekly "Ask Tori" column in which she answers questions about pregnancy and child care (Figure 4.19). This feature includes an archive of Tori's previous columns, which serves as a valuable and ever-growing content resource for the community.

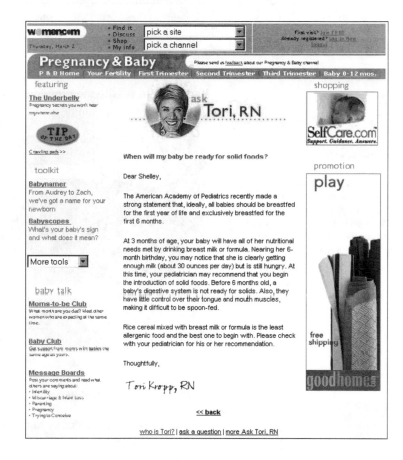

Rituals and Ceremonies

Rituals are a crucial element of community development (as covered further in Chapter 8). they keep your members involved by
forming habits, creating memorable experiences, and crystallizing
your culture. It's great when elders participate in community rituals, and even more powerful when they instigate and lead those
rituals themselves.

For instance, Lord British regularly goes into Ultima Online, and
hands out awards to distinguished players (Figure 4.20). For the
citizens of Britannia, having their king acknowledge their achievements is a powerful motivator that gives them a great sense of

pride and bragging rights and encourages them to keep playing the game. Similarly, Mary Furlong hosts a monthly conversation called "The Heart of Third Age", where she shares personal stories and stimulates discussion topics (Figure 4.21). These discussions enhance the ongoing sense of connection that Third Age members have with their founder and reinforce the values and "heart" of the community.

FIGURE 4.20
A MEETING WITH LORD BRITISH
Lord British is congratulating the Golden Brew Players after a successful performance. This visit from their "King" and the subsequent story that appeared on the Origin web site inspired the members to hone their skills and plan a series of plays in Britannia.

Maintaining a Presence

Founders are often too busy to really maintain a presence themselves, but your staff—the paid employees of your community—can help take up the slack. Even when they're newly hired, staff members will be seen as elders because they have knowledge and access to the inner workings of the community, and because (from the members' point of view) they have the power to determine how the community evolves.

The ways that your community staff interacts (or fails to interact) with the community will have a profound effect on the developing culture; other members will tend to interpret a staff person's comments as authoritative pronouncements. For this reason, you'll want to make sure that staff members understand the impact that their words and actions have.

FIGURE 4.21
HEART OF THIRD AGE

Mary Furlong, the founder of Third Age, hosts a regular discussion called "Heart of Third Age," with a different topic each month. Along with her written column, this ongoing dialogue keeps her presence alive on the site and helps her stay in touch with the members.

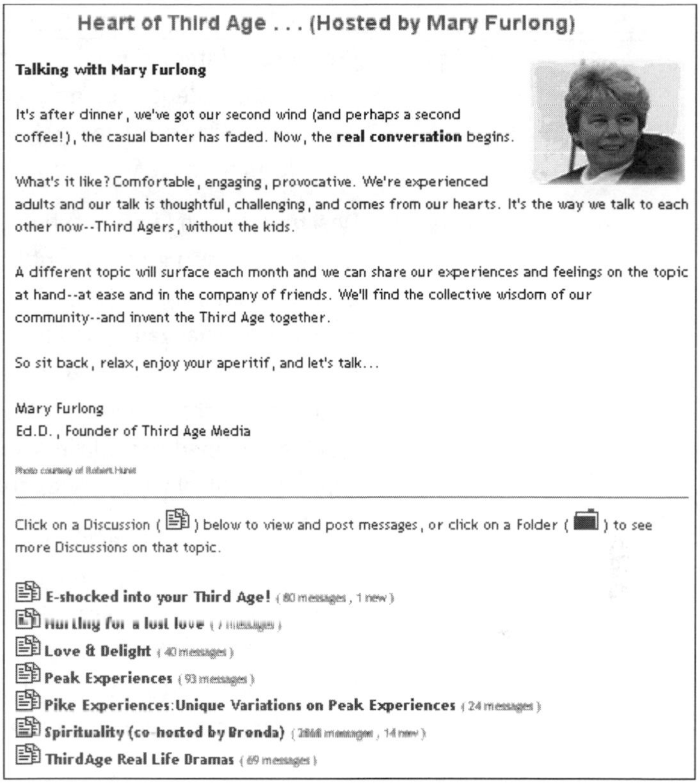

Heart of Third Age . . . (Hosted by Mary Furlong)

Talking with Mary Furlong

It's after dinner, we've got our second wind (and perhaps a second coffee!), the casual banter has faded. Now, the **real conversation** begins.

What's it like? Comfortable, engaging, provocative. We're experienced adults and our talk is thoughtful, challenging, and comes from our hearts. It's the way we talk to each other now--Third Agers, without the kids.

A different topic will surface each month and we can share our experiences and feelings on the topic at hand--at ease and in the company of friends. We'll find the collective wisdom of our community--and invent the Third Age together.

So sit back, relax, enjoy your aperitif, and let's talk...

Mary Furlong
Ed.D., Founder of Third Age Media

Photo courtesy of Robert Hurst

Click on a Discussion (🖹) below to view and post messages, or click on a Folder (▪) to see more Discussions on that topic.

🖹 **E-shocked into your Third Age!** (80 messages , 1 new)
🖹 **Hurting for a lost love** (7 messages)
🖹 **Love & Delight** (40 messages)
🖹 **Peak Experiences** (93 messages)
🖹 **Pike Experiences:Unique Variations on Peak Experiences** (24 messages)
🖹 **Spirituality (co-hosted by Brenda)** (2864 messages , 14 new)
🖹 **ThirdAge Real Life Dramas** (69 messages)

It's also important to make sure that your staff members' goals and values are in agreement with the existing (or emerging) community culture. Some Web communities thrive on debate and conflict, while others value civility and mutual support. Staff should be aware of, and prepared to reinforce, the social dynamics and core values of the community.

Role Models

What it comes down to is that community staff members are the ultimate role models, and what they do and say will be emulated. So, if you want your members to keep their profiles up to date, be sure that your staff members do. And if you want your leaders to be helpful, and treat others fairly, then staff members should demonstrate that with their words and deeds.

In practice, some of your staff will be more excited by the prospect of interacting with members than others, and some will be more adept at communicating online. Rather than requiring your staff to participate, look for ways to get the most out of the efforts of those who are interested.

Designer Dragon (a.k.a. Raph Koster, the lead designer on Ultima Online) spends a great deal of time communicating with UO players on the message boards of popular fan sites. UO is a popular yet controversial game, and has engendered many disgruntled players (www.wired.com/wired/archive/6.05/ultima.html). Raph's continuing accessibility and presence has a huge impact on the mood of the hard-core players and has nipped many a potentially explosive problem in the bud.

Another simple but effective way to make use of your staff's communication is to hold a regular "town meeting" where members have a chance to express their opinions and concerns directly. The Director of Marketing at Heat hosts a weekly chat in which he talks about new features and solicits input and ideas from the members; some member ideas have actually been implemented.

The Inside Scoop

You can also encourage your staff to share some of their insider information—within reasonable guidelines, of course. Many gaming sites feature "developer diaries," which offer an ongoing glimpse into the day-to-day struggles and triumphs of developing a computer game (see, for example, www.gamespot.com/features/index.html#diaries or staff.turbinegames.com/sean/plan.htm). Not every developer on the team publishes a diary, just those who are interested and qualified. But reading these diaries makes the community members feel like they're part of the process.

An increasingly popular feature in Web communities is the presence of staff experts, who are there to provide comfort and credibility. iVillage, for example, features experts in all of its channels (www.ivillage.com/experts), and both WebMD and drkoop.com include a variety of health professionals that lead discussions and answer questions. In fact, Dr. Koop himself is a good example of an elder whose name and image lend credibility and provide a comforting presence.

Lead On

Visitors, novices, regulars, leaders, and elders—they're all vital contributors to a thriving community. But your leaders are the members who will help you implement your vision and make sure your community fulfills its mission (or not). The next chapter deals with how to set up an effective program to make sure your leaders properly represent your interests.

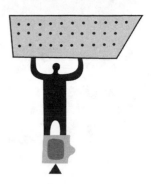

CHAPTER FIVE

LEADERSHIP:
The Buck Stops Here

Behind the scenes of any thriving community, you'll invariably find effective, dedicated leadership. Leaders breathe life into a community: they greet newcomers, coordinate events, manage programs, maintain the infrastructure, and keep the activities lively and civil.

Leaders are known by many different titles: founder, teacher, mentor, priest, counselor, coach, host, sysop, gamemaster—the list goes on. Whatever their titles, your leaders will profoundly shape your community culture, because they're your most visible role models. When newcomers arrive at your community, they'll look around for clues that tell them how to behave appropriately, and they'll view anyone who commands attention and respect as someone to emulate.

That's why it's crucial to build a strong community leader program. Well-managed leaders will keep your community running smoothly, and make it a friendly, responsive, and satisfying place to be. The key is to understand what motivates your leader, and give them the tools to do their jobs well.

In this Chapter

What's a Leader?

Unofficial Leaders

Official Leaders

Manage Your Leaders

What's a Leader?

When you enter a community gathering place, it's nice to know what roles the other people there are playing—who's a visitor, who's a novice, and who's a regular. Each of these roles plays a vital part in community life, as discussed in Chapter 4. But often, what you *really* want to know is, who's in charge here?

If you attend a Catholic Mass, a Navaho initiation ceremony, or an Elks Club meeting, it's easy to see who the leaders are because they're wearing special clothing. In the case of a bouncer guarding a club entrance, or a shopkeeper or bartender behind the counter, their location indicates their status. But the host at a party isn't so easy to spot, because party hosts don't (usually) wear a uniform or stand in a designated place. Instead, that person's role is expressed dynamically, as they welcome guests, introduce people to each other, and deal with problems that arise.

On the Web, as in the physical world, communities thrive when there's someone in charge to keep things running smoothly. As a Web community-builder, it's your job to build a strong and effective leadership program. So how do you do this? Which leadership roles are needed, and how obvious and official should they be? What does it take to select, train, and manage a corps of community leaders? Should you provide tools, rules, and uniforms, or let your leaders do their job their own way?

Get Off to a Good Start

These questions are a moving target, because leadership requirements change over time. A small message board or mailing list, for example, can be run by a single dedicated individual. But as a community grows, so does the need for more leadership infrastructure. If that message board becomes an online hot spot that's overrun with newcomers, the people in charge will need to develop mechanisms for managing the increase in traffic and members.

The most effective leadership programs (like the most successful communities in general) start small and evolve in partnership with their members. That's how many well-known Web communities—including AOL, Geocities, iVillage, Simutronics, and the WELL—developed what are now robust and dynamic leadership programs. To build a strong foundation for your leadership program, start slowly with a few well-trained leaders, and make sure that they're visible and accessible to the members.

To build a strong foundation for your leadership program, start slowly with a few well-trained leaders, and make sure that they're visible and accessible to the members.

Leading By Example

Why is this simple idea so important? Because initial conditions matter, and it can be difficult to recover from early leadership mistakes. For example, after it had been running about six months, Ultima Online announced the launch of a volunteer leadership program in an effort to provide some relief to the overburdened support staff. The popular game was quickly flooded with hundreds of applicants; the harried staff selected the most promising ones, gave them some minimal training, empowered them with the ability to "freeze" and "jail" misbehaving players, and put them to work answering simple questions and resolving minor disputes.

Unfortunately, UO's staff wasn't set up to maintain a positive presence in the game, so there was no clear leadership model for the volunteer Counselors to follow. Some of the volunteers were helpful and levelheaded, but others lost their tempers and used their new powers to help their friends move ahead in the game. The UO staff ultimately resolved these problems by instituting a more rigorous screening process and providing a more in-depth training program; but these early problems exacerbated the UO community's complaints about lack of leadership and left a lingering feeling of distrust that's been difficult to dispel.

Follow Your Members

While you can't ever completely prevent people from abusing power, you can minimize such problems by staying in close communication with your leaders and making sure that they're representing your community in a way that's consistent with your values. Official leaders are your most visible role models, and their actions can determine what kind of community you end up with. If you create an atmosphere of respect and trust and show your members what effective leadership looks like, they'll respond by showing you how your program needs to grow.

Like so many aspect of community building, running an effective leadership program involves recognizing what your members are already doing, and helping them do it better. The community staff at Simutronics learned this lesson when they ported their online games from Genie to AOL. On Genie (a now-defunct online service), they usually had around fifty simultaneous users and a few new members every week. On AOL, they were dealing with over a thousand simultaneous users and hundreds of new members *per hour*. The Simutronics gamemasters (who provided support and guidance) were quickly overwhelmed. They hired more people to help out, and streamlined their process for answering technical questions; but the games were still over-run with hordes of confused newbies, and long-time players were threatening to leave.

Running an effective leadership program involves recognizing what your members are already doing, and helping them do it better.

Then one of the product managers, Melissa Callaway, noticed that some experienced players were taking it upon themselves to welcome newcomers, show them some basic commands, and take them on guided tours of the gaming world—all tasks that the game masters had performed back on Genie. So Melissa created the Mentor program to give these volunteers some tools and special powers, and she set up a private area within the game where they could hang out with each other and coordinate their activities. Today, the Simutronics Mentor program is a driving force behind the social life in all Simutronics games and provides a great example of a member-driven, staff-empowered program (Figure 5.1).

FIGURE 5.1
SIMUTRONICS MENTOR SOCIETY
mentors.play.net

This Mentor Society Web site is a player-created resource for all Simutronics Mentors. It includes both a public area for people who are interested in joining the program (there's a program for each of the Simutronics online role-playing games) and a private area where existing Mentors can meet and share information.

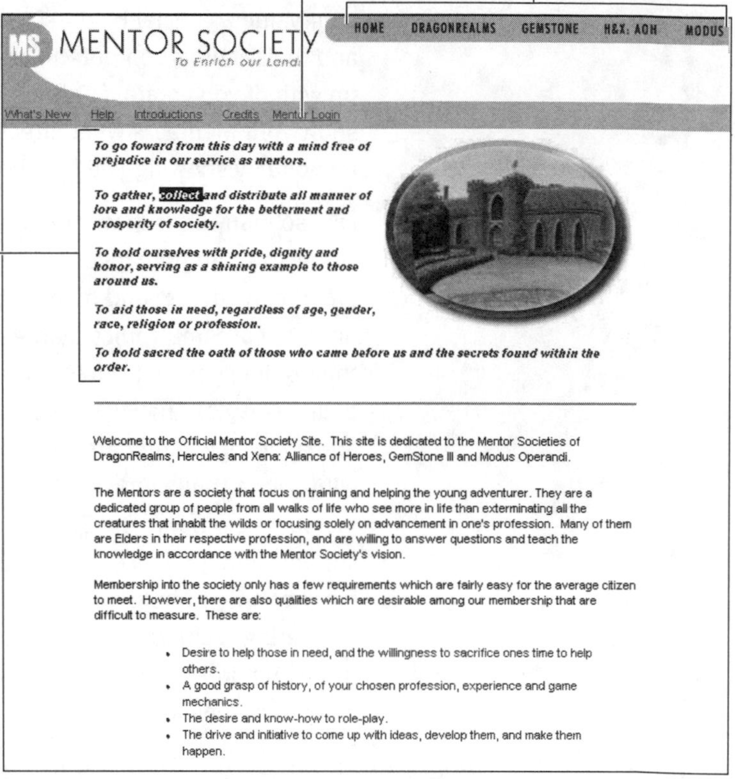

PRIVATE AREA

GAME-SPECIFIC AREAS

MS MENTOR SOCIETY
To Enrich our Land

HOME   DRAGONREALMS   GEMSTONE   H&X: AOH   MODUS

What's New   Help   Introductions   Credits   Mentor Login

To go foward from this day with a mind free of prejudice in our service as mentors.

To gather, collect and distribute all manner of lore and knowledge for the betterment and prosperity of society.

To hold ourselves with pride, dignity and honor, serving as a shining example to those around us.

To aid those in need, regardless of age, gender, race, religion or profession.

To hold sacred the oath of those who came before us and the secrets found within the order.

MISSION STATEMENT

Welcome to the Official Mentor Society Site. This site is dedicated to the Mentor Societies of DragonRealms, Hercules and Xena: Alliance of Heroes, GemStone III and Modus Operandi.

The Mentors are a society that focus on training and helping the young adventurer. They are a dedicated group of people from all walks of life who see more in life than exterminating all the creatures that inhabit the wilds or focusing solely on advancement in one's profession. Many of them are Elders in their respective profession, and are willing to answer questions and teach the knowledge in accordance with the Mentor Society's vision.

Membership into the society only has a few requirements which are fairly easy for the average citizen to meet. However, there are also qualities which are desirable among our membership that are difficult to measure. These are:

- Desire to help those in need, and the willingness to sacrifice ones time to help others.
- A good grasp of history, of your chosen profession, experience and game mechanics.
- The desire and know-how to role-play.
- The drive and initiative to come up with ideas, develop them, and make them happen.

Levels of Leadership

Not surprisingly, there's no single "right way" to run a community; after all, the skills and management infrastructure required to keep a fan club, support group, tavern, or church running smoothly are quite varied. So how do you get started? How do you set up those initial community leadership roles? What does it take to support these roles properly and grow your leadership program effectively?

To help answer these questions, take a look at the Leadership Pyramid (Figure 5.2), which builds on the ideas introduced in Chapter 4. In that chapter, we discussed the way each member will move through different stages of community involvement, each one characterized by particular needs, motivations, and rewards. In this chapter, we'll look more closely at regulars, leaders, and elders, and also at the Leadership Ritual that transforms a regular into a leader.

Figure 5.2
The Leadership Pyramid
The leadership pyramid is a diagrammatic representation of the levels of leadership that commonly occur in Web communities.

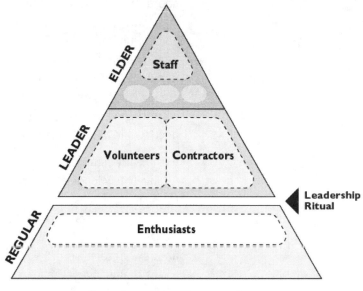

Leadership Pyramid

There are several kinds of leaders in a community:

o **Enthusiasts:** active regulars whose contributions to the community are compensated by increased attention

o **Volunteers:** unpaid but official leaders who are often compensated with a free account or gifts

o **Contractors:** official, paid leaders who are not full-time community employees

o **Staff:** official leaders who are employed full-time and receive benefits such as stock options, health coverage, and paid vacations

The Leadership Ritual, which includes selection and training, separates official from unofficial leaders (see Figure 5.11).

Roles and Responsibilities

As we saw in the previous chapter, communities need lots of different kinds of leaders, from hosts and greeters to cops and event coordinators. Figure out the leadership roles you need to fill, which will depend on what tasks need to be performed within your community. If you want to run events, for example, you'll need people to plan, promote and manage them. If you want to feature lively, focused conversations, you'll need people who are empowered to deal with disruptions, and keep the conversation on track. And if you expect your community to grow quickly, you'll need to find a way to manage your growing leadership program.

In the early "start-up" stage of a community, it's common for relatively few leaders to perform a wide variety of tasks (as did the Simutronics gamemasters on Genie). As the community grows, the leadership roles become more numerous and specialized. So as you're setting up your leadership program, think about what roles you'll need to get started and how these roles might change over time.

Defining Your Leadership Roles

To help you structure your leadership program, I've created a chart to help you think through and define the various leadership tasks that need to be performed within your community.

To get started, make a list of ongoing social activities within your community, such as conversations, games, shopping, or events. Under each activity, list the leadership and management tasks that you think are associated with each activity. After that, you'll clump these tasks into roles, and decide who will play each role and how they'll be compensated.

As you're going through this process, feel free to mix and match tasks into roles that make sense within your community. Bear in mind, though, that communities often run more smoothly when the social and disciplinary roles are separated—like the bouncer and bartender at a nightclub. That's why communities like Talk City, AOL, and CNN differentiate between Hosts—who keep the conversation lively and on track—and Cops—who remove disruptive members and/or inappropriate content. This separation allows each leader to perform their job more effectively and makes it easier for the members to understand who's doing what.

ROLE	RESPONSIBILITY	TASKS
Greeter	Welcome newcomers	Greet newcomers upon arrival
		Conduct system tours
		Answer basic questions
		Help people get into a conversation, game, other activity.
Host	Facilitate the core activities	Stimulate a conversation, keep it on topic, create and prune topics or threads
		Lead players in a game or quest
		Answer activity-related questions (e.g. how to use chat tools)
Editor	Evaluate content	Select high-quality content to highlight
		Mark inappropriate content for possible removal
Cops	Remove people and/or content that violate the community standards	Judge and remove content
		Ban a member from the system for a particular length of time
Teacher	Teach members to become leaders	Help select leader recruits
		Conduct classes and training sessions
		Offer one-to-one tutoring
		Evaluate students (through written exams or interactive sessions)
Events Coordinator	Plan and run events	Coordinate the time, place and participants in an event
		Promote the event (calendar, email, Web)
		Host or referee the event
		Post transcript or winners, participate in follow-up conversation
Support	Answer questions about the system	Answer technical or social questions
		Request changes or upgrades to the system
		Update Frequently Asked Questions list
Manager	Evaluate and support leaders	Collect and read leaders' weekly reports
		Hold group meetings
		Recommend leaders for commendation
		Discipline or remove misbehaving leaders
Director	Create and maintain the leader program	Define roles and responsibilities of leader positions
		Create and update leader documents (application, manual, code of conduct, NDA, weekly report template, etc.)
		Make policy changes as needed
		Keep leadership positions staffed

Paid or Unpaid?

Once you've determined your initial leadership roles, you'll need to decide whether to fill them with volunteers, contractors, or staff.

- **VOLUNTEERS** are unpaid but official leaders who are often compensated with a free account or occasional gifts.

- **CONTRACTORS** are official leaders who are paid by the hour, week, or month but are not full-time employees of the community.

- **STAFF** are official leaders who are employed full-time and receive benefits such as stock options, health coverage, and paid vacations.

If you're running a small, not-for-profit community like a book club or mutual support group, you'll naturally turn to volunteers. But if you've got a growing Web community that has strategic goals and quarterly budget reports, deciding who gets paid and who doesn't becomes more complicated. Some communities, like the Motley Fool, avoid the issue altogether by having all their official community leaders on staff. With paid leaders, you'll retain more control over your brand and be able to run a more professional organization because staff and contractors are legally bound to fulfil their duties. On the other hand, a struggling Web community can incur a serious financial burden if it relies solely on paid leaders.

Most large-scale Web communities—like Talk City, Ultima Online, GeoCities, Simutronics, CNN, and AOL—walk this line by developing a tiered leadership structure that includes full-time staff, part-time contractors, and shifting ranks of volunteers. If you expect to have such a mix, you should launch your leadership program with paid, experienced leaders if you can afford it. This will let you attract people who know what they're doing, avoid the ambiguities of dealing with volunteers, and get your program off on the right foot. These experienced leaders can then help you set up the infrastructure and policies for your volunteer leadership program.

Volunteering Information

Running a substantial Web community, like running a small town, requires a team of people who are dedicated to maintaining and improving the community environment. This team might include programmers, writers, artists, musicians, designers, editors, Webmasters, and technical and customer support personnel— who may be paid staff members or contractors—and also hosts, greeters, newsletter editors, and events coordinators—who might well be volunteers.

Volunteers vs. Staff

The most obvious issue is financial: using volunteers will cost less than using staff or contractors. But financial issues aside, allowing volunteers to play official leadership roles will add a personal touch that's hard to duplicate with paid leaders, because volunteers are driven by desire rather than financial compensation. Also, while paid leaders are often seen as "management," members think of volunteers as "one of us", which makes them particularly effective at communicating back and forth between management and members.

On the downside, using volunteers raises legally murky employment-law questions and is a potential source of trouble as this area of cyberspace law becomes clarified. And when you use volunteers to perform a task, you have less control than when you're using employees. It can be difficult to "fire" volunteers, for example, or ask them to behave in a certain way. It's not always clear how to discipline a volunteer who consistently shows up ten minutes late for a chat shift or posts a potentially inflammatory message to a Usenet newsgroup.

Benefits for Volunteers

People volunteer their time for a variety of reasons. For some, volunteering is a way to simultaneously establish status and give back to a community. This is what drives people to help newcomers, create free graphics, write newsletters, run clubs and committees, and contribute to the Open Source movement.

For someone who's making a career change, volunteering can be a form of internship—a way to explore an unfamiliar field, and acquire job skills and insider contacts. Volunteers have used their positions to attract clients, build their resumes, or even launch a new career: GeoCities community leaders have started Web design businesses, Ultima Online guild leaders have become managers at their day jobs, and iVillage volunteer hosts have ended up as staff members. Skills they learn as volunteer leaders—creating Web pages, managing a small group, and keeping the social climate lively and orderly—allow them to advance in their careers.

The Downside of Volunteering

There are, however, two kinds of problems. The first comes when volunteers feel underappreciated and mistreated and decide to go public with their complaints. For example, a group of volunteers brought a lawsuit against AOL contending that they were being treated like employees—punching time cards, being on call during certain hours—without having the benefits of employees, such as being able to take a leave of absence. They also contended that they were dismissed from their volunteer positions for questioning AOL's leadership practices. The real issue here isn't the job description; it's that these volunteers felt that they were treated badly and not appreciated for the work they were doing.

The second type of problem comes when volunteers do work that's more appropriately handled by employees—or that's even identical to the work done by employees. This is a tricky business, because roles can change so fast on the Web, especially in a rapidly evolving Web community.

At the heart of this debate is the question of what's "real work"— a question hotly debated among Web community builders, which will likely be ironed out in courtrooms over the next few years. Some say that hosting conversations should be paid; others say that volunteer hosts perform their tasks for love, not money, and they're being empowered to do what they'd be doing anyway. Hosts in different Web communities are sometimes volunteers, sometimes contractors (who might earn anywhere between $5 and $20 per hour), and sometimes full-time staff members.

Volunteer Do's and Don'ts

It's tough to draw the line between volunteers and paid staff; every Web community seems to draw this line in a slightly different place. In practice, using volunteers is partly a question of supply and demand. For example, thousands of college students apply for a few MTV volunteer internships because it's fun, high-profile summer job and a chance to learn skills and make connections. But a ready supply of volunteers isn't the sole determining factor; there are also legal, social and managerial issues to consider.

There are no absolutes, because every community is different. But here are some rules of thumb:

- **DON'T** use volunteers for positions that require many hours or esoteric knowledge about the inner workings of your community. Any full-time roles that are crucial for your community's functioning (such as the community manager) should be paid, as should positions that involve answering detailed technical questions about the service.

- **DO** use volunteers for part-time roles that your members might instigate themselves, such as greeting newcomers, answering basic questions, and giving tours of the environment.

- **DO** use your volunteer program as a talent pool for your community contractors and staff. It's motivating for volunteers to see that their efforts can get them noticed and result in a paid position. And someone who's hired from the volunteer ranks will know the community well.

- **DO** treat your volunteers with respect, let them know they're appreciated, and give them perks and recognition. It's in your best interest to keep your volunteers happy, because a disillusioned and angry ex-volunteer can cause damage by bad-mouthing your community in public or taking you to court.

Unofficial Leaders

Official leaders are your most visible role models, but anybody who's active in your community will be seen as a role model and a leader, even if an unofficial one. Newcomers in particular will be influenced by anyone who attracts attention and seems to be important, so it's up to you to actively highlight the role models you'd like people to follow. Attention is the currency of cyber-space, and by shining a spotlight on certain members, you'll nudge people's behavior in that direction.

Spotlight Your Enthusiasts

Enthusiasts are the most active subset of your regulars; they're excited about what you're doing and eager to be part of it. While some regulars might be readers or observers, enthusiasts contribute actively by posting thoughtful comments, building useful Web pages, creating artwork or software, or perhaps running a club or guild. By spotlighting these valuable members and their positive contributions, you're encouraging what you'd like to see more of in your community. If you give them a chance to show off and express your appreciation for their efforts, you'll be motivating them to stay involved and keep creating.

Highlighting Quality

One way to acknowledge your enthusiasts is to showcase their Web pages. The increased traffic and attention will motivate the creators to keep their pages up-to-date, and seeing high-quality pages prominently displayed will inspire other members to improve their own pages.

You can use either a centralized or decentralized editorial strategy for selecting pages to highlight; the best method for your community may change over time. In the early days of GeoCities, the in-house community staff selected which member pages to highlight, but as the site evolved, community leaders played more of an editorial role, developing a "Featured Page" program within their neighborhoods that showcased well-crafted pages. GeoCities also developed hybrid methods for selecting pages, such as Landmark Sites (Figure 5.3), which the editorial staff choose from the highest-traffic sites.

FIGURE 5.3
GeoCities Landmark Sites
The Landmark Site award was just one of many methods GeoCities used to promote members' Web sites.

You can also link to external Web sites as a way to acknowledge the efforts of your enthusiasts. For example, Ultima Online highlights the largest and most popular fan sites (Figure 5.4)—thriving subcommunities in themselves that include features such as message boards, chat rooms, and download libraries. By linking to these sites, the creators of UO both spotlight their enthusiastic members and extend the functionality of their own site.

TIP ▶ *Highlighting member-created Web sites isn't always the right strategy. For example, some eBay sellers advertise their own small-business Web sites in their eBay profiles, in order to sell their wares directly and bypass eBay's service altogether. Since eBay's business model is based on seller fees, it's not particularly in their best interest to call attention to member profiles that are essentially advertisements for a competing service.*

Figure 5.4
Ultima Online fan sites
This page from the Ultima Online Web site (town.owo.com/links.html) links to several fan sites. This approach acknowledges the efforts of fans and encourages them to keep their sites lively and up-to-date.

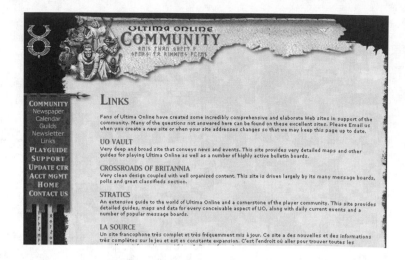

Reward their Activities

In addition to creating content, enthusiasts can play other unofficial yet influential leadership roles within your community. Some may want to become official leaders, but some won't. To keep this latter group motivated, it's a good idea to acknowledge the roles they're already playing within your community and celebrate their achievements.

From Players to Champions

If your community is built around competitive activities like games, sports, or contests, you can showcase members who perform well. To do this, you'll need to implement a rating and ranking system that keeps track of the results of sanctioned competitions. For example, Backgammon players at the Microsoft Gaming Zone can play for fun in unranked rooms; or they can play in ranked rooms and enter tournaments, which give them a chance to develop a player rating and be ranked against all the other players (Figure 5.5).

Once you've got such a system in place, you can list the highest-ranking players, as shown in Figure 5.6. Such a list creates a sense of drama and turns some players into champions (an unofficial leadership role). But any community with a rating system can have "champions" by highlighting the top performers—for example, eBay acknowledges and rewards members with the highest feedback scores. And Motley Fool uses their message board rating system to showcase members whose posts are consistently highly rated. Again, drawing attention to good performance will show all your members what success looks like and will motivate some of your most valuable members to stay involved.

FIGURE 5.5

RATINGS AND RANKINGS AT THE MICROSOFT GAMING ZONE

Players on the Zone can choose to play for fun or for ratings (upper image). The highest-ranked players are highlighted on the site (lower image), and rankings are updated every hour.

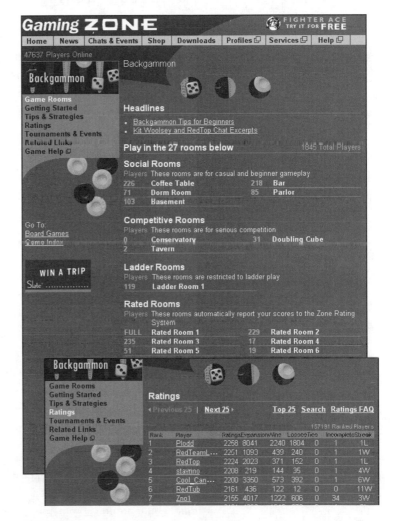

From Members to Merchants

If you're running a for-profit Web community, it's smart to set up ways for your enthusiasts to share in your success. For example, if you're running an e-commerce community like Amazon.com or eBay, think about how your members can become merchants in their own right. Like the shopkeepers in a tourist town or the proprietors at a flea market, merchants fuel the economic engine of a community and provide a focal point for members with common interests. And merchants make natural evangelists, because their fortunes are tied to yours—if you do better, they do better, which means that they have a real incentive to draw traffic and customers to your community. And nothing's more attractive than a shop owner or a barkeep who's running a thriving business on a busy corner. Just ask the merchants at eBay: they can get better rates elsewhere, but they sell their wares on eBay because it's the busiest global bazaar on the Net.

Another way to turn members into merchants is to help them set up and run their own *online store*, as Yahoo does (stores .yahoo.com). Store owners get the benefit of being on a busy, high-traffic site and being listed in a shopping directory. And Yahoo benefits by having a more places for members to shop and new opportunities for cross-promotion.

A different approach is to create an *affiliate program*, which essentially gives your members financial incentives for delivering qualified leads. The most successful and widely copied program of this type is the Amazon.com Associates Program (Figure 5.6), which gives members 5 to 15 percent of proceeds from sales that come from a link on an affiliate site. Web-based merchants such as CDNOW (www.cdnow.com) have adopted similar programs, and large Web communities such as Tripod and GeoCities provide tools that make it easy for their members to participate in these programs.

Another option is to provide classified ads or auctions where your members can buy and sell items. Even if your community isn't primarily built around commerce, you can still incorporate selling, as AOL does with its classified ads (www.babycenter.com/classifieds)

and Yahoo does with auctions (auctions.yahoo.com). This gives your members another activity to engage in and another role to play.

FIGURE 5.6
AMAZON AFFILIATE PROGRAM
The Amazon.com Associate Program page (upper image) includes instructions for joining the program, which allows anyone with a Web site to easily set up a store that generates leads for Amazon.com purchases. Amazon.com also highlights high-quality affiliate sites (lower image) to reward efforts and encourage all of their merchants.

Advise and Consent

Web communities are a great place to do market research (see Chapter 1) because you can get such direct feedback. You may want to do market research with various segments of your membership, both old-timers and newcomers, but you should also consider creating an advisory panel for members to participate in. Some Web communities—including Third Age (Figure 5.7) and BabyCenter—extend this opportunity to all members, while other communities, like iVillage, send out special invitations to their most devoted members. Either way, becoming an advisor gives your enthusiasts another role to play, and another way to contribute to the community.

ThirdAge Research

ThirdAge Advisors

Hello!

Until now, you've visited our site, posted in forums, and read our articles. Now we'd like to give you the opportunity to play an even greater role at ThirdAge.

We'd like to invite you to join a new group we're putting together: ThirdAge Advisors, a select group of people whose role is to advise us on how to better serve the needs of the community we represent.

ThirdAge Advisors will share their opinions and recommendations via the Web through online surveys, opinion polls, and forums. You will contribute greatly to our online community and sponsors.

ThirdAge Advisors will be privy to ThirdAge Research as part of our online community of close friends.

Thanks for your interest in ThirdAge Advisors.

Mary Furlong
ThirdAge Founder

LINK TO ADVISOR APPLICATION ——————— Join ThirdAge Advisors

A Critical Eye

In a lively and growing community, your enthusiasts' contributions can provide a continuous source of fresh content. But the quality of this member-generated material will likely be all over the map, which can make it difficult to find the gems. Much like a gallery owner might showcase the works of talented local artists, you want to locate and highlight the best efforts of your members, which might be comments, stories, Web sites, or even member profiles (as described in Chapter 3). To find these treasures, you'll need to set up some sort of editorial process.

You can get started by using automated tools (described in Chapter 2) that pinpoint high-traffic areas using statistics like page hits, posting activity, or hours logged into the system. You can even use these statistics to highlight popular areas, as the Motley Fool does with its "The Best of the Boards" (boards.fool.com/topboards.asp) and RemarQ does with its Top 50 Discussions (www.remarq.com).

But selecting the best content is a task for which you'll also need a human editorial eye. The easiest way to do it is to assign an editor or editors (either paid or volunteer) to choose what to highlight. At iVillage, for example, community staffers select well-written posts from a message board about "Chick Flicks" and elevate these member-written movie reviews into a regular feature on the site (Figure 5.8). And at the Motley Fool, "Hot Threads" are chosen by community staffers, who scan high-traffic areas for interesting posts.

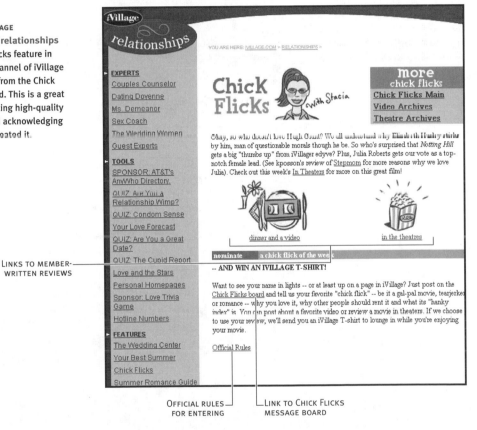

FIGURE 5.8
CHICKFLICKS AT IVILLAGE
www.ivillage.com/relationships
The weekly Chick Flicks feature in the Relationships channel of iVillage highlights postings from the Chick Flicks message board. This is a great example of spotlighting high-quality member content and acknowledging the members who created it.

LINKS TO MEMBER-WRITTEN REVIEWS

OFFICIAL RULES FOR ENTERING

LINK TO CHICK FLICKS MESSAGE BOARD

Rather than appointing an official content editor, you could take a more decentralized approach and include your members in the editorial process. For example, members reading the Motley Fool message boards can rate any post as good or bad, which automatically generates a "Top 25" list (Figure 5.9). These ratings help the editors select a post of the day, and identify and remove inappropriate posts. Slashdot's moderator system (**www.slashdot.org/moderation.shtml**) randomly transforms established Slashdot members into temporary editors who rate other people's comments on a 5-point scale.

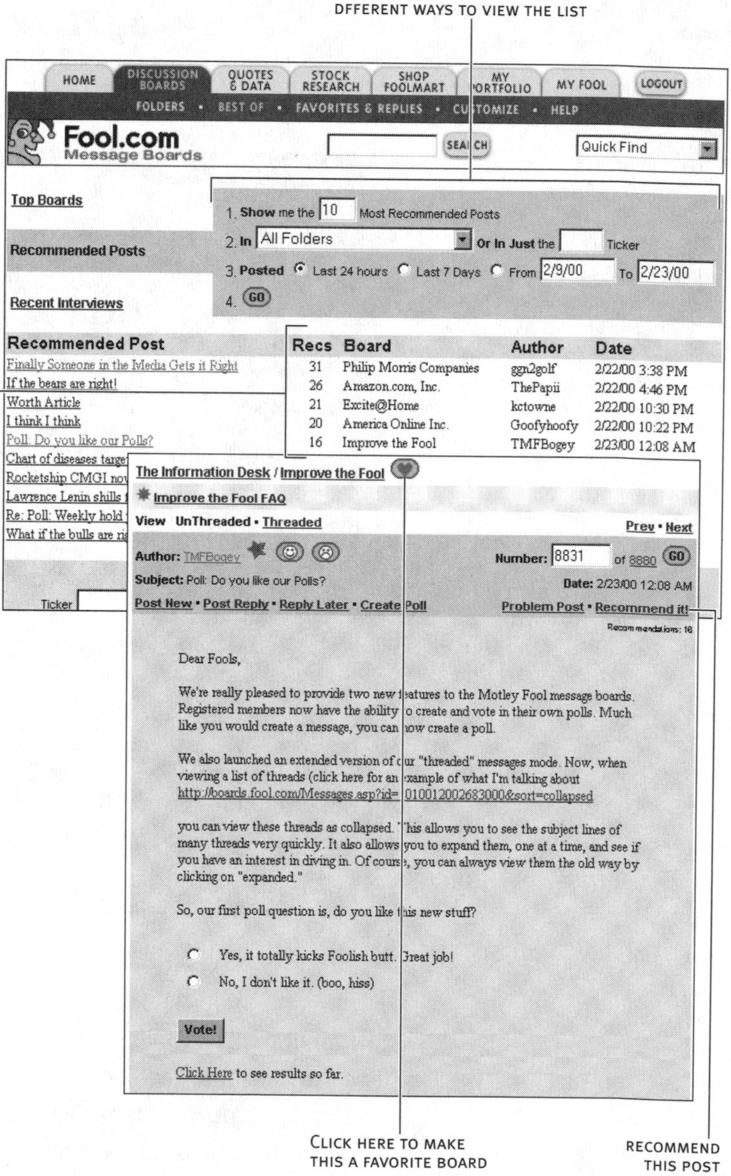

FIGURE 5.9
RECOMMENDING POSTS AT THE
MOTLEY FOOL
boards.fool.com/topboards.asp
Posts on the Motley Fool have buttons that other members can use to recommend the post or mark it as a problem (lower image). The results are fed into the system's database and are used to automatically generate a list of top 25 posts (upper image).

DFFERENT WAYS TO VIEW THE LIST

NUMBER OF RECOMMENDATIONS

CLICK HERE TO MAKE
THIS A FAVORITE BOARD

RECOMMEND
THIS POST

Whichever approach you adopt to highlighting member posts, you should give your editors some clear guidelines to follow. Slashdot editors, for instance, are instructed to rate member posts on relevancy, humor, and depth of analysis. Also let your members know what the standards are for the highlighted content. For example, the rules and judging criteria behind the weekly Chick Flicks contest (www.ivillage.com/relationships/articles/0,4097,18102~189,00.html)and the Slashdot Moderator system (slahdot.org/moderation.shtml) are clearly explained on the sites. Even when you post your standards, you'll still hear grumbling from disgruntled members, but that's to be expected with any sort of subjective rating system.

Official Leaders

Unofficial leadership is valuable and important; but if your community is growing, eventually you'll encounter situations that call for trained, empowered leaders. Your may get a surge of naive newcomers, for example, who need handholding and guidance. Your message boards may become overrun with chronic malcontents or self-promoting spammers whose impact needs to be contained. Or you might decide to start running regular events like support groups, interviews, or tournaments that require planning, coordination, and follow-up.

Although enthusiasts often take it upon themselves to greet newcomers or keep a conversation on track, leaders are far more effective when they have training, tools and support. For example, the helpful Simutronics enthusiasts who were greeting newcomers had no special powers, insider knowledge, or guidelines to follow. But once they became official Mentors, they gained "teleportation" powers that allowed them to take newcomers on guided tours of the vast gaming world. They also received training and guidelines, which gave newcomers a more consistent experience.

Power to the People: The Slashdot Moderator System

Rob Malda (a.k.a. CmdrTaco, founder and head honcho of Slashdot) had a dilemma. His homegrown Web site, Slashdot, was taking off fast. Every day brought more posts, more page hits, more press coverage, more enthusiastic members signing up. Everything was going great—except that Rob was being lobbied by two distinct special interest groups, with diametrically opposed needs. Many loyal Slashdot readers were longtime Usenet geeks, who considered the comments associated with each Slashdot story to be a newsgroup and thus felt obligated to read every post. But Slashdot was also attracting an increasing number of busy and influential people who wanted to skim the cream and read only the best comments. And Slashdot was growing bigger and busier, so the good stuff was becoming increasingly hard to find.

Rob needed a fair and impartial way to weed out the dross and highlight the best posts, and he wanted a system that could grow along with the site. He'd already hand-picked a few loyal Slashdot members to mark the best and worst comments, but the volume of activity was fast outstripping the abilities of his volunteer editorial team. And he didn't want to get into the endless cycle of finding, training, and managing new moderators for a rapidly growing site.

So Rob wrote a program that gave moderator access to 400 Slashdot members who'd posted good comments. Some people ignored their new duties, but about half of the newly minted moderators began rating posts. When people (inevitably) abused the system, Rob removed them from the pool of potential moderators. Today, Slashdot's moderator system is still being tweaked, but it's settled into a groove. Here's how it works:

○ After a thousand posts, a program randomly selects a group of moderators from the set of qualified members that represents a broad cross-section of Slashdot readers and posters, excluding newbies and known troublemakers.

○ Moderators see a special view of the message boards on their screen when they log on(Figure 5.10). Each newly-minted moderator is allotted five "tokens," each of which represents the chance to rate one post. The ratings are accumulated by the system database, which attaches an evolving score to each comment within the system. After five ratings (or three days), their moderator shift is over; but if they didn't abuse their powers, the system can choose them again from the pool. So a regular reader might be a moderator every few months, while for a regular poster it might be every few weeks.

○ Slashdot members can set their preferences to view only those posts that rise above a certain score. So using this system, the Usenet geeks can set their preference to -1, which allows them to read every post, flames and all; people who want only the top quality can set their cutoff level at 5, which will show them only the best posts.

STORY SUMMARY
AND LINK

TOTAL NUMBER OF
COMMENTS [253]

CURRENT THRESHOLD

LEVEL 5 COMMENTS, AS RATED
BY SLASHDOT'S MODERATORS

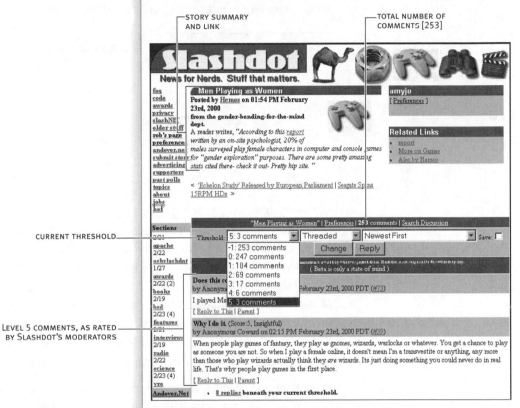

FIGURE 5.10 (slashdot.org) "Just-in-time" moderation at Slashdot

Screen Your Candidates

Because your official leaders will have special powers and insider knowledge, you'll need to take extra care in choosing people to fill these roles. To locate qualified candidates, it's important to create a selection or screening process—the first step in creating your Leadership Ritual (Figure 5.11).

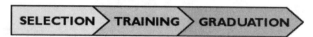

FIGURE 5.11
THE LEADERSHIP RITUAL
The Leadership Ritual consists of selection, training, and graduation, which prepare official leaders to perform their duties and play their new roles.

An Invitation to Lead

In the beginning, it's best not to open the doors too wide, but rather to handpick a few service-oriented members who are eager to continue their efforts in a more official capacity. You'll know they can do the job, because they've already (more or less) been doing it. For example, the first message boards hosts at The Motley Fool were enthusiasts who regularly posted long, thoughtful comments, and encouraged others to do the same. And the first official Community Leaders at GeoCities were people who were already helping newcomers build their Web pages.

Even after you've got an official application process in place, inviting enthusiasts to fill leadership roles can still be a valuable part of your recruiting process. When a WELL host relinquishes the role, for instance, he or she will often invite an active member of the conference to become the host. And the chat and message board hosts at iVillage often encourage active members to become official community leaders.

Once you've established your program and put a training process and management infrastructure into place, you can offer leadership opportunities to a wider segment of your members. As your community grows, you'll need to develop a way for your members to apply for official positions without being asked. Most Web communities offer a single application that lets the applicant indicate what position they're interested in. For example, Third Age offers a variety of official leadership positions, and provides a single Web-based form for all applicants (Figure 5.12).

FIGURE 5.12
LEADERSHIP ROLES AT THIRD AGE
www.thirdage.com/community/
leaders/
The Third Age leader recruitment page outlines what it takes to be a community leader and offers links to a description of the required skills and background for each role and a link to the application.

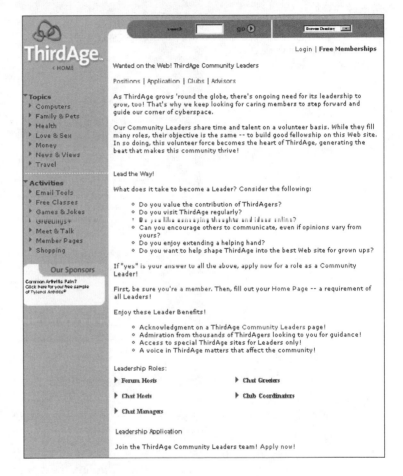

Sorting through applications takes time, so make sure to communicate clearly what's required of the position and to describe the skills and attitude you're looking for. Be sure to include any objective criteria, such as minimum age or length of membership. For example, Ultima Online explicitly states that volunteer leaders must be eighteen years old and have a clean record of online behavior (Figure 5.13). And the leader application at iVillage (www.ivillage.com/boards/how2bleader) provides a series of questions that help applicants decide if they're cut out to be iVillage leaders.

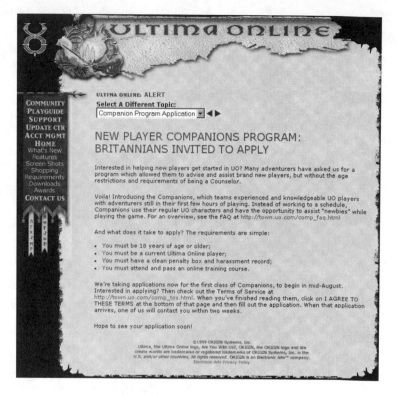

Teach Your Leaders Well

Once you've selected some likely candidates, you need to teach them how to perform their new roles. The training period is the second stage in your Leadership Ritual (see Figure 5.11), but it's a good idea to continue the screening process during these initial training sessions, because not every applicant will make an effective leader. For example, AOL requires potential community leaders to attend online meetings, during which they're given an overview of the training program and encouraged to ask questions. Some drop out voluntarily once they realize the time, dedication, and scrupulousness that's required of an AOL community leader. Other applicants are dismissed by the trainer for demonstrating a lack of maturity or inability to follow the rules. In either case, these sessions help filter out applicants who are obviously not suited to being an AOL Community Leader.

In order to feel comfortable in a community, members need to develop a sense that their leaders are consistent and fair, and that's one of the primary purposes of the training you provide. Consistent doesn't mean faceless and devoid of opinions or personality, however. On the contrary, the most effective community leaders often have a strong and memorable personal style. Some great WELL hosts, for instance, are aggressive and witty, while others are calm and scholarly. But there's an underlying code of ethics and shared social rituals that gives the community a consistent feel.

The Personal Touch

As part of your leadership program, you'll want to provide direct training and guidance, which can be as simple as a Q&A chat session or as sophisticated as a series of classes with entrance requirements and written exams. A small and intimate community can often get by with an informal program, especially if the rules and guidelines are well-documented and an effective screening process is in place. For example, the WELL doesn't provide formal training to new hosts; instead, each host is given a copy of the extensive and thorough WELL Host Manual (www.well.com/confteam/hostmanual) and is assigned a mentor who can answer hosting questions and provide informal feedback. This system works in part because the WELL is fairly small (fewer than 10,000 members) and because everyone who hosts a public conference must first be an active participant familiar with the culture and protocols. In general, WELL members are assumed to be fairly sophisticated and able to hold their own in a spirited debate—a different audience might require more handholding, and in that case the leaders would need more intensive training.

At the other end of the spectrum is the official training program for AOL Community Leaders. This program is highly structured and formalized; it includes a strict admissions policy, an orientation session, a series of self-paced online classes, and live role-playing sessions to test the abilities of the new recruits. The training program for the Kids area is even more rigorous and carefully controlled. Newly anointed community leaders are paired up with trainers or mentors (see sidebar: The Value of Mentors), who join them during their first few assignments and offer detailed feedback about their performance.

Don't let these examples intimidate you: both communities started off with simple, informal programs and policies, which gradually evolved to meet their changing needs. You can't build up a robust leadership program overnight, but if you put the time and effort into developing your training program, you will eventually be rewarded with a strong and consistent group of community leaders.

By the Book

To promote this consistency, even when your community is small, you'll want to develop a Leadership Manual—a set of written guidelines that ensures that everyone is following the same standards. This manual should outline what behavior is considered acceptable and unacceptable and describe how to handle the variety of situations that leaders are likely to confront. A good manual will reduce your training overhead and help your leaders present a united front. Some communities, such as GeoCities, have tested trainees on their knowledge of the manual before allowing them to assume leadership positions.

Your manual may start as an ad hoc collection of documents— tip sheets, system commands, and FAQs—but it's useful to develop a working version as early as possible, so that you'll have a place to document your growing experience. As you add new leadership roles, you can develop different sections of the manual (or even separate manuals) that offer specific guidelines for those positions. For example, a chat host must sometimes react quickly and decisively and thus needs to be well versed in what procedures to follow when specific social disruptions occur. By contrast, the host of a message board can take some time to compose a thoughtful response to a provocative posting and often has more leeway in how to handle disputes.

It's impossible to predict all the situations that will arise, so you'll be continually updating the manual to incorporate your growing knowledge. To help you get started, here are some basic points to cover:

- Provide a clear description of your community values and the style of leadership that's appropriate. Also include a code of conduct for leaders that states what behaviors will be considered grounds for dismissal.

- Include your Member Agreement, Code of Conduct, and Privacy Policy in an appendix and/or summarize the key points (see Chapter 6 for more about these documents). Make sure that your leaders have read and understood them.

- Ask your leaders to sign a nondisclosure agreement—an agreement not to reveal what they learn about your operation—if they'll be privy to insider company information

- Provide descriptions, instructions, and tip sheets for any tools and/or system commands that leaders need to perform their duties.

- Include a list of common situations, along with suggestions for how to handle these situations appropriately. Outline the proper escalation path for dealing with situations that require higher-level intervention.

Be sure to mention any subcommunities that require a special approach or that are governed by a different code of conduct, such as a Kids or International area. These subcommunities may also require their own training program or behavioral guidelines.

The Value of Mentors

A mentor is someone assigned to a recruit to help guide and evaluate that person throughout his or her training process. Even when a program offers classes and written documentation, a one-to-one relationship with an experienced leader is one of the best ways to develop well-trained community leaders—and many successful community leader training programs are based around this relationship. Depending on the program, a mentor might:

- answer questions and provide moral support
- let a recruit "shadow" them during their online shifts
- role-play with recruits (posing as a problem user, for example)
- coach recruits during initial assignments, and check in occasionally afterwards to see how things are going
- attend their graduation ceremony and/or announce the recruit's success at completing the program
- A mentor program will also help you build closer relationships among your community leaders, because recruits often maintain a friendly relationship with their mentors long after the training is finished.

Completing the Program

Once your recruits have made it through the training process, they're ready to be "ordained" as full-fledged leaders—the third and final step in your Leadership Ritual. To accomplish this, you'll need some kind of ceremony or ritual in which new leaders are granted their powers and welcomed into the ranks (see Chapter 8 for more about initiation rituals).

Celebrating the Event

The graduation takes place in a "backstage" gathering place, such as a mailing list, message board, or chat room. The event doesn't even have to be an actual event; for example, new hosts at Moms Online are announced in a leaders-only mailing list (Figure 5.14), while new leaders at the Zone are introduced weekly in a leaders-only message board. These announcements are typically followed by congratulations, welcome messages, and offers of help by the other leaders—all of which makes new leaders feel welcomed into the ranks.

FIGURE 5.14
MOMS ONLINE NEW LEADER ANNOUNCEMENT
Whenever a new Moms Online host joins the ranks, it's announced by a welcome letter that's sent to a hosts-only mailing list. The image of geese flying together symbolizes the philosophy of their leadership program.

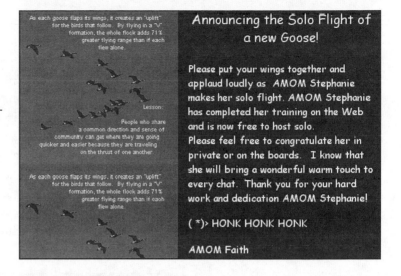

If your community includes a chat room or virtual world, you could hold a real-time graduation ceremony for your new leaders (as well as message board announcements). This ceremony would probably include fewer people than the wider announcement. New EverQuest leaders undergo a secret initiation ceremony, during which they receive their powers and swear to uphold the laws of the land (Figure 5.15).

FIGURE 5.15
EVERQUEST GUIDE INITIATION CEREMONY
In the elaborate EverQuest initiation ceremony, volunteer leaders encounter a magical winged horse, (shown here) and follow it to their death, after which they are resurrected as newly anointed Guides.

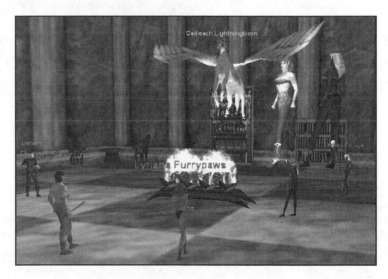

Wearing the Uniform

However it's announced, a new leader's change in status should be clearly reflected in his or her member ID and public profile (see Chapter 3). Whenever possible, you should give your official leaders some kind of "uniform" that communicates their role—a reserved prefix, a special icon, or some unique attire. For example, official leaders at Talk City have a prefix included in their name, while the "uniform" worn by official leaders in the role-playing game Asheron's Call is a magical-looking sparkly effect (Figure 5.16). For security reasons, you'll need to make sure that these markers can only be worn by designated leaders, which means you should ensure that leaders' accounts can't be hacked.

FIGURE 5.16
LEADER "UNIFORMS" AT ASHERON'S CALL
Asheron's Call offers a rich 3D design environment, so leaders can be designated with a special sparkly graphical effect.

Manage Your Leaders

Once you've selected and trained your community leaders, the ongoing task of managing them begins. Whether they're volunteers, contractors, or staff members, these people are doing real work, and they need guidance, feedback, and support to perform their duties effectively.

Keep Them in the Loop

You can avoid a whole host of problems (no pun intended) by putting some management infrastructure into place early in the process. For starters, you'll need to set up some ongoing feedback loops that allow you to both communicate with your leaders and assess how they're doing.

Meet Me Backstage

One essential ingredient in a management program is a private gathering place for leaders, like the Zone's leaders board and the WELL's Backstage conference mentioned above. This meeting place is like the break room in an office, the kitchen at a restaurant, or the wings and dressing rooms of a theatre. It's where the people who keep the show running prepare to play their roles and relax during their breaks. It's also where they can discuss topics that they wouldn't (and shouldn't) in front of members. Leaders are often faced with difficult situations, and they need a place to get advice, swap strategies, or simply let off steam.

Your backstage could be a private mailing list, message board, chat room, virtual building, buddy list, or some combination. At the Zone, for instance, leaders check in regularly at their designated area message board, receive announcements on several broadcast-style mailing lists, run into each other casually in private leaders-only chat rooms, and stay in touch with other leaders using the Zone's proprietary buddy list system. EverQuest Guides hold regular meetings in a leaders-only area of the game and use a private message board to file daily reports on what happened during their shift.

Evaluating Leader Performance

Because official leaders have special powers and insider knowledge, you also need ways to keep track of what they're up to. The most important information will come from your members, so make sure they know how to register both complaints and praise for community leaders. A special email address for comments about volunteer leaders will let members know that you're interested in feedback.

Staying in Touch with Buddy Lists

Buddy lists (described in Chapter 4) are a especially useful for community leaders. In many popular Web communities—including GeoCities, Ultima Online, and eBay—the official leaders use Internet-wide buddy list systems like ICQ (www.icq.com), while other communities—including AOL, Talk City, and the Zone— encourage their leaders to use a proprietary system that limits each person's list to people within that one community.

So should you choose proprietary or nonproprietary? Watch out—this is one of those issues where the goals of the owners may be in conflict with the desires of the members. From an owner's perspective, a proprietary buddy list reinforces the community's identity and keeps people there, while an Internet-wide buddy list pulls them away. But most people have an online life that transcends the boundaries of any single Web community, and it's inconvenient and annoying to have their buddy list limited to a single Web community. Be aware, however, that Internet-wide buddy lists can pose a security risk. For example, an Ultima Online volunteer leader who was using ICQ had his account hacked, which caused some consternation among the players. After this episode, Origin discouraged their official leaders from using ICQ.

Yet another option is to license and "brand" an Internet-wide system for use within your community, as iVillage did recently with PeopleLink (www.peoplelink.com). This approach will make more sense once there's a standard in place and the security holes in these systems have been ironed out. In general, I'd advise against using a proprietary system unless there's a really compelling reason, such as special features that you're offering within a high-end gaming environment. Your own policy will depend on how much power your community leaders have and how mischievous and technically savvy your members tend to be. (Gaming sites, beware!)

When you receive feedback from members, look for patterns in the complaints, especially if your community is large. An isolated complaint could be a disgruntled member with a bone to pick, but if you start to see a pattern of complaints about a particular leader, than you'll know you need to take steps to fix the problem.

You'll also want to find out what your leaders think about how things are going, and one way to do that is to ask them for weekly status reports that summarize their activities and bring up any concerns. These reports don't replace direct managerial contact, but they can be a great way to keep a finger on the pulse of the community and get an early warning about potential problems.

When Good Leaders Go Bad

As your leadership program grows, it's almost inevitable that you'll have problems with some of your leaders, which could range from habitual lateness to gross abuse of their powers.

The punishment, of course, should fit the crime—and the code of conduct you develop for leaders will evolve over time to cover these situations and their consequences.

Once you've determined that an official community leader has indeed abused his or her powers, it's important to deal with the situation swiftly and publicly. Many Web communities make the mistake of removing the errant leader with no apology or explanation, which can lead to speculation and paranoia. It's generally more effective to be up front about what happened and to apologize to the community for the lapse in service (because that's essentially what it is). It's also good to let the community know what steps are being taken to prevent such occurrences happening again, such as a better filtering and training process or new and improved techniques to monitor community leaders. By publicly admonishing leaders who misbehave, you'll be showing your members, vividly and directly, that actions have consequences.

The Informed Leader

Feedback loops should flow in both directions: in addition to keeping tabs on your leaders, you'll want to keep them up to date about what's happening within the system. You could set up one or more leaders only mailing lists for announcements and updates and then automatically subscribe leaders to the appropriate list(s). You could also use this mailing list to send out a weekly newsletter about what's going on in the community—a step that will be especially appreciated by volunteers, who love to feel like they're "on the inside."

Watching the Numbers

You can also use statistical analysis tools to watch what your leaders are doing. For example, you can get a feel for someone's hosting skills by looking at the traffic patterns in that person's areas. Gail Williams, the community manager on the WELL, spends time every month reviewing the conference traffic statistics and uses the information to help identify problem areas, which she then investigates in more detail. A host might be going through a personal crisis that is causing him to neglect his duties. Or a host might be trying hard but having trouble getting her conference off the ground. In either case, the statistics help Gail and her staff keep the conferences running smoothly and provide support to the volunteer leaders when it's needed.

Issues that require more extended discussion can be brought up in a leaders-only message board, online meeting, or some other form of group get-together. For example, the community staff members at GeoCities used to host a monthly conference call with all the GeoCities Community Liaisons, to keep them informed about what's happening inside the company and answer any pressing technical or social questions. Key members from every department are invited to attend and answer questions about their area of expertise. These meetings let the Liaisons know they were valued, and helped promote consistency by making sure everyone heard the same message from the top.

Tools for Leaders

Leaders also need tools to do their job, appropriate to the task they're performing. Someone who's hosting message boards may need to control access to the gathering place and edit or remove content, and a chat host will need a way to silence or remove disruptive members and communicate one-on-one with individual members.

Some message board and chat packages don't include much in the way of hosting tools—which can limit your leadership program's growth—so you should consider these issues when you're choosing your communications software, or deciding where to host your community. One AOL member found a financial opportunity in these tools, by developing a widely used program called Powertools (**AOL keyword: Powertools**) that offers many powerful features for chat hosts.

Reward Their Best Efforts

In addition to keeping an eye out for problems, you'll also want to find ways to acknowledge leaders who are doing a particularly good job. This is especially important for volunteers, who thrive on feeling needed and appreciated, but positive reinforcement is important for all of your community leaders.

A Celebration of Excellence

You can start by noting those occasions when your leaders contribute something special to the community, such as starting a newsletter, writing an FAQ, or handling a particularly difficult situation gracefully. This acknowledgement can take place in private, via email or phone, but it's even more powerful when it takes place in front of the leader's peers. For example, you could acknowledge special contributions in the weekly leaders-only newsletter, or post a note of appreciation on a leaders-only message board.

You could also create a public program to acknowledge leaders who go above and beyond the call of duty, like the Adobe Featured Host program (Figure 5.17). Hosts often take great pride in being acknowledged like this, so if you do institute such as program, it's a good idea to add a badge or medal of some kind to that person's public profile to enhance their participation history

Moving on Up

As your leadership program grows, you may need to create some layers of management to keep everything running smoothly. Some leaders will be eager to take on a more senior role with increased responsibility, visibility, and power. To help you select the best possible candidates for these roles, you'll want to keep a record of each leader's performance—not to watch their every move, but to keep track of any awards and commendations they've received, problems they've had performing their duties, and any member complaints. Ideally, your choices about who to promote will come from day-to-day contact with your leaders, but in practice that's not always possible. In the fast-changing world of Web communities, a recently hired staff member may be making the decision about who to promote, and the performance records of community leaders can help them make an informed decision.

FIGURE 5.17
ADOBE'S FEATURED HOSTS
Each month, the Adobe User's Forum
highlights a volunteer message board
host who's doing a particularly good
job. The page also lists previously featured hosts.

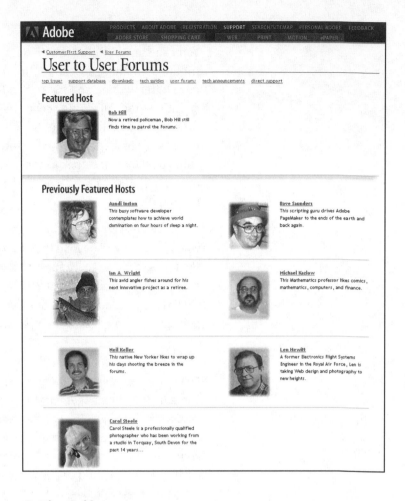

FIGURE 5.17

ADOBE'S FEATURED HOSTS

Each month, the Adobe User's Forum highlights a volunteer message board host who's doing a particularly good job. The page also lists previously featured hosts.

Getting Paid

At some point, as your community grows, you'll want to actually pay people to keep things running smoothly. Some communities elect to pay their community managers and leaders from the start; others establish a volunteer organization first and then elevate people into paid positions.

In general, you should try to fill your paid community positions with volunteer leaders or enthusiasts who have demonstrated their dedication to the community. It's very motivating for the community to see that volunteers can get hired—not to mention the benefits to you of drawing from such a pool of good candidates. Many of my clients have told me that their best community staffers have risen through the ranks of their community leader program.

The Community Manager

The most important leadership role in your community is the Community Manager, the person who is ultimately responsible for keeping the community running smoothly. In a small community, this role is often played by the founder—the person who set up the mailing list, message board, or online club. In a larger community, the Community Manager might be a full-time staff member who's responsible for things such as:

○ Defining key leadership positions (and the powers and responsibilities associated with each position)

○ Creating social and legal policies for leaders and members

○ Setting up a training program for each leadership role

○ Overseeing the creation (and continual updating) of a leadership manual

○ Defining the compensation (financial or otherwise) for community leaders

○ Creating feedback mechanisms for evaluating the effectiveness of community leaders

○ Training and managing a community staff

The number of people the Community Manager has to manage, that is, the people needed to handle these duties, will grow along with your community. For example, the GeoCities Community

Leaders program was initially launched by a single staff member, Erika Kerakas, who handled recruitment and training and developed the initial guidelines in collaboration with the first wave of Community Leaders. At the time it went public, GeoCities employed over a dozen full-time staff members to manage and develop their leadership program, which had grown to include several thousand Community Leaders.

A Clear Chain of Command

Among your community leaders and staff, it's useful to develop a clear chain of command, so that everyone knows what they're responsible for, and who to call on for help if they run into a problem that they're not equipped to handle. This is especially important in a real-time, chat-based environment, because things can get out of hand very quickly—the damage will be minimized if front-line community leaders are able to handle situations quickly and consistently. For example, Talk City chat hosts are empowered to handle minor skirmishes between members, but if someone starts seriously harassing another member, or using hate speech, the host will immediately page a CSA (Community Standards Advisor, the "cops" of Talk City). And if a CSA believes that someone needs to be permanently banned from the system, they'll refer the problem to the Community Manager, who can then consult the Director of Community about policy issues if need be.

Communities run more smoothly when there's someone who's ultimately in charge—someone who's available to handle crises, empowered to solve problems, and invested in (and respected by) the community. This might be the founder; but it might also be the community manager, the CEO, the Director of Customer Support, or the Head Wizard. In any case, that person should be seen to be involved in the community in order to retain the confidence of the members. This was made vividly clear on the WELL back in 1995, when a period of social unrest and upheaval led to the formation of a spin-off community called The River (www.river.org). The new owner was inaccessible during this time; regardless of whether or not he could have actually *done* anything, his absence during this crisis dealt a fatal blow to his already shaky credibility as a leader.

Who's Responsible?

To foster an atmosphere of accountability and trust, you may want to not only make it clear with whom the buck stops, but also bring this person more vividly to life. One way to accomplish this is through a welcome letter, such as the iVillage MoneyLife letter shown in Figure 4.5. You could also provide background information about your "uber-leader," such as the bio for the Talk City Community Manager (Figure 5.18) or the Slashdot founder's page (Figure 5.19). In fact, you could provide profiles for all your community staff members, like Talk City, which gives the community a friendly and accessible feel. The downside to this approach is that staff turnover will become more public, and these people will become more accessible to recruiters. You'll need to weigh all these factors as you're deciding how visible you want your community staff to be.

Another way to promote a sense of accessibility is to publish email addresses for key staff members, as Talk City does (www.talkcity.com/about/whodoeswhat.html). If you do this, however, be sure to tell your members what they can expect in the way of response, so they don't get angry if they don't receive a prompt reply.

Smooth Sailing

With a strong group of trained, empowered leaders, you'll stand a much better chance of maintaining the standards of behavior that you'd like to promote. These standards are the etiquette of your community, and you need to be clear and consistent about what you expect from all members. The next chapter covers how to establish a set of ground rules and enforce them when necessary.

Jenna Woodul

Vice President Community and
Co-Founder
Talk City, Inc., Inc.

eMail:
jenna@corp.talkcity.com

Jenna Woodul is the Vice President, or perhaps better said,
the team leader of community at and a co-founder of Talk
City, Inc., a new Internet content studio. Talk City, Inc. is
the only Internet studio focused on bringing community and
audience participation to high quality original programming
for the consumer market.

In her role at Talk City, Inc., Jenna leads and supports a
virtual team of conference hosts and community creative
talents located in many countries around the world.
Although many have never met in person, they share a
common passion for people, respect for individuals and a
love of shared experiences. It is from the energy of this
virtual team that Talk City, Inc., and its mission to bring
people together through Internet services, was born.

Jenna Woodul began her on-line career in 1984, heading up a
group of editors for AppleLink, Apple Computer's business
communications service. She was a core member of the team
that sought to develop a customer, community-oriented
version of AppleLink. Known as AppleLink Personal
Edition, that project eventually evolved into the service and
company that became America Online.

Jenna managed the Apple interactive events staff. She soon
discovered the joys of talking about books while tending to
small children, of attending computing lectures without
hassling for parking space, of participating in lively social
functions with a transcontinental flair. Fascinated by the
potential of the medium, she showed up at Apple again in
1993, angling for the charter to develop on-line community
for eWorld.

FIGURE 5.19
SLASHDOT FOUNDER'S HOMEPAGE
cmdrtaco.net
Slashdot's main menu has a link to the home page of Rob Malda, the founder. This page helps to communicate the values and attitude that underlie Slashdot's culture.

Welcome to CmdrTaco.net, the Home Away from Home of Rob Malda. This is the place where you can sit and stare in slackjawed amazement at my collection of Amazingly Stupid Stuff that I actually sat down and took the time to put online. Be afraid.

For your convenience, my Amazingly Stupid Stuff has been divided into 2 convenient easy-for-me-to-screw-up categories. Why are they easy to screw up? Well, because in my world, these categories tend to overlap a tad. Keep reading, you'll see why.

Linux What? You haven't heard of Linux? It's an operating system created by Linus Torvalds, and a band of hacks scattered accross the globe. You can check out My Linux Page if you want some more information, or My Stuff if you are looking for code that I've slapped together over the years. This includes the home of the amazingly outdated ascd, asmixer, asmodem & ascdc (a series of Afterstep and now WindowMaker docklets) as well as some screenshots and configs for some of my Afterstep and Enlightenment desktops.

Slashdot I guess I should just fess up and take the blame- I created Slashdot a long time ago, and now it seems to have grown into something pretty amazing. Come on down and check it out for news about Linux, Open Source Software, Legos, Games, Star Wars, Science, Technology and pretty much anything else that falls into the "News for Nerds, Stuff that Matters" umbrella.

Java Invaders if you came looking for Invaders, then tough beans. Sun asked me to change the name because it contained their highly protected top-secret, we'd tell you, but then we'd have to kill you word: Java. They own Java now. Look out StarBucks. To bad- it used to be a cute Space Invaders Clone. I was always sorta worried Atari would bitch- who knew Sun would.

Raytracer I wrote a cheesy raytracer for a Graphics class back when I was still a part of that whole college education thing. I have here a few of those stereotypical chrome-sphere-rendered-over-checkerboards online to prove that I once actually did some math.

Duckpins Behold my first feeble attempt at the world of Computer Animation in the form of Duckpins. Created during Jan-Feb of 96, I wrote, produced, directed animated edited and catered a 60 second CGI short. Download. Watch. Laugh (please?).

Hamster Havoc Following up a smash hit like Duckpins is no easy task, but I'm the only person obsessive enough to try. During the summer of 96, Rob Malda Films brought Hamster Havoc to to net. You can see exciting stills or even download the whole dang clip. It's the story of a boy, a hamster, and- awh nevermind. Who am I kidding? It barely has a plot. Download it- I think its funny.

Literature? Barely. But I might even be considered a writer. Of course, those who consider me a writer are legally blind. Anyway, Here is a little I wrote called Nerds, Unix, and Virtual Parenting. Here's another little essay I wrote about my recent obsession with Juice. Since I wrote those, most of my writings have moved to Taco Hell. I occasionally rant there about anything that is on my mind. Check it out if you like. Or don't. What do I know?

Cartoons I've scanned in and posted a small collection of Cartoons that I drew during high school. It's a desperate attempt to convince myself that I'm more than a Code Jockey- underneath this pocket protector clad exterior beats the heart of starving artist. Anyway, you can view these various works of mediocrity that I am so ashamed of, that I've placed them here for public ridicule.

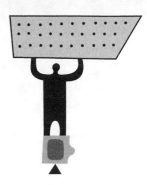

CHAPTER SIX

ETIQUETTE:
Rules to Live By

Etiquette refers to a set of behaviors—or community standards—that a group of people has agreed to abide by. These standards bring a community's beliefs and values into focus by celebrating what's admired and letting people know what won't be tolerated.

In a medium as fluid and flexible as the Web, establishing and maintaining community standards can be challenging. Online culture has long been anti-authoritarian, and people in Web communities routinely do and say things they'd never dare to in a face-to-face encounter. To complicate matters further, the tools for enforcing community ground rules are still primitive, and the laws governing cyberspace are in their early formative stages and changing rapidly.

Nonetheless, communities need clear social boundaries to thrive—so if you want to build a substantial and lasting Web community, you'll need to create some basic ground rules that are tailored to your audience, and set up systems that let you evolve these rules to meet the changing needs of your community.

In this Chapter

DEVELOP YOUR GROUND RULES

ENFORCE YOUR POLICIES

EVOLVE YOUR RULES

Develop Your Ground Rules

How do you figure out how to behave in a public gathering place? In the physical world, you look at the furnishings and decorations of a place, the way people look and act, and the official roles they're playing to assess what kind of situation you're in. Even if you're new in town, these cues help you to quickly figure out how to behave appropriately in a run-down neighborhood tavern, or an upscale downtown bar.

On the Web, it's much harder to read a social situation. All AOL chat rooms, for instance, look identical (save for an unobtrusive title)—yet while one room might host a supportive chat for arthritis sufferers, another serves as a raucous hangout for forty-something flirts, and still another functions as a place for kids to play word games. If you were to wander through all these chat rooms one evening, it would be challenging to figure out each room's etiquette standards at a glance.

Mark Your Social Boundaries

Because so many of the social cues we depend on in the physical world are missing online, you'll need to find more explicit ways to set the tone for your gathering places. You can start by creating a strong brand identity (as discussed in Chapter 1), and then marking the boundaries among different gathering places (see Chapter 2). You can also express the character of your community by designing member profiles that reflect your values (see Chapter 3), and by drawing attention to members and leaders who embody what your community is all about (see Chapters 4 and 5).

Show Me a Sign

All these cues are helpful—but if you want to build a robust and thriving Web community, you'll also need to develop and display some written ground rules. Like the "No Shirt, No Shoes, No Service" sign at a business entrance, posting your ground rules will help people know what kind of the place they're entering, and how to behave. Depending on the size and style of your community, these guidelines might be as simple as a friendly welcome letter, or as complex as a collection of legally binding contracts. Along with visual and navigational cues, your ground rules mark the social (and legal) boundary between your community and the rest of the Net.

Just as a town has local ordinances, but establishments within the town may post their own signs, your community may also include subcommunities that need their own rules. In that case, you'll need to mark your internal social boundaries as well. For example, the AOL Terms of Service (TOS) defines the line between AOL and the rest of the Net and applies to all AOL members and publishers. But some areas within AOL—such as places where kids hang out, or where people go for medical advice—post additional rules and guidelines (Figure 6.1).

FIGURE 6.1

AOL TERMS OF SERVICE AND LOCAL ORDINANCES

The AOL Terms of Service (top image) is an ever-evolving document that articulates social and legal guidelines for all AOL members. Some internal communities with special etiquette issues—like the Kids area (middle image) and the Better Health support groups (bottom image)—have developed "local ordinances" that apply only within those areas.

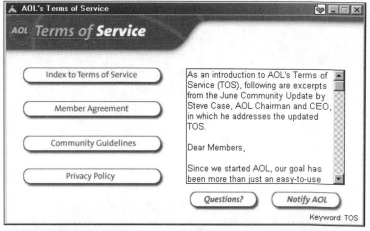

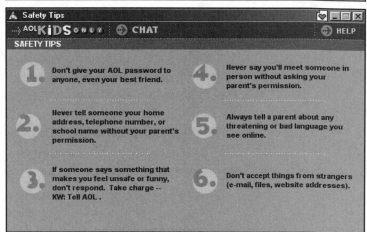

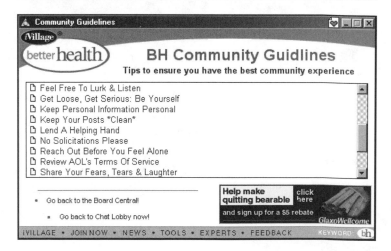

The Etiquette Cycle

Posting written ground rules is a good step, but it's only the beginning. Once people are inside these well-marked areas, the ground rules are subject to interpretation (see sidebar: What Are Community Standards?). And in a fast-changing medium like the Web, your rules may quickly become outdated and need to be revamped.

That's why, in addition to creating ground rules, you'll also need to develop mechanisms for interpreting and enforcing these rules and evolving them to keep pace with the changing needs of your community. This process can be broken down into three basic and reoccurring steps (Figure 6.2):

- You **CREATE** documents that spell out the ground rules for participation in your community

- You **ENFORCE** these ground rules, so that people take you (and the rules) seriously.

- You **EVOLVE** your ground rules to answer questions, clarify ambiguities, and address emerging social and legal issues.

FIGURE 6.2
THE ETIQUETTE CYCLE
These three steps form a continuous cycle of development for your community standards. Once you create your standards, you'll need to enforce them; this will bring about the need to develop and evolve your standards. The larger and more successful your community grows, the more intensive this process will become.

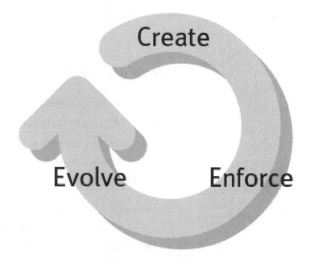

I call these steps the *Etiquette Cycle*, because the process of creating and refining your ground rules is an ongoing cycle. Whether you're launching a new Web community or fine-tuning an existing one, it's a good idea to consider each of these steps early, while you're building your community platform. Things change fast on the Web—and more successful you are, the more important it will be to have a process in place for managing this ongoing cycle.

What Are Community Standards?

When a group of people coalesce into a community, they develop a unique set of *community standards* that reflect their needs, interests, and values. Depending on the community, these standards may be expressed *explicitly* as rules, laws, and guidelines or *implicitly* through everyday social dynamics.

In general, the larger and more diverse the community, the greater the need for explicit rules with clear and enforceable consequences. In the United States, for example, our basic rights and responsibilities are defined in the Constitution (and its amendments), which are updated and enforced through a complex and multi-layered legal system.

While useful and necessary, explicit rules can only go so far in expressing and reinforcing the prevailing etiquette. Each community develops its own unique flavor, which is maintained through friendliness, ridicule, gossip, and bragging rights. For example, two bars that have the same sign at the door: "No One Under 21 Allowed" can either encourage brawling or evict fighters. Same explicit rules—different community standards.

Although bars and other places in the physical world offer visual clues as to the prevailing community standards (the body language and clothing style of the patrons, the decor and general ambiance of the interior, the type of vehicles parked outside), Web community builders often don't have such clues available, so they must express their community standards more explicitly than might be called for in the offline world.

Create Your Documents

Your first step in developing robust community standards is to create documents that outline your ground rules for participation. These ground rules will address the basic social and legal issues involved with participating in your community, such as ownership, liability, privacy, civility, and censorship.

You'll be updating these documents to keep pace with a rapidly changing world, so for both social and legal reasons, it's best to have something in place when you first launch your community. You might wonder, "How do I create ground rules for a community that doesn't yet exist?" You can't answer all your questions, of course, or anticipate every situation—but you can set a tone right from the start that expresses your purpose, goals and values. For example, the WELL launched with the phrase "You own your own words," which was later elaborated into a more comprehensive form (see Figure 6.4). This simple statement had both social and legal implications, and it has had a profound impact on the WELL's social dynamics and policy decisions.

You can't anticipate every situation—but you can set a tone right from the start that expresses your purpose, goals and values.

The Fine Print

Before addressing social issues, you'll want to make sure that your bases are covered legally. This means creating a document that's a contractual agreement between you, and the people who visit and/or join your community.

There are two basic types of legal documents for Web communities: *Terms of Use* (AKA Terms and Conditions, User Agreement), and *Terms of Service* (AKA Service Agreement, Member Agreement). Both are legally binding contracts—and while these agreements may contain overlapping provisions, Terms of Use generally address rights and responsibilities of anyone who visits or uses the site, while Terms of Service address rights and responsibilities of members, or anyone who receives an ongoing service through the community.

Which type of document will you need? That depends on how you're running your community. If you're using the services of a community aggregator such as Yahoo, Topica or Talk City, your activities will be governed by its posted legal tems. Be sure to familiarize yourself with any legally binding documents before you sign up, because these rules can affect your ability to develop your community in the future.

If you're running your own community site, you'll want to post a Terms of Use agreement before allowing visitors to access your site. If you're running a membership-based community and/or delivering an ongoing service, you'll want to create a Terms of

Service agreement that clarifies the legal arrangement between you and your members. Although most sites only have one Terms document, some sites such as E*TRADE (www.etrade.com) include both types of agreements—a Terms of Use for the entire site (which applies to both visitors and members), and a Terms of Service for the members-only community areas.

The exact contents of your Terms document will depend on which features your community offers. Whatever the contents, try to make the tone and formality of your legal documents reflect the style and purpose of your community. For example, the Nickelodeon Terms document contains enough legal language to protect a high-profile media company but also speaks directly to kids—and in doing so, reinforces the central tenet of the Nickelodeon brand (Figure 6.3).

The easiest way to get started creating your Terms is to find a similar document and tweak it to meet your needs (see companion Web site, www.naima.com/community). As you look through several Terms documents, you'll get an overview of topics to address and learn about some issues that you wouldn't necessarily think of in advance. I strongly encourage you, however, to work with a lawyer who's familiar with cyberspace law to finalize this document. Even if you think your community is low-key and immune from lawsuits, you'll want to have your bases covered if something should happen—and in the fast-changing world of the Web, it's always wise to expect the unexpected.

Creating Your Member Agreement

Here's an overview of some key legal issues to keep in mind when you're creating your Member Agreement:

LIABILITY

Make it clear right up front who is liable for the content within your community. Are members responsible for their own words, Web pages, and other creations? Does the community management pre-filter member-created content? To what extent, and in what circumstances, will you be liable to a member for damages?

FIGURE 6.3
NICKELODEON TERMS AND CONDITIONS
www.nick.com/info/terms

FIGURE 6.3
NICKELODEON TERMS AND CONDITIONS
www.nick.com/info/terms
Your Terms document doesn't have to be devoid of personality; for instance, the Nickelodeon Terms document is a legally binding contract that still manages to speak directly to kids—the primary users of this site.

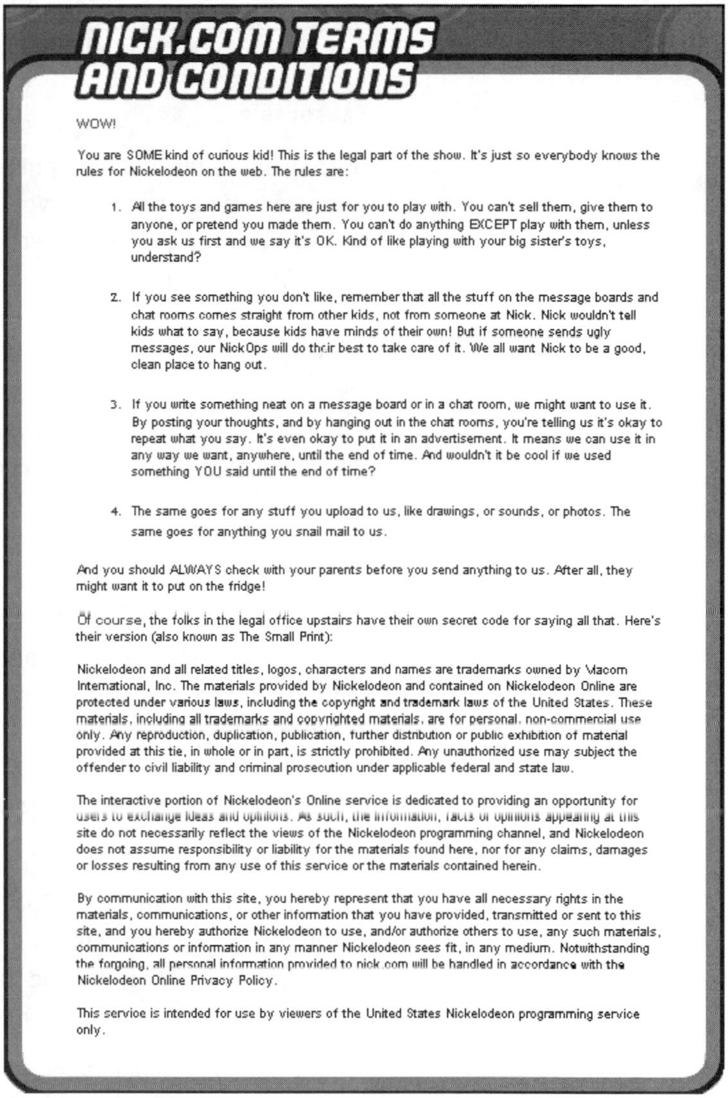

NICK.COM TERMS AND CONDITIONS

WOW!

You are SOME kind of curious kid! This is the legal part of the show. It's just so everybody knows the rules for Nickelodeon on the web. The rules are:

1. All the toys and games here are just for you to play with. You can't sell them, give them to anyone, or pretend you made them. You can't do anything EXCEPT play with them, unless you ask us first and we say it's OK. Kind of like playing with your big sister's toys, understand?

2. If you see something you don't like, remember that all the stuff on the message boards and chat rooms comes straight from other kids, not from someone at Nick. Nick wouldn't tell kids what to say, because kids have minds of their own! But if someone sends ugly messages, our NickOps will do their best to take care of it. We all want Nick to be a good, clean place to hang out.

3. If you write something neat on a message board or in a chat room, we might want to use it. By posting your thoughts, and by hanging out in the chat rooms, you're telling us it's okay to repeat what you say. It's even okay to put it in an advertisement. It means we can use it in any way we want, anywhere, until the end of time. And wouldn't it be cool if we used something YOU said until the end of time?

4. The same goes for any stuff you upload to us, like drawings, or sounds, or photos. The same goes for anything you snail mail to us.

And you should ALWAYS check with your parents before you send anything to us. After all, they might want it to put on the fridge!

Of course, the folks in the legal office upstairs have their own secret code for saying all that. Here's their version (also known as The Small Print):

Nickelodeon and all related titles, logos, characters and names are trademarks owned by Viacom International, Inc. The materials provided by Nickelodeon and contained on Nickelodeon Online are protected under various laws, including the copyright and trademark laws of the United States. These materials, including all trademarks and copyrighted materials, are for personal, non-commercial use only. Any reproduction, duplication, publication, further distribution or public exhibition of material provided at this tie, in whole or in part, is strictly prohibited. Any unauthorized use may subject the offender to civil liability and criminal prosecution under applicable federal and state law.

The interactive portion of Nickelodeon's Online service is dedicated to providing an opportunity for users to exchange ideas and opinions. As such, the information, facts or opinions appearing at this site do not necessarily reflect the views of the Nickelodeon programming channel, and Nickelodeon does not assume responsibility or liability for the materials found here, nor for any claims, damages or losses resulting from any use of this service or the materials contained herein.

By communication with this site, you hereby represent that you have all necessary rights in the materials, communications, or other information that you have provided, transmitted or sent to this site, and you hereby authorize Nickelodeon to use, and/or authorize others to use, any such materials, communications or information in any manner Nickelodeon sees fit, in any medium. Notwithstanding the forgoing, all personal information provided to nick.com will be handled in accordance with the Nickelodeon Online Privacy Policy.

This service is intended for use by viewers of the United States Nickelodeon programming service only.

WARRANTY

Define how members should interpret any content from the community staff (either created in-house or licensed). Many communities state that any information found within the site should be taken under advisement, and that the community management is not responsible for any actions that result from this information (for instance, medical advice). It is also common to see a disclaimer stating that the community site is offered "as is," and that there may be outages and downtime on occasion.

CENSORSHIP

If you want to reserve the right to edit and/or remove content that you find objectionable, you should state it as part of the Member Agreement (with reference to the Community Guidelines). This could include postings, Web pages, or other member-created content. You might also want to establish a mechanism by which members may request removal of objectionable content. In any event, if you intend to police content prepared by others, you should be clear in your Member Agreement that you do not necessarily endorse the content left up on the site.

ILLEGAL ACTIVITY

You'll want to make it clear that any illegal activity—such as copyright violation, trade in illegal substances, child pornography—is expressly forbidden, and spell out how these situations will be handled. This topic is often covered again in the Community Guidelines.

Develop Behavioral Guidelines

Some Web communities—including Nickelodeon—include behavioral guidelines within their Terms document. There's nothing inherently wrong with this—but because these documents are often written in rather dry and daunting language, you can't count on everyone reading it, much less understanding it.

For this reason, it's best to provide a separate Community Guidelines document (AKA Code of Conduct, Community Rules, Community Standards, Member Guidelines) that outlines the social conventions of your community in clear and straightforward language. This will help your members understand your guidelines and make it easier for you to maintain and update both documents as well. (You always associate these documents by referencing your Member Agreement from within your Community Guidelines—see Figure 6.4).

Home Join About Conferencing Members Services & Help Enter

THE WELL Conferencing

Community Guidelines

The free-wheeling WELL was launched in 1985 with minimal rules. The aphorism crafted to greet users at the time was:

You Own Your Own Words

Recently this now classic and carefully-tended policy has been expanded into the WELL Member Agreement with detailed explanations of the implications of "YOYOW," as members refer to it.

WELL Policies and Etiquette

The WELL, as a community, functions on mutual respect and cooperation.

Computer conferencing is quite different from face-to-face communication. Only your words travel over the network -- the facial expressions, tone of voice, and other live conversational nuances are completely absent from discussions on The WELL.

MEMBER AGREEMENT

So what should you cover in your Community Guidelines? There are three basic types of issues to address:

- **LEGAL ISSUES** like copyright violations, illegal activities, and own-ership of member-generated content. Although this information may be present in the Terms document, it's helpful to restate it here in an accessible way. Just remember to be consistent with your Terms document.

- **SOCIAL ISSUES** like swearing, spamming, posting off topic, or impersonating an employee. This document is the place to spell out what behaviors won't be tolerated, and also which behaviors will be encouraged and rewarded.

- **SUPPORT ISSUES** like how to use the tools and where to go for help. In a larger community, these issues often appear in separate documents, which can be referenced within the Guidelines (see below).

Some issues—such as prohibiting illegal activities and forbidding sexual harassment and racial slurs—are common to most communities. But the details of your social guidelines will depend on the style and purpose of your community. Some communities will accommodate, and even encourage, a wide range of expressiveness, while others have more stringent social requirements. For example, the WELL Community Guidelines offer helpful suggestions for online etiquette, while expressly allowing for different tastes and maturity levels (Figure 6.4). Contrast this with the CNN Community Standards, which proudly announce that "You may find our standards more stringent than other Web-based communities" and list specific behaviors that are forbidden, including straying off the stated topic (Figure 6.5).

FIGURE 6.5
CNN COMMUNITY STANDARDS
cnn.com/discussion/standards.html
CNN's discussions exist to foster focused discussion of newsworthy topics. Accordingly, CNN's guidelines are strongly worded, and inappropriate or off-topic postings are regularly removed from the message boards (as stated in the guidelines).

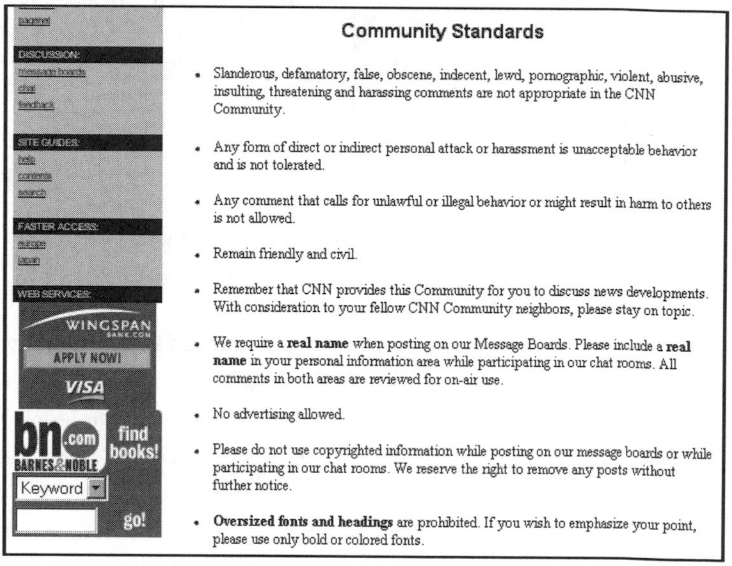

Community Standards

- Slanderous, defamatory, false, obscene, indecent, lewd, pornographic, violent, abusive, insulting, threatening and harassing comments are not appropriate in the CNN Community.

- Any form of direct or indirect personal attack or harassment is unacceptable behavior and is not tolerated.

- Any comment that calls for unlawful or illegal behavior or might result in harm to others is not allowed.

- Remain friendly and civil.

- Remember that CNN provides this Community for you to discuss news developments. With consideration to your fellow CNN Community neighbors, please stay on topic.

- We require a **real name** when posting on our Message Boards. Please include a **real name** in your personal information area while participating in our chat rooms. All comments in both areas are reviewed for on-air use.

- No advertising allowed.

- Please do not use copyrighted information while posting on our message boards or while participating in our chat rooms. We reserve the right to remove any posts without further notice.

- **Oversized fonts and headings** are prohibited. If you wish to emphasize your point, please use only bold or colored fonts.

It's generally a good idea to have a single Guidelines document that applies throughout your community and sets the overall tone, such as the WELL and CNN guidelines, or the iVillage 'Rules of Play/Community Covenant' (www.ivillage.com/boards/aux/0,3451,N~rule,00.html). But if your community includes diverse subgroups, you'll need more than one Guidelines document (as illustrated in Figure 6.1 above). If your community includes international or kids areas, or an adults-only area where language restrictions are relaxed, or support groups that require extra discretion, than you'll need to clearly mark these social boundaries and let your visitors know what's expected of them (see Chapter 9 for more about "local ordinances").

Creating Your Community Guidelines

The contents of your Community Guidelines will depend on things like the purpose of your community, the interactive features provided, and the age and sophistication of your audience. Whatever you include, you'll need to be familiar with certain common issues.

PERSISTENT AND UNIQUE IDENTITY

Most communities require their members to register using their real name (although it won't necessarily be revealed to other members) and refrain from impersonating another member, especially a leader. Some communities also ask members not to register under multiple names.

APPROPRIATE CONDUCT AND ILLEGAL ACTIVITIES

Communities differ on the boundaries for acceptable conduct. Some actions , such as hate speech, overt harassment, libel and slander, and disruptive behavior like "scrolling" in a chat room are universally forbidden. Other issues such as swearing, off-topic posting, and using pseudonyms are highly dependent on the local culture and vary from community to community. Most Web communities include a statement reminding members that illegal activities—such as copyright violations, slander and libel, posting software serial numbers, and so on—are expressly forbidden.

CONTENT STANDARDS AND OWNERSHIP

If your community offers members the ability to create persistent content (such as message board postings, Web pages or HTML-enhanced member profiles) you'll need to outline content standards that specify what kind of content is encouraged and disallowed, who own the rights to the content once it's posted on the site, and what will happen to content that violates these standards. If you decide, for liability or other reasons, that you do not want to own the content, you may want to have it licensed to you for certain specified uses. Many communities include a content standards clause about in their Terms document—but it's also a good idea to include an easy-to-understand description of your content standards somewhere in your Community Guidelines.

COMMERCIAL USE

Many Web communities—particularly free ones—forbid their members from using the interactive features of the site for commercial purposes. If the community offers a commercial program, such as an online store, the commercial areas are usually segregated, and solicitations are forbidden in other areas of the site.

Privacy Concerns

To many people, the Web looks like a scary and unregulated place—and Web communities are particularly suspect. Once you know who someone is, you can easily track their movements and transactions within your site. You can build trust with your members by giving them a sense of control over what's happening to their personal information (discussed in Chapter 3). You can take an important step in this direction by creating (and living up to) a Privacy Policy for your community that outlines what data you're collecting, why you're collecting it, and what you'll be doing with that data.

An easy way to get started is to visit TRUSTe (www.truste.org), an organization that functions as a "Privacy Provider" for Web publishers. TRUSTe offers many services to help you create your Privacy Policy, including a "Privacy Wizard" that will help you create an initial privacy statement. Going through this process is a good way to educate yourself about privacy issues—but if you want to display the TRUSTe "trustmark" on your site, you'll need to become a member of TRUSTe. As a member, you'll get help tailoring your privacy statement, and TRUSTe will review your site periodically—which gives *your* members a place to go if they feel your stated policies have been violated. (Most of the Web communities mentioned in this book participate in the TRUSTe program; a full list can be found at www.truste.org/users/users_lookup.html).

As with Terms of Service and Community Guidelines, you may need to create several privacy statements if your site contains subcommunities with special privacy needs. For example, Yahoo runs a network of sites, all of which are covered by Yahoo's basic privacy agreement—except for Yahooligans, which is directed at children and has its own privacy statement (Figure 6.6). (The issue of children's privacy on the Net is changing rapidly, so if your community includes this audience, you'll need to make a special effort to stay aware of, and compliant with, the legal requirements.)

FIGURE 6.6
YAHOOLIGANS PRIVACY POLICY
www.yahooligans.com/content/tg/privacy.html
Yahoo includes a privacy policy that covers its many related sites, but because of the special online privacy needs of children, Yahooligans has its own privacy policy.

Help!

Privacy Policy

Yahooligans! takes the issue of safeguarding your online privacy very seriously. Please read the following to understand our views and practices regarding this matter, and how they pertain to you as you make full use of our many offerings.

TRUSTe Certified

Yahooligans! is a licensee of the TRUSTe Privacy Program. This statement discloses the privacy practices for Yahooligans!. When you visit a Web site displaying the TRUSTe trustmark, you can expect to be notified of:

- What personally identifiable information of yours is collected;
- Who is collecting the information;
- How the information is used; and
- With whom the information may be shared.

In addition, Yahooligans! has also agreed to the following children's requirements when a visitor is under 13 years old. This site will:

1. NOT collect online contact information without prior parental consent or parental notification, which will include an opportunity for the parent to prevent use of the information and participation in the activity. Without prior parental consent, online information will only be used to respond directly to the child's request and will not be used for other purposes.
2. NOT collect personally identifiable offline contact information without prior parental consent.
3. NOT distribute to third parties any personally identifiable information without prior parental consent.
4. NOT give the ability to publicly post or otherwise distribute personally identifiable contact information without prior parental consent.
5. NOT entice by the prospect of a special game, prize or other activity, to divulge more information than is needed to participate in the activity.

Other Compliance Programs

If you're building a Web community that deals with a particularly sensitive or controversial issues—such as giving medical or financial advice, or offering access to violent computer games or adult material—you may want to offer your users extra assurances that go beyond the policies we've already covered. Just as your TRUSTe "trustmark" helps assure your users that their personal information is safe, you can also display your compliance with any self-regulating organizations in your field. For example, WebMD displays a "HON" icon, which links to a medical site code of conduct created by Health on the Net (www.hon.ch/HONcode/Conduct.html). Whether or not you decide to join such a program, it's wise to familiarize yourself with the policies of any voluntary compliance programs in your area, because you'll get an overview of issues and concerns that you may soon be grappling with in your own site.

Help is On the Way

In addition to drafting these three basic policy documents—member agreement, community guidelines, and privacy policy—you may also want to develop some more detailed "help" documents. For instance, if some of your members are Net newbies, and your community includes chat or message boards, it's a good idea to offer clear instructions and "Netiquette" tips, as Third Age (www.thirdage.com/help), Talk City (www.talkcity.com/help) and iVIllage (www.ivillage.com/membercenter) do.

If your community revolves around a more complex activity, like playing games or bidding on auctions, it's even more important to provide hints and tips that will help your members have a successful experience. For example, the Zone (ww.zone.com) features an extensive Help section that includes a new member tutorial, instructions for installing and using all the Zone interactive tools, and a series of steps to follow for dealing with problem players. And eBay includes a similar set of help features geared towards auctions (see Figure 6.14 below).

FAQs are Your Friend

As you collect feedback from your members, you'll noticet that certain questions come up repeatedly. You can streamline your communications by creating FAQs that address potentially confusing issues. The beauty of FAQs is that they're designed to evolve; people expect them to grow, and once in place, they're easy to modify and update. For example, when ZDTV switched their chat tool to the Palace, the staff created a FAQ about how to use the tool; when new questions came up, they simply added questions and answers to the existing document (www.zdnet .com/zdtv/interact/chatwithus/story/0,6924,2258125,00.html). If like ZDTV, you're using third-party tools, you may be able to get an initial FAQ from your tools provider that can help you kick-start this process.

In addition to any community-specific FAQs that you create, you may also want to craft a document that specifically addresses questions about cookies (see, for example, www.ivillage.com/ membercenter/cookies.html, help.netscape.com/kb/consumer/ 970226-2.html or www.nytimes.com/subscribe/help/cookies. html). This issue comes up often, because many people's Web browsers will warn them when sites place cookies on their hard drive. Some people turn off cookies permissions altogether, which can cause problems for membership-based communities. By explaining what cookies are, their advantages for the user, and how your Web community will be using them, you can alleviate some of the anxiety surrounding this technology and help your members to have a more comfortable experience on your site.

Enforce Your Policies

Creating basic ground rules is a good start, but these rules won't mean anything unless you enforce them. As we discussed in Chapter 3, build trust by keeping your promises—and your standards documents are essentially promises you make to your members about how things will be in your community. If you want to establish and maintain credibility with your members, you'll need to figure out how to enforce your ground rules with consistency and fairness.

You build trust by keeping your promises—and your standards documents are essentially promises to your members about how things will be in your community.

Power to the People

Many professionally run Web communities use trained leaders (see Chapter 5) to enforce their community guidelines. But it's also important to encourage and empower your members to manage their own interpersonal conflicts—not all communities have leaders on hand at all times. In any case, the community will run more smoothly if members are empowered to work out minor skirmishes between themselves.

Tools AND Rules

There's an old saying on the Net: "Tools, not rules," which comes out of the Net's anti-authoritarian origins. My own philosophy is "Tools AND Rules," which comes from seeing so many Web communities bicker endlessly about where the social boundaries are, and what the rules should be. Self-management tools are great, but they work best in communities where the rules for acceptable behavior are also clearly delineated.

I'm Ignoring You

One popular and well-established tool is the *Ignore Filter* (AKA Bozo Filter, Bozo List, Mute List), which allows someone to filter out the comments of specific people in a message board or chat room. If a member finds someone's comments annoying or distracting but wants to continue to frequent places where that person might show up, the member can put the annoying member on a personalized "ignore list." This feature is a great way to reduce tensions in your environment without requiring leader intervention—and if an annoying member is ignored by several of the participants in a discussion or chat, his or her comments won't drag the conversation off track.

Ignore lists are built into both IRC and Usenet, so any software that runs on top of these platforms (such as Talk City, WebMaster, or Remarq) should offer this feature. For example, the game Acrophobia (built on top of IRC) automatically offers members the ability to ignore other players (see Figure 6.7a). It's also something to look for when selecting or building message board or chat software for your own site. ETrade uses message board software from WELL Engaged that includes this feature, which they highlight in the discussions area of their site (**www.etrade. com/cgi-bin/gx.cgi/Applogic+Community?page=mylist.html**).

The downside of ignoring people is that members may lose conversational context and won't know if something's being said behind their backs. Nonetheless, it's generally helpful to provide this option to your members, and instruct them on how to use the feature appropriately.

Behind Closed Doors

Another way to help your members avoid certain people is to let them create private gathering places where they control the "door policy." For example, any full-fledged WELL member can create a private conference, and any Talk City user can create and host a private (although temporary) chat room for hanging out with friends (as shown back in Figure 4.16).

Although private gathering places can help maintain public civility, they're not automatically appropriate for every site. If you're running a large, full-service Web community like Talk City or AOL, you'll almost certainly want to offer them. If, however, you're running a site with a more focused purpose like eBay or CNN, you may want to introduce this feature judiciously, if at all. For example, private gathering spaces don't particularly enhance CNN's brand; in fact, they dilute the focus on moderated discussion and hosted events. As CNN community manager Lynn Clater says, "There's lots of places on the Net for people to have a private chat; when they're at CNN, we want them to be contributing to the public discussion."

Be careful that private spaces don't suck the life out of the more public areas of your community. If you're interested in offering private gathering places to your members, you may want to consider limiting them in some way—perhaps offering them an advanced feature for longer-term members, who usually have the greatest need for privacy anyway (see Chapter 4).

You Can't Say That Here

Another avoidance technique is the obscenity filter, which allows you to specify a list of words that will be automatically translated into an innocuous string of letters. Some Web communities include software that allows individual members to turn this filter on or off, and thus filter their own personal view of conversations. More often, community sites like Acrophobia will create both "family friendly" and "adult" gathering places; members can avoid profanity by choosing a "clean" room where the obscenity filter is on for the entire room, and they can report bad language when they encounter it (Figure 6.7b).

Although they dissuade some language abuse, in practice obscenity filters are of limited use because people can get around the filter by using alternate spellings of words. The real enforcement will come from members who understand the rules of the room and exert peer pressure on people who break those rules—with the backup and support of staff members who can be called on to handle the most egregious cases.

We're Not Gonna Take It

An intriguing approach to member self-management is to empower members to control their environment by pooling their opinions. Acrophobia, for example, includes a "complain" feature that allows the people in a chat room to vote an annoying person out of the room—essentially, to function as a "host in aggregate" (see **www.won.net/channels/bezerk/acro/afiles16.html**). This strategy is loosely related to both the Slashdot moderator system (see Chapter 5), and the eBay reputation system (see Chapter 3)—they all make use of the aggregate behavior and opinions of members. It's likely that we'll see more of these types of bottom-up systems in the future.

FIGURE 6.7A
ACROPHOBIA'S IGNORE FILTER
Players can choose to filter out messages
from a particular member.

FIGURE 6.7B
"CLEAN" OR "ADULT" ROOMS IN
ACROPHOBIA
www.berzerk.com
Acrophobia offers Keep it Clean rooms,
where the obscenity filter is turned on,
and Adult Language rooms where the
filter is off.

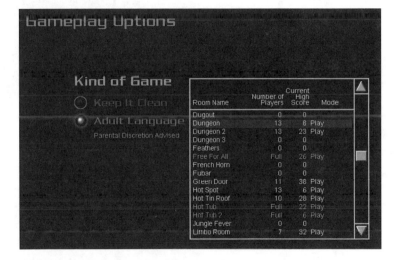

Handling Harassment

If you include any of these self-management tools in your community platform, it's a good idea to offer suggestions for how to best use them and what steps to take when handling harassment. For example, Acrophobia includes a monthly supplement to Community Guidelines called "The A Files" (Figure 6.8) that offers stories about the game, suggestions for how to play better, and a suggested escalation path for handling problem players (www.won.net/channels/bezerk/acro/afiles2.html). Similarly, eBay includes a document that outlines the steps to take when faced with a problem user (Figure 6.9).

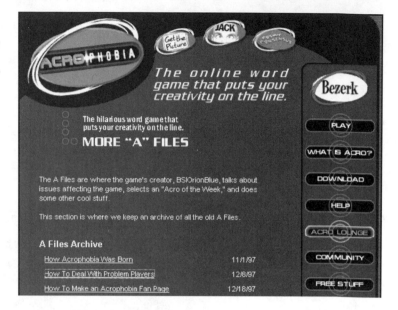

Who Ya Gonna Call?

In some communities, giving members the tools and resources to manage their own conflicts is sufficient for maintaining the community standards. But as they grow, many communities discover that this approach can result in a chaotic and unfocused environment, where the most disruptive and obnoxious people manage to dominate the scene.

You can avoid this kind of situation by populating your community with leaders who are empowered to interpret and enforce your community standards. Provided that your leaders are well trained and managed effectively (see Chapter 5), their presence will go a long way towards developing a sense of trust and security within your community.

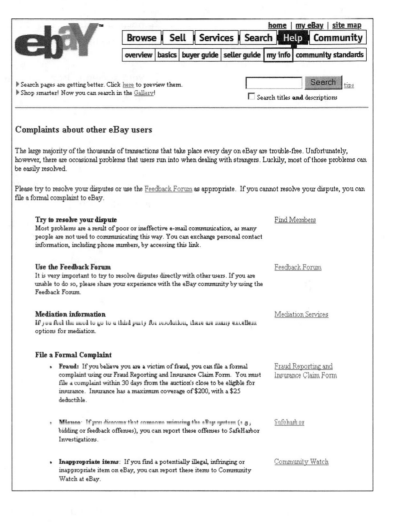

Imposing Consequences

There's a range of consequences that leaders can impose on members who violate the community standards. For example, a leader might:

○ Restrict someone's participation (gag someone in a chat room, freeze a player in a game)

○ Restrict someone's entry to a space (ban a member from particular conference, chat room, or game)

- Remove persistent content (Web pages, forum postings, uploaded files, MUD objects)

- Prevent someone from entering the community for some length of time

- Take legal action (prosecute someone for harassment, fraud or copyright violation)

These actions have increasingly severe and lasting consequences, with increasing potential for abuse. Therefore, you'll need to make sure that whoever has the power to impose such consequences is well equipped to handle the responsibility. The more severe the consequences, the more important it is to have a proven, trusted leader handle the problem. Nothing can destroy a member's trust faster than a heavy-handed leader who doesn't play fair.

Nothing can destroy a member's trust faster than a heavy-handed leader who doesn't play fair.

When you're creating your ground rules, think about what the punishment will be for violating these rules, and how you'll handle that process. Some communities like Ancient Sites go so far as to post these consequences, which drives home the message that certain behaviors that won't be tolerated (**www.ancientsites. com/xi/justice/listCode.rage**). Even if you don't make this kind of information public, you should go through the exercise of attaching specific consequences to rule violations, to make sure you're ready to enforce your rules.

To handle this issue effectively, you'll need a chain of command with a clearly defined escalation path for handling problems (as explained in Chapter 5). At each level of the hierarchy, leaders are responsible for handling specific types of problems, and have powers that are commensurate with their responsibilities. For example, Talk City has a robust and well-defined leadership hierarchy, which has allowed this community to maintain an amazingly civil atmosphere, given its size and diversity. The multiplayer fantasy game DragonRealms also features a well-developed hierarchy of leaders who know who to call on when a problem arises that exceeds their authority.

Leadership by Example

Elonka Dunkin, the General Manager of Simutronics, is in charge of the hosting programs for all Simutronics games, including DragonRealms. Because Simutronics has a robust and well-defined leadership hierarchy in place, Elonka rarely has to intervene in player affairs. But at one point, two powerful players were engaged in a vicious war of words on the GemStone message boards, and the game masters turned to Elonka for help. She contacted both players, and spoke to them at length about the effect that their actions were having on the community. Her solution was to give the combatants their own area on the Gemstone message boards to continue their flame war—the online equivalent of a bartender telling pugnacious patrons to "Take it outside, boys."

Elonka was careful not to take sides, and she wanted to avoid turning the warring parties into martyrs by banning them from the community. Her style of leadership is widely emulated within the GemStone leadership hierarchy, which is characterized by tolerance, fairness, and a supportive atmosphere

The Importance of Positive Role Models

It's important to offer avoidance tools and suggestions for handling harassment—but don't forget to shine a spotlight on members whose comments and creations embody your values, and demonstrate your etiquette standards. Although not everyone will read your written guidelines, members notice what others are doing and saying and follow suit.

This is especially true for leaders. As the designated authority figures, leaders will be observed, scrutinized, and emulated. It's important to impress upon your community leaders the ripple effect that their actions will have, and encourage them to carry out their duties with consistency and fairness. The higher up in the Leadership Hierarchy someone is, the more strongly this applies (see sidebar: Make the Punishment Fit the Crime).

Evolve Your Rules

Now that you've developed some ground rules, and put mechanisms into place to enforce them, you're ready for the third step in the Etiquette cycle: evolving your rules. This process is a natural and vital part of running your community—just like passing local ordinances is part of running a small town.

As your community grows, newcomers will arrive, features will be added, and unanticipated social issues will come up that throw some aspect of your rules into question and reveal ambiguities that need clarification. Don't be dismayed when your carefully crafted rules don't meet the needs of your growing community; just think of this process as "customizing" your community standards.

For example, when eBay was small and low-key, their standards were built on goodwill and mutual trust (**pages.ebay.com/help/ community/values.html**). As the community became more prominent, sellers posted increasingly questionable auctions on the site, so eBay has responded by adding documents that more explicitly spell out what's allowed and disallowed (**pages.ebay. com/help/community/png-items.html**). They'll continue this process as long as necessary.

Finger on the Pulse

The faster your community grows, the more important it will be to stay in touch with the changing social climate, and keep your rules relevant and up to date. To do this, you'll need to get feedback from both members and leaders, interpret that feedback, and, finally, update your standards documents and communicate any changes back to the community. Managing these feedback loops can be time consuming and somewhat tricky; but it's a necessity for maintaining a successful community in the fast-changing environment of the Web.

Listen to Your Members

One way to keep your finger on the community pulse is to encourage your members to send you email feedback about any etiquette problems they're having. These messages can help you assess how well your rules are working, and serve as an early warning system for problems before they spin out of control. For example, the message boards at Family.com include a "Notify Host" button for reporting inappropriate postings (family.go.com/Features/family_0000_01/dony/NotifyHost/NotifyHost.html).

To go even further, you could create a specific public forum where members can discuss the rules, such as the WELL's Policy conference (Figure 6.10). Unlike private email, a policy-oriented message board lets members compare notes with others in the community, and gives leaders an opportunity to engage in the dialogue and explain the rationale behind policy decisions, which can be extraordinarily helpful in managing disagreement and dissent.

Be warned: you may get a disproportionate number of comments from chronic malcontents who have nothing better to do than complain about your shortcomings (see sidebar: Interpreting Feedback). If your only feedback mechanisms are problem-oriented, you'll develop a skewed picture of what your members think about your community. To balance this out, make an effort to solicit feedback from the "silent majority" (the people who neither love you nor hate you) by using periodic surveys, polls, and focus groups (described in Chapter 1), or by offering a form on your site to gather members' input, as the Palace does (Figure 6.11).

Really *Listen to Your Leaders*

These same communications channels—email, message boards, surveys, polls, feedback forms—can also help you stay in touch with your community leaders (although leader communications take place in private). More than anyone, these people know what's going on within your community. They're on the front lines, dealing with newbie confusion, interpersonal conflicts, and policy thrashes on a daily basis. Due to the nature of their role, community leaders can offer you a distilled overview of how well your rules and tools are working, which can help you to filter and interpret the raw input you're getting from members.

FIGURE 6.10
THE WELL'S POLICY CONFERENCE
This is the front page of the Policy
Conference (www.well.com/conf/
policy), where changes to the Community Standards are discussed, and
various issues can be raised directly
with the community staff.

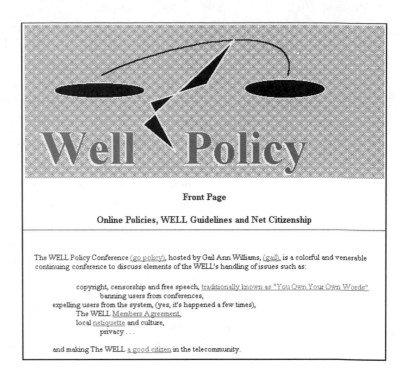

Front Page

Online Policies, WELL Guidelines and Net Citizenship

The WELL Policy Conference (go policy), hosted by Gail Ann Williams, (gail), is a colorful and venerable continuing conference to discuss elements of the WELL's handling of issues such as:

copyright, censorship and free speech, traditionally known as "You Own Your Own Words"
banning users from conferences,
expelling users from the system, (yes, it's happened a few times),
The WELL Members Agreement,
local netiquette and culture,
privacy . . .

and making The WELL a good citizen in the telecommunity.

As your community grows, you may want to introduce more structured ways of soliciting feedback from your community leaders, such as regular meetings and status reports (discussed in Chapter 5). For example, all Ultima Online volunteer leaders submit a weekly report summarizing the week's events and raising any relevant problems or issues. These reports give the community staff a good overview of what's going on in the game and alerts them to any policy issues that need to be addressed.

The Power of Public Hearings

When people have the chance to participate in the process of evolving the rules, they're much more likely to embrace, understand and uphold them. This is the basic idea behind representative democracy—and although the reality often falls short of this ideal, the mechanisms for promoting public discussion of policy issues are part of this political system.

Figure 6.11
User Feedback at the Palace

At the Palace, users can offer feedback via a form (www.thepalace.com/help/servfeed.html) that helps the community staff process and sort the feedback. Notice that this form clearly states that users should not expect a response to their feedback—an important part of managing users' expectations.

Feedback response statement

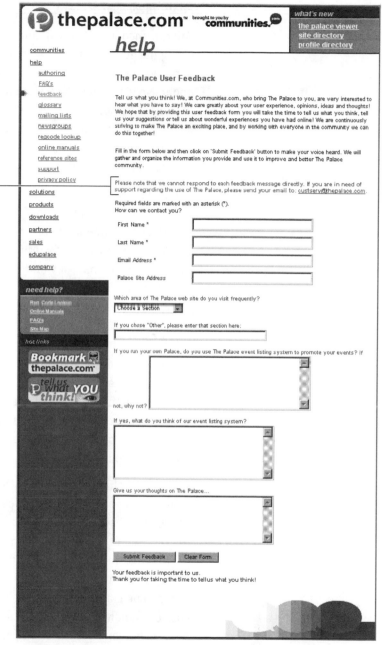

Public Involvement—Pro...

You can encourage this dynamic in your own community by providing the equivalent of town meetings, where community members and leaders can discuss policy changes and offer feedback about evolving community standards. These public meetings can take place in message boards, chat rooms, or even on a mailing list. Although such meetings can be contentious, they'll give you valuable feedback and ideas, and help your members buy in to the inevitable policy changes that your community will undergo.

The WELL's public Hosts conference (www.well.com/conf/hosts) illustrates this idea in action. For example, when the WELL Member Agreement needed major revisions, the community director, Gail Williams, posted a draft in the Hosts conference and told the participants that they had one month to voice their opinions and concerns. The ensuing discussion helped her shape and refine the agreement.

...and Con

The downside to this dynamic is that it's time consuming and can lead to unrealistic expectations of a fully democratic process for policy decisions. For pragmatic reasons, Web communities are not usually run as democracies: they are labors of love, benevolent dictatorships, or for-profit business ventures that must answer to the owners and shareholders.

While it's useful and necessary to find ways to involve your members in shaping your policies, it's crucial to set realistic expectations about the decision-making process and to carefully consider the amount of time and energy that it takes to engage your members in an ongoing dialogue. For example, although Gail Williams considers the Policy and Hosts conferences to be extremely valuable, she also finds that policy discussions among members can be a huge time sink and often devolve into endless nitpicking and rehashing of old, tired issues. These days, Gail and her team usually update WELL manuals without posting them for discussion, simply because they don't have the time or energy to engage in a lengthy debate.

Interpreting Feedback

Although member feedback is important and useful, it can be challenging to interpret and manage. Often, the support staff of a Web community find themselves overwhelmed with email that they aren't prepared to respond to. Furthermore, it can be tricky to differentiate between a valid complaint from a well-meaning member and an inflammatory diatribe from a perennial malcontent. All too often, these challenges result in the community support staff either ignoring most of the feedback they receive or giving too much credence to the vocal minority with an axe to grind.

You can avoid some of these pitfalls by learning how to manage and interpret feedback effectively. Here are some guidelines to help you get the most out of your feedback loops:

○ **Set expectations that you can meet** for responding to email, and participating in discussions. Let your members know who will be reading their feedback, and if they can expect a reply.

○ **Look for patterns in the feedback,** especially in regards to particular people or features. Often, the community will react negatively at first to changes in the interface or the rules. If possible, give the issue some time to settle out— if you're still getting a lot of negative feedback, consider making some changes.

○ **Communicate your reasoning** about policy issues and changes. You can go a long way toward alleviating people's concerns by providing clear explanations about your policy and feature decisions, and by encouraging community leaders to participate actively in discussions.

○ **Adopt tools that help you respond efficiently** to feedback, such as form letters, FAQs, and macro programs. Not every email demands a complex response; often, a quick note will solve the problem, and the positive effect of getting a response will strengthen the member's loyalty to the community.

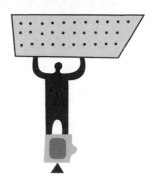

CHAPTER SEVEN

EVENTS:
Meetings, Performances and Competitions

Every long-lasting community is brought together by regular events: family dinners, weekly card games, monthly club meetings, annual celebrations. These gatherings help define the community, and they remind people of what they have in common and what their community is all about.

Successful events don't just happen; they require careful planning, skillful facilitation, and timely follow-up. To get the most out of your events, you'll need to understand the basic anatomy of an event, and then develop an events plan that reinforces your purpose and values while meeting the changing needs of your members.

In this Chapter

Event Planning 101

What communities do you belong to? You might think first of your neighborhood or town, your church or school, or maybe your workplace or favorite local hangout. You might also think about your extended family or the people who attend the same business conference with you every year. Perhaps you play in a softball league after work or belong to a regular book club or movie group.

In each case, your sense of belonging is reinforced by participating in scheduled events—town meetings, church services, professional receptions, amateur games, and so on. These regular gatherings help to cultivate communities by bringing people together and helping them stay in touch. A mailing list, message board, or chat room can do those things, too, but an event is more structured—it occurs at a specific time and place, and has a beginning, middle, and end. You can chat with your kids anytime, but Sunday dinner is an event. Similarly, while the "Positive Reflections" chat room on AOL is open for conversation 24 hours a day, the Thursday evening support group meeting is a regular event. These gatherings give people a community experience they can count on and plan their schedules around.

Like a Saturday night card game, church on Sunday, or even appointment TV, regular events can help to make community participation a habit.

What's Going On?

Events also infuse a community with a sense of liveliness and purpose and reflect what it's about. Take a look at the events calendars from Mplayer.com (Figure 7.1) and iVillage (Figure 7.2), for instance. Both seem to be lively places, with a lot going on, but what different places they are!

In each community, the event programming reflects the needs, interests, and daily rhythms of the people who hang out there. iVillage is targeted at women who are juggling multiple roles and responsibilities, with schedules as varied as their multifaceted lives. Mplayer's core audience is young, competitive guys who love gaming and carve out time for their hobby after school or work and on the weekends. By glancing at each calendar, visitors can quickly get a sense for what's going on in that community and whether or not they'd fit in.

FIGURE 7.1
MPLAYER EVENTS CALENDAR
www.mplayer.com/cal
This weekly calendar shows all ongoing events at Mplayer, which include chats, launch parties, and tournaments. By clicking on a gaming genre, users see a filtered view that shows only genre-specific events.

GENRE-SPECIFIC EVENTS

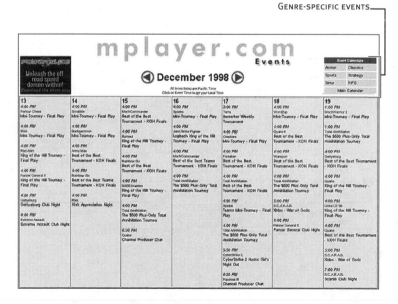

FIGURE 7.2
iVillage Events Calendar
www.ivillage.com/chat/today
This daily calendar displays all ongoing
events at iVillage, which include topical
chats, support group meetings, and words
games. By clicking on a channel, users
see a filtered view that shows only
channel-specific events.

Friday's Chats
At-a-Glance

Click on any title to enter the chat room. All times based on Eastern time zone. For
Pacific time, subtract 3 hours. For Greenwich Mean Time (UTC), add 5 hours.

chat channels
book club
career
fitness & beauty
food
health
money
parenting
relationships
travel
work from home

chat search

We have thousands of events each month.
To find chats for you, type in a keyword or
phrase and hit "go!"

[Go]

CLICK TO SEE A
FILTERED VIEW

Time	Chat Name	Channel
4 am	KidzCan Parents Chat (4:30am)(8pm Australia)	Better Health
9 am	Domestic Abuse	Parent Soup
9 am	Rise and Shine!	Relationships
9 am	Schooltime At Home	Parent Soup
9 am	Dr. Greene's Office Hours - December 18	Parent Soup
10 am	Join the Relationships Fun!	iVillage
11 am	Breastfeeding Support Group	ParentsPlace.com
11 am	Codependents Support Group	Relationships
12 pm	Financial Fundamentals	Armchair Millionaire
12 pm	Your "Home" at iVillage	Parent Soup
12 pm	Just Hanging Out	Parent Soup
1 pm	The Lunch Hour	Career
1 pm	Lively Lunch Chat	Fitness & Beauty
2 pm	Coffee Break	Relationships
2 pm	How Do You Balance Family and Work?	Work from Home
3 pm	Cartoon Break	Parent Soup
3 pm	Romantic Travel	Travel
3 pm	Mothers and Teens: Let's Talk	Relationships
4 pm	June '96 Playgroup	ParentsPlace.com
4 pm	"Coffee Break"	Work from Home
5 pm	Afternoon Delight	Relationships
7 pm	Walking for Health	Fitness & Beauty
7 pm	TGIF Happy Hour	Career
8 pm	Calgon, Take Me AWAY! 24 hours Pain Free Chat!	Better Health
8 pm	Kick Butt Quitters Club!	Better Health
8 pm	Beauty Buzz	Fitness & Beauty
8 pm	Alcohol & Drug Recovery -- All are Welcome! 8-10pm ET	Better Health
9 pm	Yoga Chat	Fitness & Beauty
9 pm	Parents of Newborns (0-3 months)	Parenting
9 pm	Work At Home Ideas	ParentsPlace.com
9 pm	Pregnancy After a Loss	ParentsPlace.com
9 pm	Military Families	Parent Soup
9 pm	It's Friday! Kick Back and Relax	Food
9 pm	Friday Night Live	Relationships
9 pm	Investing Basics	Armchair Millionaire
9 pm	Campfire Chronicles	Parent Soup
9 pm	January '97 Playgroup	ParentsPlace.com
9 pm	Parents Of Newborns and Babies	Parent Soup
10 pm	Fireside Chat	Food
10 pm	Sex After Kids	Parent Soup
11 pm	Parents of Uncircumcised Children	ParentsPlace.com
11 pm	Late Night Soup	Parent Soup
11 pm	HTML	Parent Soup

Something in Common

Once someone is attracted to a community, events can help that person build relationships, the glue that holds a community together. An iVillage newcomer, for example, might join the "Kick Butt" support group, looking for motivation and support to quit smoking. As she attends the meetings, week after week, she'll share her struggles and triumphs with the group—and may very well develop some lasting friendships that transcend the meetings.

At Mplayer, a Quake tournament serves a similar purpose for a different audience. Over the course of several weeks, hundreds of players compete fiercely against each other; they brag about their achievements, cheer on their clanmates, and check the winners page to see who's made it to the next round. Though different in purpose and scope, both events bring people together who have something in common and provide a structure within which they can get to know each other better over time.

Varieties of Events

There are three basic types of events: *meetings*, which are small-group gatherings that emphasize participation; *performances*, which are larger, more structured gatherings focused around a performer or presentation; and *competitions*, which give members a chance to compete for prizes or glory (see Figures 7.3–7.5). Each kind of event places different demands on your community platform.

Meetings are essentially chats that take place at a specific time and place. To run them successfully, you need a chat environment that includes:

- a consistent place to meet (such as a room with a reserved name)

- the ability to display the current topic in the interface (and link to ancillary materials)

- ○ moderator powers that include "muting" people or barring them from the space

- ○ macro capabilities (either built-in or added on) that let the moderator post standard blocks of text quickly and easily

FIGURE 7.3
THE STRUCTURE OF AN ONLINE MEETING
A meeting consists of a small group with a designated leader (the large figure) who starts and ends the meeting and keeps the conversation on track. Online meetings usually take place in chat rooms (or other chat-enabled gathering places).

Performances (such as celebrity interviews, executive briefings, and training sessions) run best in an auditorium or similar environment that includes, in addition to the above features:

- ○ distinct areas for the stage, backstage, and audience

- ○ a mechanism (such as rows or rooms) to divide the audience into groups

- ○ the ability to allow or disallow the audience to chat amongst themselves during the presentation

- ○ a "question queue" that funnels questions from the audience into the backstage area, and another to funnel filtered questions to the stage

- ○ the ability for the performer to display visuals or other media types

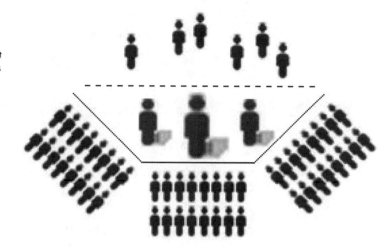

FIGURE 7.4
THE STRUCTURE OF AN ONLINE PERFORMANCE
A performance consists of an audience that may be divided into groups or "rows," plus a stage area with a performer (the large figure) and often one or more facilitators (smaller figures on stage). Performances may also include a backstage area where more facilitators work to keep the event running smoothly.

Some competitions—such as contests—take place asynchronously, while others—such as multiplayer games—require a real-time gathering place. Regardless, all competitions need an environment that includes:

○ a mechanism for participants to enter the competition

○ a way for spectators to enjoy the competition (such as watching an ongoing game or viewing contest results on the Web)

○ a structure for judges and/or announcers to view the competition

FIGURE 7.5
THE STRUCTURE OF AN ONLINE COMPETITION
Whether synchronous or asynchronous, simple or complex, a competition always includes participants (in the center) and spectators (surrounding the arena), and may include judges or referees.

You'll want to focus on events that meet your strategic goals, which might be to attract new members, turn novices into regulars, or enable members to run their own events. You'll also want to offer events that serve the needs and interests of your members, which might be to form intimate relationships, get help with a problem, or escape into a fantasy environment.

Create Your Events Plan

Facilitating events is a key part of long-term community building, but successful events don't just happen—they're the result of careful planning, ongoing facilitation, and thoughtful follow-up efforts. To use your resources wisely, it's helpful to create an *events plan* that outlines:

- what types of events you'll be facilitating and why

- what infrastructure, policies, and training you'll need to make those events happen

- who will initiate, coordinate, and moderate the events

- who will attend the events, and what existing needs are being served

- what role your members will play, and how that role will change over time

- what kind of follow-up efforts will be needed

- what results you expect to achieve, and how those results will be measured

You won't have all the answers at first, but asking these questions up front will help you focus your efforts and create a solid framework for your events programming. (See The Three Phases of an Event for more on these issues.)

Follow Your Members

Your event plan will give you a starting point and a strategic vision, but it's not a fixed blueprint. As usual, it's best to start small and flexible and see what your members respond to. In the planning stage you can make educated guesses; once your events are up and running you can directly assess how people are responding and use feedback mechanisms like attendance statistics, exit polls, and email suggestions to tune your events accordingly.

The Three Phases of an Event

Most people think of an event as a shared activity, whether a meal, a company meeting, or a play or concert. Yet most of what goes into an event takes place behind the scenes, both before and after the activity itself.

Phase I: Planning

This is where the bulk of your work takes place. We'll talk more about specific event types later in this chapter, but details aside, here are some basic guidelines to help you create your event plan:

o **FORMULATE A STRATEGY.** First, you need to define what types of events you'll be running and why. Each type of event makes a different contribution to a community, and each has its own infrastructure and staffing needs.

o **CHOOSE A LOCATION.** Next, you'll need to select an appropriate gathering place. Small-scale events like topical chats, word games, and support-group meetings can be comfortably held in chat rooms, while larger events like celebrity interviews, online conferences, and gaming tournaments require a more structured gathering place like an auditorium or arena.

o **BUILD YOUR INFRASTRUCTURE.** You'll need a shared calendar for coordinating and publicizing the events, along with an event database and the tools to enter and update events. With these elements in place, you can develop a more sophisticated promotional infrastructure like targeted mailing lists and personalized Web pages that remind people about upcoming events.

o **ASSESS YOUR STAFFING NEEDS.** At minimum, an event requires a trained host or moderator to keep things running smoothly. Larger events require auxiliary support staff—such as ushers, question screeners, talent coordinators, or contest judges—who may need specialized preparation and training.

o **PREPARE YOUR DOCUMENTS.** Events need clearly stated rules and behavioral guidelines, which could be incorporated into your Community Standards (see Chapter 6) or offered as a separate document. Some events require auxiliary documents—such as a speaker bio or meeting agenda—to be prepared and distributed prior to the event.

o **CHOOSE A TIME AND PLACE.** You'll need to select a specific date, time and place for each event. Timing is crucial for success, so you'll want to take the existing habits (and time zone) of your audience into account.

continued ⋯⟩

Phase II: Facilitation

If you've done your planning and preparation, you'll have a well-attended event with a clear purpose and a trained staff. Now your job is to make sure the event runs smoothly. To do this, you'll need to:

○ **Display Information About the Event.** To keep the event on track, it's helpful to display basic information such as the title, topic and moderator as "signage" in the interface. This will let people know where they are and help them know how to behave. It's also helpful to provide links to background materials like speaker bios and agendas.

○ **Make Sure the Event Is Adequately Staffed.** In addition to assigning enough people to cover the event, you'll need a way to know if they actually showed up. You'll also need a backup plan for what to do if an events staff member can't make it.

○ **Be Prepared for Troublemakers.** For the event to run smoothly, you'll need leaders on hand who are trained to handle any problems that crop up. Audiences attract troublemakers, so it's especially important to train and empower event leaders to deal with disruptive people in real-time.

Phase III: Follow-up

After the last person has left the gathering place, the real-time portion of the event is over, but the follow-up phase is just beginning. During this phase, you may want to:

○ **Offer a Place to Continue the Discussion.** If an event generated a lively discussion, you may want to provide a message board or mailing list where people can continue talking.

○ **Post or Distribute the Results.** If the event produced results—such as interview transcripts, tournament winners, or action items from a team meeting—you should publish these results as soon as possible after the event.

○ **Plan for the Next Gathering.** If an event is held regularly, you'll want to do some planning and promotion for the next event. This could involve announcing an upcoming discussion topic, taking questions for an upcoming speaker, reminding team members about the next staff meeting, or notifying tournament participants that they're eligible for the next round.

Meetings: Bringing Groups Together

It's the end of another week, and the Net is buzzing with conversation. Over at BabyCenter, the "Balancing Work and Family" chat is just getting underway. On the Heat gaming network, the Friday Afternoon Chat regulars are barraging the community staff with interface suggestions. And in a few hours, the Ultima Online counselors will be meeting in a private IRC channel to discuss a new game patch, while the eBay doll collectors will be gathering at their regular time to discuss the upcoming Barbie convention.

All these events are examples of meetings, which are essentially regularly scheduled chats. Like all events, meetings can add a sense of liveliness to your community, but their true power lies in their ability to create habits and routines, which help people who already know each other maintain their relationships. Work groups, for example, use weekly meetings to disseminate information, raise issues, and solve problems together, while the members of a hobby club might get together monthly to take care of club business.

Meetings can also help a novice form new relationships. A newcomer to iVillage, for example, who checks out the Breastfeeding Support Group and finds sympathetic answers to some of her questions is likely to return again and again. Pretty soon she's a regular for whom the meeting is a habit, like a favorite TV show.

Topical Chat

One common type of meeting is a topical chat (or chat group), a hosted gathering where people discuss a topic that's related to the community's purpose. At Moms Online, for example, you can discuss toddler discipline strategies, while over at Third Age you can talk about saving for retirement, and at iVillage MoneyLife you can swap tips about debt management. These meetings bring like-minded people together on a regular basis (most often weekly) and give them something focused to talk about. While some people may prefer the ease of dropping by a "hangout," others will enjoy the focus and continuity of attending a meeting with a clear purpose, that's run by a leader who's empowered to keep things on track.

Where Are We Meeting?

If you want to hold chat group meetings, you'll need to choose a venue. If your community platform includes chat rooms, you can host these meetings on your own site. Some Web communities—AncientSites, for instance—use internally developed chat software; others use third-party tools like iChat or Webmaster (see Chapter 2 for more on chat software). If your community is hosted on an aggregator's site, such as Talk City, AOL, or YAHOO Clubs, you can use your host's built-in chat tools.

If your own community site doesn't offer chat rooms at all, you could sign up for a free, permanent chat room at Talk City (**www.talkcity.com/irc/apply.htmpl**), or create a Yahoo club that includes a chat room (**help.yahoo.com/help/clubs/cfound/cfound-09.html**—see Chapter 9 for more on Yahoo clubs). In either case, you'll need to become a member of that site to get a permanent room, and all participants will need to register to reserve a permanent member name (although at Talk City, non-members can visit your chat room as a guest). You'll receive a URL for your room that you can direct participants to by including it in an email or via a link on a Web page.

What Are We Talking About?

Once you've settled on where the meeting will be held, you'll need to choose some topics. It's best to start with a few open-ended topics and then expand your schedule as you learn more about what your members are interested in. A general topic can spin off more specific chats; for example, an attachment parenting support group might evolve out of a general parenting chat. You can get initial ideas for topics from your partners, staff, and sponsors, but soon you'll want to solicit new topic ideas from your members via email or message boards.

When's the Meeting?

Now that where and what are nailed down, you need to decide when. Consider the habits and lifestyle of your audience. When do they have time to meet—after school? During a work break? After the kids are asleep? Many chat groups have floundered due to bad timing, so if you want your meetings to be well attended, schedule them at a convenient time for your intended audience. (Remember the differences between figures 7.1 and 7.2.) The "Breastfeeding" chat at BabyCenter, for example, really took off when it was moved from Saturday noon to Friday evening, because that's when the participants were eager for some socializing. As with the topics, make some educated guesses about timing beforehand and modify them by observing and listening to your members.

Along with nailing down times, you'll want to create an events calendar to let your members know when the meetings are happening. If you're running your chats on an aggregator's site, there may already be a calendar (public or private) that you can enter your events into; if you're holding meetings on your own site, you'll need to build your own. Communities with few events per week can get by with a manually updated HTML page, but if you're running lots of events, you'll want to create a more flexible calendar that can pull information from a database. And if your community is subdivided into thematic areas, it's especially helpful to offer a filtered events view for each area, as Moms Online does (Figure 7.6). (The iVillage and Mplayer calendars shown in Figures 7.1 and 7.2 also provide this feature.)

FIGURE 7.6
TOPICAL CHATS AT MOMS ONLINE
As in many large communities, the Moms Online chat calendar is divided into channels. Here we see the weekly chats for the "Ages and Stages" channel (upper image), and the listing for a specific chat about home-schooling (lower image), which includes the date, time, and host name.

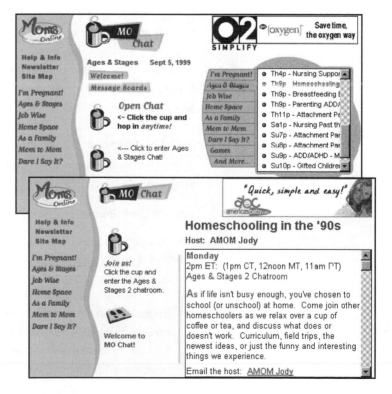

Who's Our Host?

You'll need to line up some hosts to greet participants and keep the conversation lively and focused. These people will have a lot to do with the success of your meetings, so you'll want to select and train them carefully. You can start by using hosts who've had previous experience and then set up a system for selecting and training new ones once your chat program is underway (see Chapter 5 for details). As your chat programming expands, you can recruit new hosts by asking your current hosts to keep an eye out for "talent" and putting up a application for interested members to fill out. You may also find that the members who suggest new topics can be persuaded to host those groups. Hosts can develop a following, so it's a good idea to display the host's member name, along with other event information (see Figure 7.6).

As for training your hosts, remember that there's no one right way to facilitate a meeting. Some communities, including iVillage, Talk City and Moms Online, cultivate a friendly and relaxed atmosphere; others, such as CNN, are stricter about keeping discussions on topic and quickly remove disruptive members. Some communities train their chat hosts to greet everyone who enters a room; others find this ritual to be intrusive and forced. Although you'll inevitably see stylistic differences between hosts, you can avoid many problems by thinking ahead of time about the atmosphere you want to create, developing clear policies to support that atmosphere, and training your hosts to be consistent about enforcing these policies.

Beyond Chat Groups

Once you've got the infrastructure and staffing in place to run scheduled chats, you can start to expand your programming by holding similar types of events, such as:

- **OFFICE HOURS:** a scheduled time when an expert or support person is available to answer questions. For example, the resident financial planning expert at iVillage MoneyLife holds online office hours every Tuesday at 4 PM.

- ○ **MEET THE STAFF:** an event during which members can meet the people who run the community. For example, every Wednesday at Parent Soup, members have an opportunity to chat with the community staff.

- ○ **SHARE YOUR IDEAS:** a meeting that's dedicated to collecting people's feedback on the community. For example, every Friday afternoon the director of marketing at Heat hosts a Suggestion chat, during which members can tell him what they think of the site and what's on their wish list for future enhancements.

You may also want to set up one or more associated message board topics where regular chat participants can continue their discussion between meetings. You may find that some of your members prefer chatting while others like to communicate via message boards, so don't be surprised if two separate interest groups develop. Parent Soup, for example, hosts both a weekly chat (www2.parentsoup.com/pschat/full/index.html#4433) and a message board (boards.parentsoup.com/messages/get/psalternativerel31.html) on the subject of alternative religions. To encourage crossover, have the same person host the chat and the message board, mention the message board during the weekly chat, and post a chat reminder on the message boards.

Support Groups

Like topical chats, support groups meet regularly and have a set topic, but they serve a different purpose for the participants. People come to chats to relax, have fun, and shoot the breeze, while they are drawn to support groups during difficult times—when they're struggling with a problem and want to connect with others who know what they're going through.

If people are coming to your community during transitional times looking for information, advice, and support, it can make a lot of sense to feature and facilitate support groups. For example, many health-oriented communities—including allHealth, Thrive, WebMD, and drkoop.com—prominently feature support groups for people who suffer from various illnesses.

Support groups are also great for people wanting to connect with others who share their worldview, whether about religion, politics, or child rearing. For example, Moms Online features an attachment parenting support group, where participants discuss this controversial child-rearing method and swap tips about how to handle disapproving friends and relatives.

As a medium, the Internet is particularly well suited to foster support groups. Online conversations have a peculiar blend of anonymity and intimacy that encourages people to reveal themselves—and similarly, the privacy ground rules of support groups help people feel safe enough to discuss difficult personal issues that they might not otherwise reveal.

As you might imagine, the line between a support group and a topical chat can be fuzzy; depending on the topic, a chat could easily evolve into (or spin off) a support group. For example, the HOPE infertility support group at allHealth emerged from a regular chat on fertility drugs. So if you're running topical chats on your site, you may want to keep an eye out for emerging support groups and give them their own meeting space (see Chapter 9 for more on this dynamic).

Supporting a Support Group

Support groups have similar infrastructure and planning requirements to chat groups: you'll need a venue, a calendar, and a leader. But the behavioral ground rules will generally need to be more specific and structured than chat guidelines, with the exact content dependent on the type of support group you're running. For example, the "Transformations" support groups at Talk City (www.talkcity.com/transformations) model their rules and structure on Alcoholics Anonymous, while the allhealth support groups are more loosely structured while still including specific guidelines (Figure 7.7).

Likewise, a support group requires special leadership skills. The people in a support group are in physical or emotional pain and are frequently dealing with a crisis situation, so the leader needs to be familiar with the problem that's shared by the group and may also need special training. Support group hosts at iVillage receive specific guidelines—including referrals to local resources—for handling someone who's going through a personal crisis. Although written guidelines are helpful, it's ultimately up to the leader (and other regular members) to communicate and reinforce the group's particular etiquette standards in meetings.

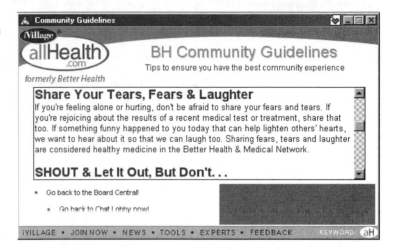

Like topical chats, support groups often benefit from having a place to continue the discussion between meetings. The HOPE support group at allHealth, for example, hosts several infertility-related message board topics in addition to daily support group meetings (Figure 7.8).

Remote Workgroup Meetings

More and more these days, people who work together are physically separated, and your community will likely have staff members who work remotely. You can all stay in touch via email, message boards, and buddy lists; but when a group is physically dispersed, regular online meetings can help them bridge the distance and stay in sync.

For example, both Talk City and iVillage hold weekly remote staff meetings in private areas of their sites. At these meetings, the participants compare notes, raise issues and concerns, discuss upcoming features, and swap strategies for dealing with troublemakers. Such meetings typically take place in a private chat room, led by the group's manager.

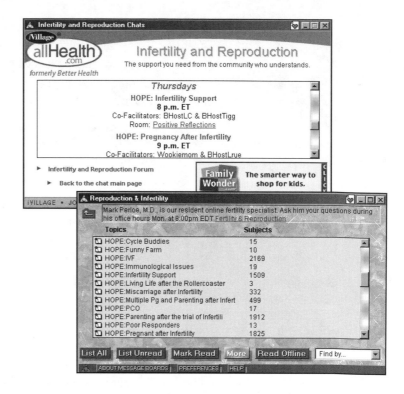

If your community platform doesn't include chat rooms or isn't
well suited to this type of meeting, you could hold the meetings
in a different venue. For example, the Ultima Online volunteer
counselors hold weekly meetings in a private IRC channel. In theory, they could log into a private chat area of the game, but that
involves more overhead, and IRC offers them a more streamlined
environment.

Visually Enhanced

You have several options for adding visuals to your online meetings. For example, Microsoft's NetMeeting (www.microsoft.com/
windows/netmeeting) is built into Windows 98 and available as
a free download for Windows 95. (It doesn't run on other platforms.) This tool allows up to eight people to share images, files
and even live applications, but it require you to set up and configure the software yourself. The current version doesn't work

well across a firewall, so it's most suitable for Intranet or VPN (virtual private network) applications.

Alternatively, you could use a meeting service like PlaceWare (www.PlaceWare.com), which runs well across a firewall and supports Windows, Unix, and later-model Macintoshes. After you and your group log into PlaceWare's servers, you can show slides, use a shared whiteboard, and even show live software demos. (PlaceWare's software is also available for licensing). Talk City offers a similar service, with simpler features, build around their EZTalk software (www.talkcitymeeting.com). I'll discuss these services further in the next section.

Just Because You Can, Doesn't Mean You Should

These days, easy-to-use chat rooms are cheap and widely available, so it's possible for just about any community to hold regular online meetings. But just because you *can*, doesn't mean you *should*. It's a big waste of energy and resources to set up and run meetings that aren't needed and aren't well attended. To avoid this trap, ask yourself the following questions about your community members:

- **Do They Already Meet in Person?** If your members see each other often in the physical world, they may not need (or want) regular online meetings. For example, a book club might use online tools to plan their monthly in-person meetings; similarly, people who work together in the same office may usually communicate using email, but they'll probably hold staff meetings in person. A distributed workgroup or virtual book club, on the other hand, would probably benefit from regular online meetings.

- **Do They Prefer Asynchronous Communication?** Many people who participate in mailing lists and message boards prefer the convenience of communicating when they want; they simply don't have a desire for real-time online meetings. For example, I enjoy reading WELL conferences at odd hours; if these communities required real-time meetings, I probably wouldn't participate.

- **Does an Open-All-Hours Chat Room Better Serve Your Audience?** Some people prefer to drop by a topical chat room at their convenience rather than attend scheduled meetings. For example, day-traders tend to be online all day, so they typically use chat rooms as hangouts rather than as a place to hold scheduled meetings. And my teenage niece has never attended a scheduled online event, but she often hangs out in AOL chat rooms with her friends after school.

In practice, the best way to decide whether to have online meetings is to listen to and observe your members. If they request a meeting space or start to hold meetings on another site, they're expressing a need—and you can encourage them to stay loyal to your community by filling that need. For example, the Dolls message board at eBay developed an avid group of regulars who began to hold daily meetings. Many of them eventually grew frustrated with trying to hold real-time meetings in a message board and went elsewhere in search of a more appropriate meeting space.

Performances: Up on Stage

It's Monday morning, the beginning of another week. At Talk City, the special events coordinator is reviewing the celebrity interview schedule for the coming week. At Charles Schwab, the CEO is reviewing his slides in preparation for an online conference with his top managers. And over at CNN.com, the regulars are gathering in the TalkBack Live chat room for their daily simuchat fix.

These Web communities are using online performances to educate, inform, or entertain their members. Unlike meetings, where everyone's participation is encouraged, performances feature some main attraction, which might be a technical training session, an executive briefing, a celebrity interview, or a live Webcast. Attendees might ask questions or chat with each other, but the focus is on whoever's "on stage."

Puttin' on a Show

A performance is a show, which naturally involves more planning, coordination, and resources than a simple group meeting. A celebrity interview might involve booking the guest, doing background research, screening the questions, and editing the final transcript. An online training session could require lining up a venue, preparing slides, and evaluating students.

Because of this extra overhead, its important to be clear about why you're hosting performances and what you're hoping to gain by running these events. Online performances bring people together and give them something to talk about, just as a play, movie, TV show, or lecture can stimulate conversation among a group. Like any show, a performance can add excitement to your community, and recordings or transcripts of performances can become an attractive part of your site's content archives.

Train Leaders

Many Web communities—including Talk City, AOL and the Zone—offer ongoing classes for community leader recruits. In addition to teaching recruits how to perform their roles, these classes also serve to weed out those who misbehave in class, don't show up, or who for other reasons would be inappropriate as community leaders. During a leadership class, the teacher will present basic material and lead a question-and-answer session. Trainees can sign up for classes that fit their schedule, and they're often encouraged to continue the discussion on message boards or mailing lists. (For more on training leaders, see Chapter 5.)

Teaching and Training

Classes, seminars, and training sessions are among the most useful and easily produced kinds of performances. These events can help you train your staff, instruct novices in how your community works, make presentations to your salespeople—in general, communicate important information to the people you want to hear it. Classes need not put much strain on your resources; small classes are often held in chat rooms, with a teacher in place of a host. If you've already got chat rooms and a calendar, adding some classes is straightforward: you line up an instructor, develop some material, and put the classes on the schedule. For larger classes, you might need an auditorium, which will probably call for more time and staff.

What Does "Interactive" Mean?

In pre-Web days, I worked at the West Coast arm of a big media company. One day my boss gave a presentation to some East Coast executives, during which he said: "We really understand 'interactivity' out here, because we make CD-ROMs, which are far more interactive than plain old software." I cringed when I heard that, because it was clear that my boss didn't understand what interactivity really meant.

Suppose you're talking with an intriguing woman at a party; she's smiling, nodding, looking into your eyes, responding to your comments—feels pretty interactive, right? Earlier, at this same party, you talked briefly with a well-dressed man who seemed distracted, or you spent what seemed like forever with a young man intent on delivering a monologue about government conspiracies. Those conversations felt very different, didn't they?

What irked me about my boss's pronouncement was that while our CD-ROMs contained richer media, they were actually less responsive to user input than "plain old software." Conversations feel interactive when you know the other person is aware of your presence and responding to you. If you want to create the same feeling in your events, acknowledge the presence of your audience and let them know that their comments and questions are being heard.

Help Newbies

If your community includes a lot of Internet newbies, you might consider offering classes that teach some basic community skills. For example, both Third Age (**www.thirdage.com/chat/schedule.html#mon**) and Talk City (**www.talkcity.com/calendar/events/event4835.htmpl**) offer introductory classes on building Web pages. Depending on your focus, you could offer classes on how to set up a buddy list, configure a Start page, or list an item for auction. Such classes can supplement your written documentation by offering newbies a safe place to practice their skills, as well as an opportunity to meet other community members and leaders (as discussed in Chapter 4).

One-Room School

If you decide to incorporate chat-based classes into your events programming, make sure that you have a macro facility in place; this will make your teachers' jobs easier by letting them post a lesson with one keystroke. If your chat platform is IRC-based and your instructors are comfortable using a standard IRC client, you're all set, because most IRC clients include this feature. Alternatively, you could use a popular shareware package like TypeIt4Me (Macintosh) or Keyboard Express (PC), which can be downloaded from **www.shareware.com** or **www.tucows.com**.

If education plays a central role in your community, you could develop more robust, multiweek classes that involve lesson plans, office hours, reading lists, and tests. Distance learning organizations like ZDU (**www.zdu.com**) and DigitalThink (**www.digitalthink.com**), for instance, offer classes targeted at Web developers and technical professionals. Besides providing information and giving exams, these classes offer students the ability to connect directly with the instructor or teaching aide—and with each other—through a combination of message boards, chat rooms, instant messaging, and email; each class has the potential to be a short-term community. Look to these programs for ideas about how to structure such classes in your community.

An Auditorium with a View

Chat rooms can work well for classes of up to a few dozen attendees, but once these gatherings grow beyond that size, you'll want to hold them in an auditorium. Auditoriums are a more structured chat environment and offer specific features for managing large groups. In an auditorium, you could hold larger and/or more formal classes, such as a training session for your entire staff. These events are usually structured around a presentation (which is what makes them performances), followed by a Q&A session. In more formal classes, row chat is turned off during the presentation, although attendees can send in a question at any time. I'll discuss auditoriums in greater detail in the next section.

Virtual Conferences

The meeting services I mentioned earlier that let you incorporate visuals in meetings—PlaceWare and Talk City—also offer online conference rooms. These rooms provide structured chat facilities like those of an auditorium, along with the ability to simultaneously broadcast images to everyone in the room (Figure 7.9). These features allow for larger and more formal presentations, such as a quarterly executive briefing or a product training session for sales staff. These types of meetings often take place as a supplement to a conference call; for example, the CEO of Charles Schwab conducts a quarterly managers briefing using the PlaceWare Auditorium to show slides and queue up questions, while simultaneously explaining the slides and answering questions on the telephone. This setup allows the CEO's support staff to filter and prioritize the questions, thus eliminating redundant or off-topic queries.

These services (and others in the new Web-based presentation field) offer different levels of support. Talk City will facilitate presentation events with its internal staff, for instance, while PlaceWare offers a meeting place and some online training but assumes that you'll staff the event yourself. Full-service event planning companies like Envoy (www.envoyglobal.com) will run your online event using the PlaceWare software platform. And both PlaceWare and Talk City offer multimedia recordings (similar to transcripts) that allow someone who missed the event to view the slides, hear the commentary, and see the questions and answers from the meeting.

FIGURE 7.9

PLACEWARE ONLINE CONFERENCE ROOM
PlaceWare allows a presenter (in the photograph) to display a series of slides to a group of attendees, who can chat among themselves and send in questions. One or more facilitators can manage the question queue.

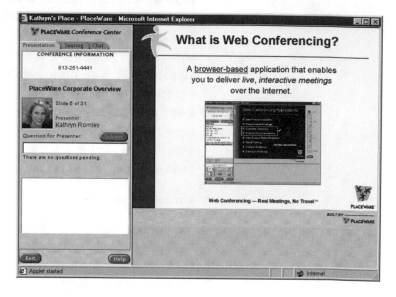

Interviewing Special Guests

The interview is one of the most popular types of online performances. An online interview is a moderated question and answer session between community members and a featured guest. Depending on the topic and guest, these events can attract hundreds or even thousands of people who are eager to be "in the same room" with and interact directly with a well-known person.

Used appropriately, interviews can add spice and excitement to your events lineup. If your community is tied to an existing media property, such as MTV, CNN, Newsweek, or Fortune, celebrity interviews are a natural extension of the brand. For example, CNN features interviews with politicians and authors (www.cnn.com/chat), while MTV hosts interviews with popular musicians and on-air talent (Figure 7.10). If your community offers information, advice and support, as iVillage, WebMD, and ZDNet do, then expert interviews can complement an existing lineup of topical chats and group meetings.

FIGURE 7.10
CELEBRITY INTERVIEWS AT MTV
www.mtv.com/mtv/live/arena/
tranny.html
MTV holds celebrity interviews on AOL;
later the transcripts are posted both on
AOL and on the MTV Web site, making the
content available to the widest possible
audience.

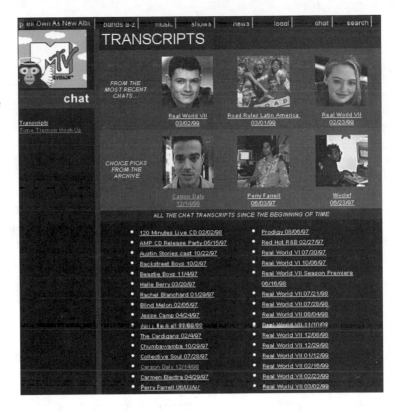

By associating your community with a well-known name, interviews can help you attract new members and keep your current members interested and involved. Although celebrity events are exciting, they can also be distracting, so you'll want to think carefully about how these events contribute to your community-building efforts.

On the one hand, many community builders (particularly those with a PR background) use celebrity events to create a "buzz," and attract media attention—which raises the overall level of awareness about the community. On the other hand, dealing with celebrities often involves a lot of extra overhead and expense, and the results may be short-lived. If you have limited staff and budget (and who doesn't?), celebrity events can end up diverting your resources and distracting you from higher-priority tasks without necessarily contributing to your long-term community development.

More Than a Chat Room

In practice, online interviews are sometimes held in (gasp!) plain-vanilla chat rooms, like any other meeting. This is fine for a small or casual event, but chat rooms can't gracefully handle large numbers of attendees. And although a chat room moderator can mute or ban disruptive attendees, there's no way to stop someone in advance from posting rude or inflammatory comments, which can upset your featured guest and ruin the mood of your event.

That's why it's usually best to hold interviews in an auditorium, which functions like a group of linked chat rooms: there's a stage area for the performers, a backstage area for the event coordinators, and an audience area for attendees that's divided into rows or rooms (as diagrammed in Figure 7.4). Questions from the audience are collected, screened for quality and appropriateness, and then passed along to the stage. This structure allows more people to attend the event and ensures that the guest answers the best questions, which makes for a better experience for everyone present.

Where to Hold Interviews

The easiest way to get started with interviews is to use an aggregator like Talk City, YAHOO, or AOL, who run events on their sites using their own auditorium software; they can coordinate your event, promote it to their audience, and provide a transcript afterwards. You can have your own staff run the event or make use of the aggregator's in-house event facilitators. Some sites like Talk City will even create a customized interface specifically for your event (Figure 7.11).

With all those services available, using an aggregator can be a great way to test the waters and run events without incurring a lot of overhead. You won't have to purchase and set up software or worry about load-balancing your servers. On the downside, you can't tweak the software platform to suit your particular needs, and your attendees won't be able to use their member identity within your community to participate in the event. In fact, at YAHOO and AOL, they'll need to join the aggregator's community to participate in the event (visitors can attend some Talk City events). You're also at the mercy of the aggregator's schedule—during busy times, your events may not be at the top of their priority list.

FIGURE 7.11

TALK CITY CUSTOMIZED AUDITORIUM
For an extra fee, Talk City will create a customized look for special auditorium events, like this interview with the rock band Our Lady of Peace. Attendees can ask questions using the input box at the top of the screen and talk with others in their section before and after (but not during) the event.

CLICK HERE TO TALK TO OTHERS IN THE ROOM

QUESTION INPUT BOX

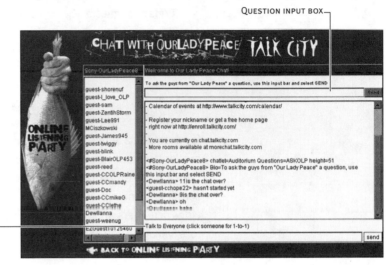

You can get more control and integration by running interviews on your own site. To do this, you'll need to build your own auditorium software (as YAHOO and Talk City did), or license software from a company like iChat (www.koz.com) or WebMaster (www.webmaster.com). Unfortunately, current auditorium software packages aren't as full-featured as what you'll find at the aggregator's sites, but hopefully there'll be better choices in the future.

Who's Running the Show?

A live interview requires a larger and more specialized staff than a group meeting. In addition to booking the featured guest, you'll need to fill some or all of the following roles:

○ **GREETERS** (AKA hosts or ushers), located in the audience to greet attendees, help them get settled, and answer any questions they have about the event

- **QUESTION SCREENERS,** who are located backstage and sort through audience questions, choosing the best ones to forward along

- **MODERATOR,** usually onstage (or on the phone) with the guest, who starts and ends the event and passes questions to the guest

- **TYPIST,** for guests who don't type in their answers directly

- **PRODUCER,** who makes sure that everything runs smoothly and may be in different locations during the event

These duties may be parceled out in different ways depending on the scale and style of the event. During a small, low-key interview, for example, a single person might be able to handle the producer, moderator, and screener roles. Aggregator sites tend to staff their events differently; for example, Talk City provides greeters, screeners, and a producer, but no moderator, while YAHOO provides screeners and a moderator but no greeters. Most aggregators will allow you to integrate your own staff into the mix, which is a good way to learn about facilitating an interview.

An aggregator will have a event management process in place that will include estimating staffing needs and assigning people to fill those roles. For example, a large-scale celebrity interview at Talk City might involve about a dozen greeters, five or six question screeners, and a producer and typist who are on the phone with the celebrity. The greeters arrive early and stay late, the screeners make sure that the questions are appropriate and not redundant, the typist relays the questions to the guest and types in the answers, and the producer makes sure that the guest is comfortable and fills in if staff members need extra help.

The Next Best Thing to Being There

After the interview is over, you'll want to post a transcript of the proceedings so that people who weren't able to attend the live event can find out what they missed. Interview transcripts are often very popular and can become valuable content assets for your site. Aggregators usually maintain a searchable archive of past events, and some (such as Talk City and YAHOO) will deliver transcripts as part of an events package. Whether or not you're using the services of an aggregator, you should include an events archive on your own site, as MTV does for their AOL interviews (see Figure 7.10). If you decide to edit your own transcripts you'll need to hire and manage editors to take care of it.

Simuchats: Look Ma, I'm on TV

A simuchat is a live chat that's held simultaneously with a broadcast show or event, such as a concert, a football game, or a TV or radio show. If you're building a Web community that's associated with an existing show or event, running a simuchat can enhance and extend the broadcast experience and develop closer ties with the event's audience. And if the simuchat is hosted by someone who's "live" at the event—such as a sports-caster, concert promoter, or talk show host—the Internet audi-ence will feel more involved in the event. For example, during the MTV Video Music Awards, an MTV community staff member sits backstage and hosts an online chat—making comments, cracking jokes, and passing along audience questions to celebrities.

Running a Simuchat

As far as tools, infrastructure, and staffing goes, running a simuchat is very similar to running either a topical chat or audito-rium interview. Depending on the scale and formality of the event, you'll need a gathering place, some instructions or ground rules for the participants, and one or more people to facilitate the event. You could hold a small, casual simuchat in a chat room, with a single moderator. For a larger and more formal event, you'll need an auditorium and various people to greet the audience, screen questions, and host the event. Additionally, the participants will need some way to watch the event; this could be a program on TV or radio or an audio or video Webcast. (Instructions for doing a Webcast are beyond the scope of this book.)

Interactive TV

Some simuchats actually incorporate comments or questions from an online chat room into the event itself. For example, CNN hosts a daily simuchat in conjunction with *TalkBack Live*, the long-running political talk show (www.cnn.com/talkback). In addition to the on-air host, guest, and live studio audience, there's also a live Web audience, who gather in chat rooms on CNN's site to talk about the show while watching it on TV (or viewing a live Webcast). CNN staffers moderate the chat room, making sure the conversation stays civil and on-topic. The TalkBack executive producer is also logged into the chat room, and whenever he sees a comment that's particularly thoughtful, provocative, or relevant, he can select it for one of the "bumpers" that appear before and after commercial breaks.

This event is a simple yet effective form of interactive TV—and it's truly interactive (see interactivity sidebar above), because the participants get clear feedback about their comments. In a sense, this simuchat has become more of a game for the participants than a conversation, with the object being to make comments that end up on the air.

Competitions: Members in the Spotlight

It's early December, a time of holiday preparations and year-end activities. Over at Hecklers Online, the weekly Digital Graffiti contest has taken on a decidedly Christmasy tone. At iVillage, the community staff is choosing a holiday-themed Chick Flick of the Week, and wrapping up the Make a Tradition community challenge. And over at Heat.net, the staff is gearing up for HellCamp III, a post-holiday series of member-run tournaments.

All these communities are using competitions to build excitement and anticipation and to highlight the skills and accomplishments of their members. Like performances, competitions can attract an audience, but unlike performances, which focus on a featured person or event, competitions feature your members and encourage them to earn a place in the spotlight.

Competitions Build Character

Competitions allow your members to "build character" (as discussed in Chapter 3) by providing a way for each person's talents and contributions to be acknowledged and expressed. Once someone's achievements are made tangible and quantifiable, they can become part of that person's evolving identity. For example, many of the badges and awards that decorate so many GeoCities pages are a result of competitions (see Figure 2.21), while at Heat, each member's Trophy Case shows what that person has accomplished (see Figure 3.11). By contrast, when someone participates in a support group or attends an interview, they're building relationships, but these activities don't (usually) extend their member profile—any contribution to that person's identity exists only in the memories of the other participants.

One of the best reasons to display someone's participation history is that it builds loyalty (what some people call "stickiness"). The more developed someone's online persona becomes, the more invested that person becomes in maintaining his or her identity and staying involved in the community.

Try to focus on integrating *meaningful* markers into your profiles, though, or things may get cluttered. At Heat, for instance, the ThunderHammer trophy identifies a fearsome and skillful player, but the Shamrock trophy is awarded to everyone who logged in on Saint Patrick's day—it doesn't convey anything meaningful about the players who display it (see Figure 3.11). Such easy trophies are intended to encourage and reward beginning players, but they also clutter up the profiles of more advanced players. This trophy system could be improved by better distinguishing between real accomplishments and mundane behavior.

Bragging Rights

People generally like to measure how they're doing against others, and so get a sense for where they fit in. Competitions offer community members one way to establish status and earn some bragging rights. They also give others a way to evaluate that person's skills, and know something about them right off the bat. For instance, when new Heat members look at someone's profile and see an impressive collection of game rankings and tournament trophies, they'll know they're dealing with a skillful player who can probably hand them their hats—and maybe teach them something.

Contests: You Could Be a Winner

The simplest kind of competition to run is a contest; they work on any platform, whether e-mail, message board, or live; and they needn't require much extra staff (though they can, as discussed later). Whether small and low-key or large and high-profile, contests can help you raise the overall participation level within your community and highlight your most talented members. For instance, when Talk City ran a home-page building contest, they were able to spotlight a number of high-quality pages—and the contest motivated hundreds of members to create their first Talk City home page.

Long-Term Value

Many communities run contests to raise interest and attract new members, but the most effective contests contribute to long-term community building as well by reinforcing a community's purpose, values, and brand identity. For example, MetaCreations sponsors an Image of the Day contest that highlights digital artwork created with their software tools (Figure 7.12). The contest establishes MetaCreations as a company that empowers and appreciates digital artists.

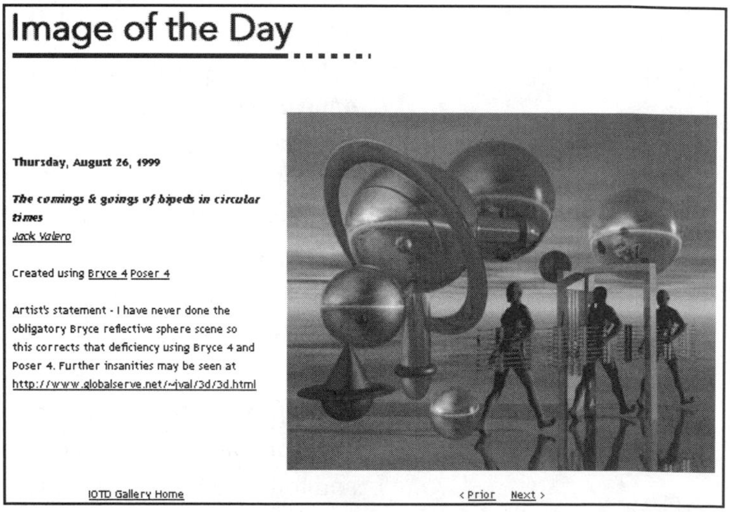

FIGURE 7.12
IMAGE OF THE DAY AT METACREATIONS
www.metacreations.com/iotd.html
MetaCreations selects a member-created image to highlight each day, which provides an ongoing artistic showcase for people who use MetaCreations' tools. The winner's page (shown here) includes a list of the tools used to create the image, a statement from the winner, and a link to the archive of all previous winners.

For a different take on what people like to do with image-manipulation software, check out Hecklers Online (www.hecklers.com), a highly participatory humor site that features a contest called Digital Graffiti (Figure 7.13). Each week, the image of some celebrity is posted on the site for players to maul using their favorite image-editing program. Hecklers also features a text-based daily contest called the Interactive Top Ten, where members concoct clever responses to a topical question. These contests do a good job of expressing the Hecklers culture, which revolves around irreverent wit.

FIGURE 7.13
DIGITAL GRAFFITI AT HECKLERS ONLINE
www.hecklers.com/Digital_Graffiti
The weekly Digital Graffiti contest at Hecklers Online invites members to mangle a celebrity photo in a humorous and irreverent way. The winning entries are posted each week, along with instructions for entering the next contest and links to the contest archives.

Same Time Next Week

The contests at Hecklers and MetaCreations have a cyclic rhythm that helps to build habits and generate repeat business: viewers return for the fresh content, and participants return to see if their entry was chosen. Regular contests are also a great way to improve the overall quality of member contributions—members can see in the contest winners what the community staff is looking for. For example, at Hecklers Online, the contest judges make a point of rewarding cleverness and originality while ignoring entries that are lewd or hateful, which encourages people to mimic the winners and reduces the number of "undesirable" entries.

Running a Successful Contest

Unlike most events discussed in this chapter, contests don't require a specialized gathering place or a complex ratings system. Running a contest is fairly straightforward: you need a challenge, a means of collecting and judging the entries, and a way to announce the winners and award prizes (see the sidebar on the WELL's Annual Writing Contest) Within this simple framework, here are some basic guidelines that can help your contest be a success:

○ **KNOW WHY YOU'RE RUNNING THE CONTEST.** Define your purpose—be clear about what you hope to get out of the event. As mentioned above, it should express your community values, and should also be designed to meet your goals, which might include generating high-quality content, attracting new members, or increasing the involvement of existing members.

○ **DETERMINE YOUR ENTRANCE REQUIREMENTS.** Early on, decide who can enter your contest. Members only, or also prospective members? Do entrants have to be over eighteen? Do they have to be U.S. citizens? Your answers will be shaped by your contest goals and by any legal restrictions involved in giving away prizes (such as whether employees, children, or non-US citizens are eligible).

- ○ **ARTICULATE YOUR JUDGING CRITERIA.** Tell contestants what you're looking for, and (whenever possible) let them know who the judges are—if not by name, at least by background and position.

- ○ **THINK THROUGH YOUR STAFFING REQUIREMENTS.** The technical requirements for contests are minimal—a few Web pages, some associated documents—but staffing needs can be substantial, especially if the contest generates a lot of entries. In addition to judges, you may also need additional people to sort through the entries and pass along the best ones. You'll also need people to post the results and notify the winners.

- ○ **OFFER A MEANINGFUL PRIZE.** For some contests (especially those that run daily or weekly), the glory of winning is the only reward. This is especially effective if you can integrate the results into their online identity, as described above. It's even better to offer a tangible prize, which can be as simple as a company T-shirt or as elaborate as a car.

- ○ **COMMUNICATE CLEARLY AT EVERY STAGE OF THE CONTEST.** Publicize the contest ahead of time and clearly articulate the entrance requirements and judging criteria. Announce when the submissions are closed, and when to expect the final results. You should also be prepared to answer any questions that come up about contest rules and results. And be sure to publish the results in a timely manner and leave them up long enough so that everyone who's interested gets a chance to check 'em out.

- ○ **USE THE CONTEST AS A SPRINGBOARD FOR OTHER ACTIVITIES.** If you integrate your contest into your community environment, the event can have a greater community-building impact. For example, you could create a message board for discussing that contest, hold a post-contest chat, or offer the winners a judging role in the next contest.

The WELL's Annual Writing Contest

At the WELL, high-quality writing is greatly valued; therefore, the WELL sponsors an annual contest to honor the online writing talents of its members (www.well.com/user/contest). This low-key event (the grand prize is $500) is a good example of how to create a fun and appropriate competition on a shoestring budget.

Like many contests, the WELL's writing contest requires only minimal technical preparations—a few simple Web pages and an email account for receiving submissions—but the staffing requirements are more substantial; member volunteers must be recruited to sort through the entries, and potential judges must be contacted and interviewed. Two months prior to the submission deadline, the community staff posts a call for entries along with the contest rules, submission guidelines, and the judges' names and bios.

Once the submission deadline is reached, volunteers filter the entries and pass the best ones along to the judges, who consult with each other to make their final decisions. On a specified date, winners are notified via email and asked to write "acceptance speeches" that are posted alongside the winning entries in a virtual "awards ceremony"—a simple idea that gives the entire contest a whimsical yet comfortably familiar sense of closure.

Fun and Games

Contests are active and fun, but for the most part, each contestant labors in isolation to produce an entry. Games, on the other hand, are inherently social; they provide a structured way for people to relax, have fun, and learn more about each other in the process. Wherever you find people getting together with free time on their hands—in a tavern or coffeehouse, after a family dinner, in a graphic chat room—you'll find people playing games.

There are a dizzying variety of multiplayer games on the Web — everything from chat-based trivia to fast-action shooters to large-scale virtual worlds. Some communities, like Ultima Online or Heat, are built around gaming, while communities like iVillage or Talk City use games to spice up their events programming.

Let the Games Begin

Here's a quick overview of some common types of online games and what's involved in running them:

WORD GAMES

Once you've developed the infrastructure for group meetings, it's easy to include word games like trivia or "Name That Tune" in your community. You'll need to write up some rules, line up a host, and promote the game within your community. For example, Moms Online features a variety of weekly word games, each with its own rules and host (Figure 7.14). You could also combine a word game with a topical chat; at Talk City, for example, the @Music community hosts a weekly music trivia game as part of a hosted chat about rock music (**www.talkcity.com/calendar/ events/event3634.htmpl**). You can amplify the community-building power of these games by introducing the hosts and celebrating the winners, as Moms Online does in its Hall of Fame (see Figure 7.14).

FIGURE 7.14
WORD GAMES AT MOMS ONLINE
Moms Online features a variety of word games in its regular chat rooms, hosted by the volunteer community staff (upper image). The Hall of Fame (lower image) showcases especially clever entries and highlights talented regulars.

Games schedule

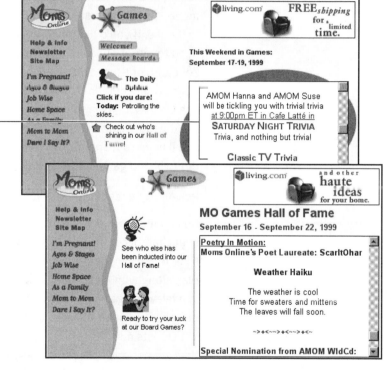

BOT GAMES

You can create a more sophisticated chat-based game by writing a "game bot," which is an automated program that greets players, runs the game, and keeps score. To create a bot game, you'll need to have access to a chat room that you can control programmatically, such as an IRC channel. For example, Talk City (which runs on top of IRC) hosts several different text-based bot games (www.talkcity.com/games/botgames). If you have the resources, you could also create a graphic-style bot game, such as Berkeley Systems' Acrophobia (www.won.net/channels/bezerk/acro).

Card and Board Games

Many Web communities—including YAHOO, Excite, Lycos, and AOL—have spiced up their services by offering online card and board games. These games are familiar, lightweight, and highly social, and they're a natural addition to a public social environment—the online equivalent of cards and board games in a coffeehouse. If you'd like to add such games to your site, you'll need to either build (or buy) your own gaming platform as the Zone did, or license it from a games provider like Pogo.com (www.pogo.com) or Go2Net (www.go2net.com), as have portals like Go (www.go.com), Lycos (www.lycos.com), and YAHOO. To get the most community-building power from these games, you'll want to foster regular events and develop a ranking ladder (which a games provider may or may not offer).

Hybrid or Crossover Games

Some media outlets have begun to feature games that, like a simuchat, occur in conjunction with events taking place offline. NFL.com, for instance, has a game for sports fans who want to play along with their team, in which players predict the next play in a televised game and earn points for the accuracy of their predictions. And in a version of traditional fantasy sports leagues, YAHOO lets members select college basketball teams to play on their squads and earn points based on the teams' performance in several statistical categories (http://basketball.fantasy.yahoo.com/collegehoops). MTV, meanwhile, has launched an online game show called WebRiot, in which online players answer the same questions, at the same time, as the in-studio players (www.mtv.com/sendme.tin?page=/mtv/tubescan/webriot/).

These kinds of game can enhance a community by offering sports or entertainment fans a new way to actively participate in their area of interest and gain public recognition for their performance.

The Main Event

Unlike a coffeehouse, where games are a background activity, some communities coalesce around games as a primary activity. Gaming-centric sites like Mplayer, Heat, and the Microsoft Gaming Zone support a variety of games and foster subcommunities that spring up around individual games. These gaming aggregators provide features like calendars and ranking ladders that are shared by all games, and provide the infrastructure and support needed to run events.

Another type of game-centric community is an ongoing, persistent gaming world, such as Ultima Online, EverQuest, or Dragon-Realms. In these worlds, players live out a virtual life in an immersive fantasy environment—developing their characters, going on adventures with their friends, earning recognition and status, and running clans and guilds. These gaming worlds typically host a wide variety of events, including games and tournaments, club meetings, and even life-passage events like weddings, funerals. and initiation rituals. (We'll take a closer look at some of these events in the next chapters on Rituals and Subgroups)

Tournaments

If you're developing a gaming-centric community, you're probably already thinking about tournaments. A tournament is a structured competition based around a series of progressive elimination rounds. In the early rounds lots of players sign up and play against each other; the winners then move on to play other winners, and so on until the final competition, from which a champion emerges.

It's a cross between a game and a contest, but a tournament involves more players, draws bigger crowds, and offers greater rewards to both the players and the community. Like any game, tournaments allow players to test their skills against others, but on a larger scale. And like most contests, tournaments offer prizes to the winners and allow lots of people to participate; but they unfold over a longer time frame.

Not for Everyone

Tournaments aren't for everyone; they require more planning and overhead than simple games, and may not be worth the resources and effort. But every community builder can learn from tournaments—they're an exceptionally effective way to get lots of members interested and involved as players, spectators, commentators, and fans. Think of a tournament as a large-scale, culturally important community event that unfolds over time, with a dramatic arc that involves much of the community. Even if your community isn't gaming-centric, I'd encourage you to think creatively about how to adapt the structural elements of a tournament into your event strategy. If you can do this in a way that reinforces your community's core identity and purpose, you'll be creating new types of events that can build your community in a truly powerful way. (see the sidebar on the iVillage Community Challenge)

What Does It Take to Run a Tournament?

Tournaments require more planning, infrastructure, and resources than a simple game or contest. They're built from smaller-scale competitive events; so to run a tournament, you'll first need to create the infrastructure and process for running games or contests. Like contest rules, tournament rules should clearly state:

- **ENTRANCE REQUIREMENTS**: who is eligible to enter the tournament, and receive prizes;

- **JUDGING CRITERIA**: who will judge the event, what criteria they'll use;

- **PRIZES**: what the winners will receive for their efforts;

- ○ **RESULTS:** how the results from each phase will be tabulated, registered and displayed; and

- ○ **RULES OF PLAY:** how the tournament will run, how many rounds there are, where the competitions will take place, and any other applicable rules.

You'll also need to select a venue. If the event is small, it can probably be held in the same chat rooms, at the same aggregator, or in the same virtual world where you hold your regular games and contests. But a larger, more extended tournament really demands an arena—a place that can accommodate not only several players and contests at once, but also spectators from the rest of the community—and the technology doesn't yet exist for providing such a venue online. At that point, you may need to find an offline place to host some of your tournament. For example, the qualifying rounds of the recent Female Frag Fest tournament (www.femalefrag.com) took place in the game rooms at Heat.Net, while the final round took place in New York City, with all the finalists flown in to participate in person.

Planning and Promotion

Once you've created your rules and chosen your venue, you'll need to start planning and promoting your tournament, taking care of staffing and infrastructure needs, lining up prizes and/or sponsors, and selecting the judges or referees. At this stage, it's helpful to create a special Web site (or page) to display all the necessary tournament information in one place, just as you would for a contest. For example, to prepare for an upcoming Quake tournament, the Heat staff created a Web site with the entrance criteria, rules of play, and tournament prizes, along with entry instructions (Figure 7.16a). They also set up tournament-specific lobbies and ladders (a mechanism for keeping track of players' relative rankings), and created a new trophy to place on the winner's profile.

The iVillage Community Challenge

In keeping with the iVillage core purpose of helping busy women solve real-world problems, the site features a highly popular multiweek event called the Community Challenge. Each Challenge focuses on making real and lasting lifestyle changes, such as quitting smoking, improving one's sex life, creating a family tradition, or launching a new career. The first Challenge was instigated by Susan Hahn, an iVillager who was struggling to discipline her teenage son. Noticing that many other iVillagers shared her frustration, Hahn recruited an expert who'd written a book called *How to Behave So Your Kids Will, Too* and worked with the iVillage staff to create a 10-week program that included reading assignments, weekly chats, an ongoing message board, and interviews with the book's author (Figure 7.15).

The event was a great success, and Community Challenges are now a key part of iVillage's events programming. Each challenge takes place over a number of weeks and is often structured around a book and/or an expert. The event begins with a kickoff chat, followed by weekly meetings and a message board where participants can swap stories, boast about their progress, and lend each other support. At a concluding expert-led chat, the participants summarize what they've learned and accomplished. After each Challenge, the iVillage community staff archives the message boards and chat transcripts and summarizes the results by selecting representative comments from the participants.

The Community Challenge is a hybrid event that incorporates the continuity of weekly meetings (like a topical chat), the presence of an expert (as in a performance), and the multiweek structure of a tournament. The lesson here is to think creatively about your events and don't feel locked into one category; feel free to combine elements that make contextual sense within your community. And remember that an iVillager sparked the first Community Challenge—so listen to your members and your volunteers, because they may come up with great ideas that would never occur to you.

FIGURE 7.15
iVILLAGE COMMUNITY CHALLENGES
www.ivillage.com/challenges

You'll also need to decide how to structure your event. Many tournaments involve several phases, with the top players from earlier phases proceeding to the next. Heat's Quake tournament, for example, started with a qualifying round; the top 64 players from this phase then competed in the tournament round, and then the top two players competed for the grand prize, the Intensor gaming chair (www.imeron.com/products/products_LX.html), made by the tournament's sponsor. A few days after the final game, the staff posted the results in the News section of their site (see Figure 7.16)—and similarly, you should be sure to publicize the results of your tournament in an appropriate way.

Keep Them Coming Back

We talked a lot in this chapter about the value of repeated, regular events for creating habits and building loyalty among your members. The rituals of greetings, celebrating birthdays, and so on are another class of repeated events that have an equally powerful effect; they will be discussed in the next chapter.

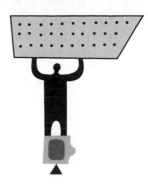

CHAPTER EIGHT

RITUALS:
Handshakes, Holidays,
and Rites of Passage

From the mundane to the magical, rituals help guide us through the transitions of life. Whenever we attend a wedding or funeral, light the candles on a menorah or birthday cake, or greet our friends at the office, the tavern, or the church, we're engaging in a familiar and comforting sequence of actions that remind us of who we are, what we value, and where we belong.

If you incorporate such familiar and time-tested community rituals into your Web community, you'll help your members feel at home. By reflecting seasonal changes, celebrating holidays, and acknowledging personal milestones, you'll be laying the foundation for a true online culture.

In this Chapter

The Power of Ritual

What does it feel like to belong? What defines that moment when you cease to be a tentative newcomer and start to feel that you're part of a community? In your neighborhood, that moment might come when you first ask for "the usual" at the local tavern (and get it), or when you're invited to join an ongoing book club or card game. In a Web community, it might be when a leader remembers your name, or when you're invited to join a private message board or mailing list.

We Are Gathered Here

Each of these "moments of belonging" is a type of community ritual—a stylized and meaningful sequence of actions that binds people more closely together. Whenever we say grace at mealtimes, stop by the pub after work, gather around the table for Thanksgiving, or attend a wedding, graduation, or funeral, we're participating in a timeless and universal event that reminds us of who we are and where we belong. Rituals are similar to events (see sidebar: What is a Ritual?)—but while some events take place only once, a ritual occurs repeatedly; for example, the WELL's first potluck dinner party was an event, but now these monthly gatherings are a well-established ritual. And unlike events, rituals can also be private, such as when I log into my favorite online gathering place every morning to kick-start my day.

Meaningful Transitions

Whether we're shifting gears after a long workday or mourning the death of a loved one, rituals can help us navigate the transitions of life by giving us something familiar and comforting to do. Within a community setting, any meaningful transition has the potential to be ritualized (and therefore become more powerful). Some community rituals are simple, everyday events, like saying hello to one's coworkers in the morning or dropping by the gym after work. Other rituals are seasonal and social, like a Thanksgiving dinner, a May Day dance, or a tailgate party at a football game. Still others are associated with major life transitions, like a wedding, funeral, baptism, briss, or graduation.

Any meaningful transition has the potential to be ritualized

Whether simple or elaborate, all community rituals have the power to reinforce group identity and strengthen the bonds between members, as we'll see in the rest of this chapter. That's why incorporating some familiar and time-tested rituals can help your members develop a sense of belonging and add power and depth to their community experience.

What Is a Ritual?

Throughout our lives, we encounter systems of belief that bind us together, and give our lives structure and meaning. The most important lessons are usually acted out in the form of rituals and ceremonies — small, scripted dramas that, in the words of anthropologist Victor Turner, "communicate our deepest values ... and inscribe order in the hearts and minds of participants." Although rituals can be private, the most powerful community-building rituals are held in a group setting and serve to strenghten the group's identity by giving the participants a shared, meaningful experience that they can look forward to experiencing again.

Personal Acknowledgments

At the most basic level, a community is a place "where everybody knows your name." It's also a place where, for better or worse, people learn things about you — your personal history, special talents, social reputation, and peculiar quirks — and incorporate that knowledge into their interactions with you. The bartender at the local tavern might greet you by name on your second visit, but eventually she'll be inquiring about your family, asking how the job's going, or chuckling over your vacation photos; she's built up a context that allows her to communicate with you in a more personalized way.

Welcome Your Members

Acquiring this sort of personal context is what "becoming known" is all about, and it's part of what draws people back to a community setting. As a community builder, you can initiate the process by welcoming people as they arrive. As discussed in Chapter 4, it's a good idea to greet new visitors right away and lead them to an informative Visitor's Center. But your members will have a persistent and unique identity (see Chapter 3), which means that you can get to know them better over time and use this knowledge to welcome them in an increasingly more personalized way.

Hello, It's Me

Creating an effective welcome ritual can be tricky. The right kind of greeting can encourage your members to keep coming back, but if you use member information gratuitously, you can easily put people off or even scare them away. For example, if you overuse a member's name in your communications with them, you'll come off sounding as insincere as an unctuous telemarketer.

You'll want to create a greeting ritual that's personalized, appropriate, and (most important) informative. When you log on to AOL, for example, a voice says "Welcome" and perhaps "You've Got Mail" (Figure 8.1). This simple greeting acknowledges a member's arrival and provides individualized information that's appropriate for AOL's core audience, many of whom use the service primarily for email. These sound bytes might seem corny, but they can pack quite an emotional punch—ask any AOL member who's longed to hear that familiar phrase. (You could also introduce a parting ritual as well—see sidebar "The Power of Goodbye").

The Power of Goodbye

Developing a welcome ritual is great, but leave-taking also offers an opportunity to ritualize the community experience. Many scheduled chat events, for example, are brought to a close by the participants saying goodbye, exchanging virtual {{{{hugs}}}}, and making plans for the next gathering. Similarly, someone who decides to stop participating in a particular message board will often post a message giving the reason. Such parting rituals can be incorporated into your Community Guidelines (see Chapter 6) and your host training program (see Chapter 5).

Automated farewell rituals are a bit trickier. On the Web, it's not always possible to know when someone is logging out of your community—they may just be visiting a different site for a while. Accordingly, some Web communities offer their members the opportunity to click a Goodbye button that leads to a special area of the site that announces upcoming events. In contrast, Web communities that use a custom client— such as AOL—have the control over the logout process and thus have an opportunity to invoke an exit ritual, such as AOL's automated Goodbye screen (Figure SB-1).

In theory, a goodbye ritual can give each person's visit to the community a sense of completion, and can even become another branding or advertising opportunity. In *practice*, however, people don't want to be slowed down when they're ready to leave—so if you do create a goodbye ritual, make sure that it's not more of an annoyance than a pleasure. You can do this by making it optional (such as clicking a button), or by delivering personalized information that the member is likely to find valuable.

FIGURE 8.1
AOL's WELCOME RITUAL
When an AOL member logs in, a disembodied voice says "Welcome," followed by "You've Got Mail" when there's email waiting. The email icon is redundant but necessary, since some users may have the sound off.

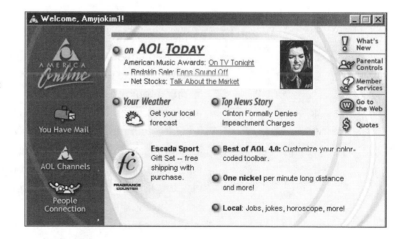

Just What I Want to See

Another way to welcome back returning members is to offer them a customized Start page, which can be any customized view of content and activities that members see when they first arrive. For instance, when I log onto the WELL, I'm greeted with my own personal conference list, and an indication of which conferences have new postings (Figure 8.2). Similarly, my personal Start page at the Motley Fool (Figure 8.3) includes stock quotes and news headlines, and shows me how many new posts there are in conversations I'm following. Some communities, such as the Motley Fool and YAHOO, automatically recognize returning members using cookies, while others like AOL and the WELL require returning members to log in.

FIGURE 8.2
THE WELL'S CUSTOMIZED CONFERENCE LIST
When WELL members log in, they see a list of their favorite conferences (like my personal list, shown here), with icons that highlight new postings.

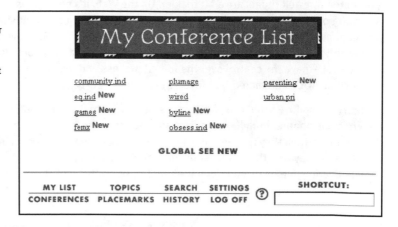

While these Start pages allow a member to customize what appears on them, they lack the ability to automatically evolve in response to the member's behavior. No matter how avidly I'm following a topic on the WELL, the conference it's in won't appear on my Start page unless I explicitly add it to my settings. That's why, if you're going to implement this type of Start page, it's a good idea to make it easy for your members to change their preferences. For example, the Motley Fool's message board interface includes an icon that allows the reader to add that board to their preferences with a single click (see Figure 8.3). (The Motley Fool is able to achieve this integration because their message boards and Start page technology are custom built in-house).

Add the Personal Touch

Being greeted with useful information is great, but it doesn't really make people feel like someone's getting to know them. As we discussed in Chapter 4, each member's experience changes over time, and your welcome ritual can be even more powerful and effective if it incorporates your evolving knowledge about each member.

FIGURE 8.3

"FAVORITE BOARDS" AT THE MOTLEY FOOL
The Motley Fool's personal Start page lets members create a list of their favorite discussion topics and then see the number of new postings in each topic (upper image). Members can add a new topic to their list simply by clicking on the heart icon while reading that topic (lower image).

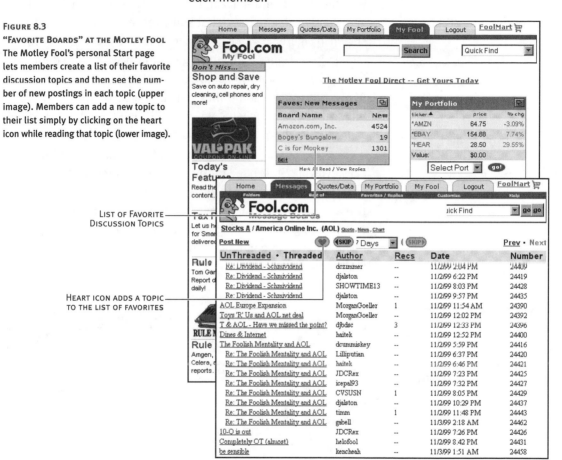

LIST OF FAVORITE DISCUSSION TOPICS

HEART ICON ADDS A TOPIC TO THE LIST OF FAVORITES

Leverage the Community Database

One way to create an automatically evolving welcome is to use a software technique called *collaborative filtering*, available from companies like Net Perceptions (www.netperceptions.com/product) and Macromedia (www.andromedia.com/products/likeminds). This approach recommends items a member might be interested in based on what he or she has previously expressed interest in and on what other members with similar interests have selected. The more preferences the member reveals, the more personalized these recommendations can become over time.

Whenever I log onto Amazon.com, for example, I'm greeted by name and invited to check out some recommended books (as shown in Figure 3.15). I can then view and refine these recommendations (Figure 8.4), which gives the system more detailed information about my tastes. This is a relatively unobtrusive form of personalization, somewhat similar to a bookstore clerk's getting to know you and what you might like. Although this style of welcome ritual is most appropriate for a transaction-based community, you could apply the same ideas to create an automatically evolving Start page for other types of communities. For example, a Singapore-based community named CoolConnect (www.coolconnect.com) uses Net Perceptions' personalization software to greet returning members with movie, music and restaurant recommendations that are based on their stated tastes, rather than on their purchase behavior.

FIGURE 8.4
REFINING RECOMMENDATIONS AT
AMAZON.COM
Amazon.com encourages members to rate the recommendations the system generates, and then feeds this information back into an evolving portrait of each person's tastes.

Interact with a Person

When someone enters a real-time social space like a chat room, there's another opportunity for a greeting ritual—one that's performed by a person. Many Web communities—including Talk City, iVillage, and Moms Online—train their chat hosts to greet everyone who enters the room. If you enter a chat group at Moms Online, for example, the host will post a message that welcomes you into the conversation and tells you the topic (Figure 8.5).

This style of greeting can help newcomers feel welcomed, and keeps the conversation on track. But it's not for everyone—as you're designing your greeting ritual, be sure to consider who your members are, and what style of interaction they'll appreciate. For example, Internet newbies will often enjoy being welcomed by name into an unfamiliar social space, but the computer science students in my graduate seminar (www.naima.com/CS377B) were put off by the chirpy, cheerful greetings they encountered at places like Talk City and Moms Online.

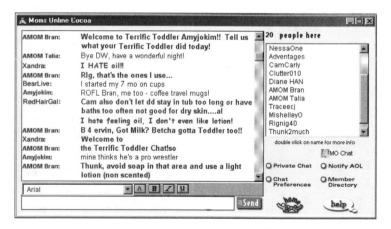

FIGURE 8.5

AUTOMATED GREETINGS AT MOMS ONLINE
On AOL, Moms Online chat hosts send an automated greeting to every person who enters the chat. Here, the host named AMOM Bran greets me as I enter the Terrific Toddler chat.

If you want to welcome people as they enter a chat room, your job will be easier if you use macros, which allow a host to prepare a welcome message in advance and send it with a few keystrokes. (Some hosts prefer to compose each greeting afresh, so you shouldn't force the issue.) Programs like Powertools (on AOL) and Pirch (a powerful IRC client—see Chapter 2) offer built-in macros, or you could use the shareware packages described in the previous chapter.

Like a bartender greeting her regulars, hosts will naturally want to greet regular participants in a more personalized way than with a standardized message. At Moms Online on AOL, for example, many chat hosts will send an automated greeting to everyone who enters the room, and then send a more personal greeting to returning members. Both types of greeting are seen by everyone in the room (due to an inhernent limitation in AOL's hosting tools)—and like a stranger who enters a boisterous neighborhood bar, enthusiastic greetings between old friends can make a newcomer feel awkward and left out. Accordingly, you may want to look for tools that support sending chatroom greetings that only the recipient can see, and suggest to your hosts that they greet old friends privately, as Talk City does.

Leave a Note

It's also possible to have a personal greeting that's doesn't happen in real time. If your community includes message boards, for example, you can use an Introductions topic (described in Chapter 4) as an asynchronous welcome ritual to greet newcomers and ease them through the potentially intimidating transition between lurking and posting. If you include such a topic, it's a good idea to train your hosts to respond to newcomers who introduce themselves, so that person has the satisfaction of having their post acknowledged. In a lively conference, other members will often chime in as well, which helps the newcomer feel welcomed and encourages them to post again.

Remember Special Days

All of us have birthdays and anniversaries that are personally meaningful, and we feel closer to people who remember these special days. If your friends at work surprise you with a birthday cake, for instance, you'll feel acknowledged in a very personal way. In your Web community, celebrating birthdays and anniversaries (when appropriate) can evoke the same feelings and make your community feel a little bit more like an extended family.

Happy Birthday to Me

If you're already collecting your members' dates of birth when they register, you could consider sending them a congratulatory email or Web-based birthday card. For extra impact, you could even include a small gift—a discount coupon or company T-shirt, for instance. Like welcome letters, birthday wishes are most effective if they at least appear to come directly from one or more community leaders, such as a founder, community manager, or host.

Even if you don't know people's birthdays, you can still encourage members and leaders to celebrate informally. For example, the WELL staff doesn't automatically send out birthday greetings, but individual conferences (which are subcommunities in themselves) often have a special topic for wishing Happy Birthday to their regular participants.

A Meaningful Anniversary

Another way to make a member feel known and special is to acknowledge personal anniversaries that are meaningful within the community context, such as the date that person joined. For example, you could send an appreciative email on their one-year anniversary, or even place a marker or badge in their profile.

In a small group setting, these personal anniversaries can be celebrated in a more public way, which gives them more community-building power. For instance, twelve-step groups often celebrate the anniversary of each group member's sobriety, which reminds everyone of their community's purpose and the group's shared goal. You can tap into this power by publicly celebrating the day that someone achieved a sought-after goal, such as living free of pain (in a health-oriented community) or getting out of debt (in a finance-oriented community).

Community Holidays

If you think of the special times when you were a kid, what events come to mind? You probably remember holiday gatherings, especially ones that involved some sort of ritual or ceremony. For example, I vividly remember celebrating Passover at the home of my grandparents: each year we'd see the same people, hear the same stories, recite the same prayers, and eat the same symbolic foods. These yearly gatherings helped me get to know my extended family and indelibly shaped my sense of cultural identity.

Seasonal activities like religious holidays, harvest festivals, and even sporting events are deeply ingrained into human culture; they bring people together and remind them about what's important and valued within their community. As a community builder, you can deepen your members' sense of belonging and develop your culture by celebrating yearly events that are meaningful within the community context.

Mark the Holidays

You can start by celebrating existing holidays in a way that means something to your members. For example, in December 1998, NetNoir celebrated Kwanzaa (Figure 8.6), while Talk City hosted Santa's Workshop (Figure 8.7), AncientSites celebrated the pre-Christian holiday Saturnalia (Figure 8.8), and iVillage promoted their nondenominational Holiday Survival Kit (Figure 8.9). Each celebration both expressed and reinforced the community's unique identity.

FIGURE 8.6
KWANZAA AT NETNOIR
NetNoir's celebration of Kwanzaa places special emphasis on educational materials about the origins and background of this African-American holiday.

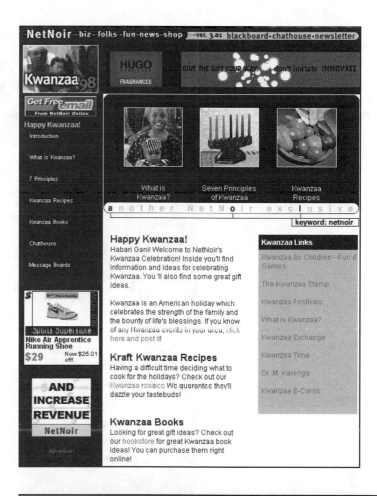

FIGURE 8.7
SANTA'S WORKSHOP AT TALK CITY
This seasonal area of the Talk City site contains a variety of simple activities and games that reinforce the community's mainstream and family-friendly identity.

ANCIENTSITES
SATURNALIA

AncientSites Saturnalia Events

Rulers - Be Crowned a Mock King or Queen for a Day! Ruler's BB.
Feast - Sacrifice a Piglet and Bring Out The Best Falernian Feast BB.
Poetry - Tributes, Verse and Epigrams Poetry BB
Treasure - Virtual Fortune in the Forum? Richest Citizens
Theater - Drama, Comedy and Especially Farce Theater BB
Oracle - Prescience, Profundity, and General Murkiness Fortune Booth
Avatar - Dressing Down for the Saturnalia Avatar's BB

"Io, bona Saturnalia!" - "Hail, good Saturnalia!" This was the traditional formula cried out by the Roman crowds as they rushed to the streets of the capital after the completion of the solemn sacrifice at the Temple of Saturn on the first day of the merry festival celebrating the Winter Solstice - a.d. XIV Kal. Jan. (17 December). These were "the best of the days", in the words of the poet Catullus. The customary, often tedious, often exacting, mode of life was turned upside down. Everyone was allowed some measure of self-abandon, men and women, masters and slaves, children and adults - and an entire week of revelry. All public activity ceased: warfare, labor, mourning, exercise of justice. Strict social distinctions relaxed, and people from all walks of life mingled in a common sentiment of joyous rapture.

The origins of that most important festival are clouded in obscurity and made a subject of learned debates, both in Antiquity and in modern times. Some Roman antiquarians attributed it to the immemorial Golden Age when humankind was ruled by the benevolent god Saturn; others, to the days of the first Rome's king Romulus, or of the last, Tarquinius Superbus. The historian Livy provides the later date, 496 B.C., shortly after the establishment of the Republic.

The Saturnalia started as an agricultural celebration and originally lasted for only one day. With time, it was prolonged to embrace two other festivals - the Opalia, dedicated to the fertility goddess Ops (Dec. 19) and Larentalia, honoring Acca Larentia, the legendary nurse of Romulus and Remus (Dec. 23), and finally acquired its classical seven-day form.

The Romans eagerly looked forward to those festivities: the Saturnalia, not unlike the medieval and even some modern carnivals, promised the release of anxieties and pleasures of self-indulgence. To dress in loose tunics instead of formal togas, to eat and drink their fill in public and private banquets, to play the fool under the orders of a mock king, to engage in pranks and practical jokes, to turn the tables on those whom they otherwise had to revere, to speak sense and nonsense, even to obey the whims of their own slaves knowing that it is nothing but pretence - all that made an experience to be treasured and fondly remembered for the rest of the next year. They were never happy that everything has an end, even the Saturnalia, and they used an expression 'Saturnalia extendere' (presumably, ad infinitum) to indicate, in a manner of wishful thinking, their own vision of an earthly bliss.

Let us prove that the Roman spirit did not die and that we are the worthy heirs of the ancients - both in their wisdom and their folly! Let us momentarily forget our worries, our careers, our taxes, our TV sets, our three-piece suits, our shopping malls, and descend on the streets of the Empire's capital on these December days, mixing with the happy crowd of Romans!

To create holiday celebrations that strengthen your community, think about who your members are and how holidays affect their lives, and then structure your celebrations to meet their needs. For example, Halloween is a big deal for most kids, which means that their parents often have a lot of preparation and work to do. Consequently, tuned-in parenting sites like FamilyPlay (www. familyplay.com), ParentsPlace (www.parentsplace.com), Parent Soup (www.parentsoup.com), and BabyCenter (Figure 8.10) feature costume ideas, safety tips, and party recipes. Online games like EverQuest and Ultima Online, on the other hand, cater to people who may have outgrown trick-or-treating but still enjoy the fantasy of dressing up and playing a role, so these sites feature in-game costume contests and storytelling events.

FIGURE 8.9
HOLIDAY SURVIVAL KIT AT IVILLAGE
Taking a pragmatic and nondenominational approach to the holiday season, IVIllage provides a Holiday Survival Kit filled with advice and support for busy women.

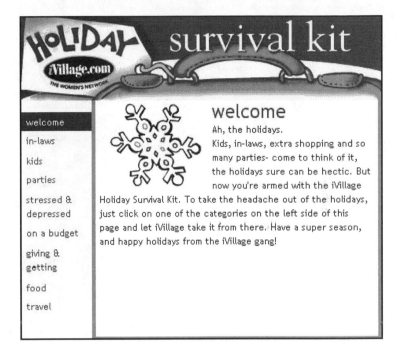

Beyond such universal holidays, look for special days to celebrate that offer an opportunity to reinforce your theme and purpose and/or enrich your backstory. For example, every year NetNoir celebrates Martin Luther King Jr.'s birthday in a special way. Similarly, a site like iVillage or Women.com could celebrate the birthdays of famous women.

Member Contributions

Although you can certainly provide holiday-themed content and activities yourself, your members will feel even more involved if you showcase and support their own efforts. For example, the October issue of the GeoCities World Report (an email newsletter for members) includes pointers to a variety of member-run

FIGURE 8.10

BABYCENTER COSTUME CONTEST

In keeping with BabyCenter's focus on highlighting member contributions, the site sponsors a Halloween costume contest that includes instructions on how to make the winning costumes.

Happy Halloween!

We have Halloween trivia, tips on how to keep your little goblin **safe and smiling** and a roundup of fun, not frightening, books.

BabyCenter Second Annual Costume Contest Winner

The Second Annual BabyCenter Costume Contest was a great success -- more than 18,000 users chose among our nine semi-finalists. The race was close, but the flowerpot costume came out on top. Click here to see the other eight semi-finalists, or click here to see last year's winner.

Flowerpot
Name: Avery
Age: 5 months

How to make this costume:

To dress up her 5-month-old daughter Avery, Chloe Tingley made a union suit out of green fleece and attached leaves around the neckline. Using fabric glue, she glued silk roses to a baby bonnet. The final touch, of course, was the flowerpot itself, which was big enough for Avery to sit in comfortably with her legs crossed while her parents carried her around.

"We got a great reaction. Total strangers were stopping us to take pictures of her and they even took a picture for the local newspaper." — Chloe Tingley

Got a great idea for a costume? Tell us about it!

Tricks and treats from BabyCenter

- Keep Halloween fun! We'll show you how to take the scare out of the big day.
- Do's and don'ts for a safe Halloween
- The best Halloween books for babies and toddlers
- Where does Halloween come from? Find out in our trivia roundup
- Discover more great costume ideas in our Baby Store's Halloween costume department
- Poll: What do you think will be the most popular costume this year?
- Poll: What candy are you most likely to steal from your kid's stash?

Halloween contests and events. Similarly, the EverQuest Web site highlights Halloween events that are created and run by players, which the game masters make a special effort to attend. Gestures like these make the members feel that their efforts are noticed and appreciated by the community staff.

In addition to running events, your members may be able to provide you with themed content. For example, the Halloween area at Moms Online is filled with member-contributed costume ideas, safety tips, and ghoulish recipes (Figure 8.11). The MO community staff builds this collection by soliciting tips and stories both before and after the holiday, which gives them an ever-growing collection of member-generated content. (After all, a good recipe or costume idea never goes out of date.)

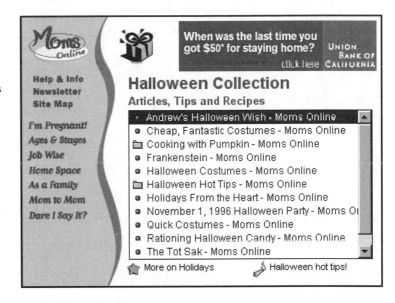

You can make these celebrations even more memorable by providing storytelling opportunities for your members. For example, many of the member-submitted Halloween tips at Moms Online include personal stories, which gives the holiday area a friendly and personal feeling. And Parent Soup members who participate in a holiday Community Challenge are encouraged to share their success stories (and their struggles) as they work on creating new family traditions (Figure 8.12).

FIGURE 8.12
CREATE A NEW FAMILY TRADITION AT PARENT SOUP

This Community Challenge took place in December and let members tell each other stories about their experience creating this tradition in the chat rooms, on the message board, and as part of the final wrap-up.

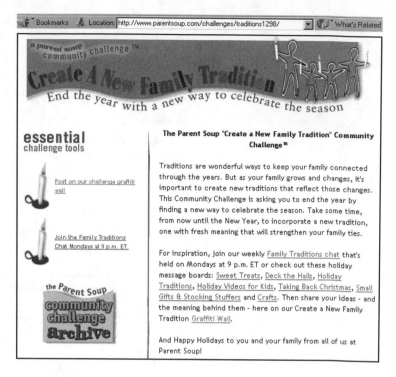

Recall Events

It's great to celebrate existing holidays, but you can reinforce your community's identity even more by creating your own holidays that honor important people and events in your community's history. Here in the United States, for example, we have special holidays that honor our Founding Fathers (Washington's Birthday) and commemorate the day that we were freed from British rule (Independence Day). For many, these holidays simply mean a day off from school or work, but they offer an ongoing reminder of our collective history, and the rituals associated with these events provide an opportunity for storytelling and education. ("Why are there fireworks on the Fourth of July, Daddy?")

Happy Birthday to Us

An easy way to get started is to celebrate the "birthday" (that is, the launch date) of the community. This is a sure-fire way to build community spirit (and won't invoke factional infighting, as religious holidays sometimes do). If possible, celebrate this event in a way that expresses your basic community values (because your members and visitors will see it as an expression of them). For example, Parent Soup celebrated its third birthday with a "family reunion" contest (Figure 8.13), while Heat celebrated its second birthday with games, contests, and an awards ceremony for "Player of the Year."

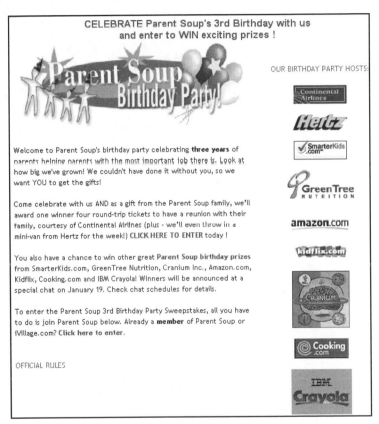

If you can arrange it so that your community's birthday falls on a day that ties into your community theme, so much the better. NetNoir, for instance, officially launched on June 19th, or "Juneteenth," which is the oldest known celebration of the ending of slavery (Figure 8.14). As a result, whenever NetNoir celebrates its birthday, it's also celebrating an important (and often overlooked) day in African American history.

FIGURE 8.14
JUNETEENTH AT NETNOIR
For its launch date, NetNoir chose
Juneteenth—an important day in
black history—which allows NetNoir
to educate people while celebrating.

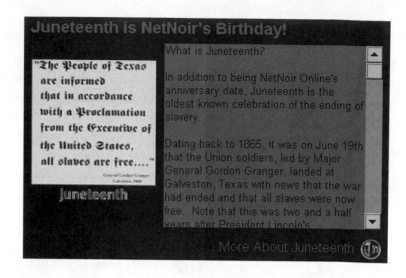

If your community contains subgroups with their own distinct identity—such as cities, neighborhoods, clans, or clubs (see Chapter 9)—you can encourage them to celebrate their own launch dates by highlighting these events or otherwise providing support and attention. For example, GeoCities showcased the PicketFence neighborhood's birthday celebration in the monthly newsletter (Figure 8.15). Similarly, a gaming community could encourage member-run clans or guilds to celebrate their launch dates, or a support-oriented community could encourage groups to celebrate their yearly anniversaries.

Celebrate Your Heroes

Besides anniversaries, you can also create and celebrate other community-specific holidays, such as the founder's birthday or a seminal event in your community's history. These holidays offer an ideal opportunity to flesh out your backstory and tell your members more about who founded the community and why. A fantasy gaming community like Ultima Online or EverQuest, for instance, could celebrate the birthdays of characters in the story or pivotal events that occurred in the fantasy world.

FIGURE 8.15
HAPPY BIRTHDAY TO PICKETFENCE
The GeoCities PicketFence community leaders organized a birthday celebration for their community as a way to promote the neighborhood and make the homesteaders feel special.

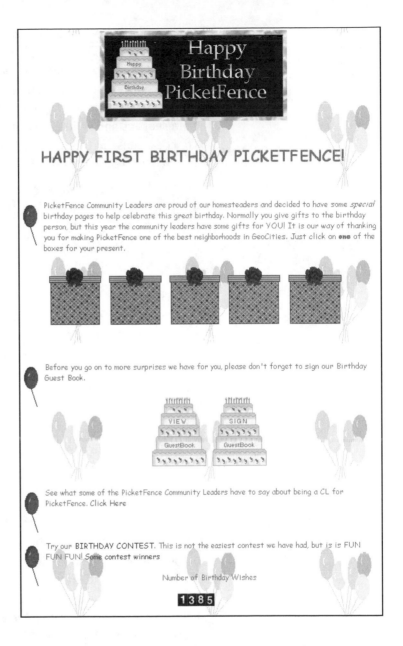

Reflect the Seasons

Holidays are meaningful and memorable, but you don't have to limit your seasonal efforts to these one-day events. All year long, you can decorate your site to reflect the changing seasons.

Much as someone might adorn their home or workplace, you can embellish your Web community with spring flowers or autumn leaves. These embellishments don't have to be fancy or take up much space; for example, the Motley Fool cycles through several different logo icons during the year that reflect both seasons and holidays (Figure 8.16). This simple technique creates a sense of time passing and makes the community feel more connected to the rest of life.

If you're working with a more graphically rich environment, you can develop these embellishments even further. For example, the now-defunct Imagination Network (a pioneering online gaming community) included four seasonal versions of the opening interface screen: flowers and greenery for spring, beach-themed summertime decorations, colorful autumn leaves, and a snowy winter landscape. The interface was automatically updated on the first day of each season—a simple yet highly visible ritual which delighted the members and reinforced their sense of belonging.

Living in a Fantasy World

If you're running a fantasy-oriented community, you can immerse your members more deeply by noting the seasons and holidays of the fantasy world rather than the physical world. For example, the citizens of Elanthia (the mythical setting for the Simutronics games DragonRealms and GemStone) celebrate four seasonal holidays that exist only within the game's fiction: Lormandu (Spring), Anlandu (Summer), Blufandu (Fall), and Geomandu (Winter). Each holiday is associated with particular events and people in the Elanthian backstory, so the celebrations help newcomers learn more about Elanthian history; they also an provide an opportunity for more experienced players to launch new in-game business ventures or hold an in-game wedding ceremony. (As with many online fantasy games, time is sped up, so a year in the game lasts only three "real" months.)

Even in such a fantasy world, you may also want to acknowledge real-world holidays. For example, if you logged into Ultima Online during the Christmas season, you'd find a special gift in your knapsack and meet an automated character dressed up as Santa Claus. Even though Ultima Online takes place in a fantasy world, these homages to existing holidays delight the players and make them feel that the game is connected to their ongoing lives.

Passages and Transitions

Rites of passage such as weddings, funerals, baptisms, and graduations are another type of celebration that brings a community together. But unlike holidays, which commemorate a historic event, these community rituals mark the transformation of an individual. Communities everywhere turn to these ancient and universal celebrations to guide their members through potentially difficult and confusing times. Getting married, graduating from college, having a baby, facing the death of a loved one—these are all life-changing events, and it's helpful to have customs and rituals that prepare us for the transformation and teach us something about how to play an unfamiliar social role.

Rites of passage are fundamentally social events, because they involve a change to not just our own role but the roles of those around us. When we have a child, for example, we become parents; but in addition, our parents become grandparents, and our siblings become aunts and uncles. That's why we celebrate these events in a community setting—to announce an individual's change in social status to the wider community and to give everyone who's affected by these new roles a chance to acknowledge the changes that are taking place.

Celebrate the Stages of Life

For many people, Web communities provide an important way to share their life transitions with others. In a page-building community like GeoCities or Tripod, for instance, you'll find thousands of member-created pages that announce births and naming ceremonies, bar mitzvahs and graduations, weddings and funerals. And in a conversational community like the WELL, you'll often see special conference topics that are devoted to announcing and discussing these transitions.

Announcing Life Transitions

Given a forum, community members will announce life transitions on their own, just as people will place birth, marriage and death announcements in their local newspaper. You can support this activity by highlighting these announcements and making them easier to create. For example, GeoCities provides members with page-building templates for baby announcements and personal tributes (**geocities.yahoo.com/members/build.html**) and occasionally highlights members' birth, death, and wedding announcements in the monthly newsletter. GeoCities could further encourage this activity by providing templates for a wider variety of life transitions and by creating special announcement areas in the neighborhoods. Another approach would be to offer a regular Community News section on your Web site or in an email newsletter and provide email or Web-based forms with which people could submit their birth announcements, wedding stories, and obituaries.

We're Having a Baby

Having a child is certainly a life-changing transition, and parenting-specific sites often note this event by highlighting birth announcements and providing a variety of resources for new parents. In a more general (or less personal) community, it would be more appropriate to highlight birth announcements as part of an overall community news area.

Baby News

Like so many life passages, having a baby is a process that unfolds over time in distinct stages. This means that you, as a community builder, have the opportunity to deliver "just in time" content and activities to someone who's going through it, because each stage has distinct needs and requirement. A great example of this idea is the BabyCenter Newsletter (Figure 8.17), which I subscribed to when I was pregnant with my son Gabriel (whom you can meet at www.naima.com/gabe). If you sign up and enter your due date, you'll start receiving weekly email newsletters with health tips, medical information, and shopping suggestions that are targeted for your stage. These newsletters continue after your baby is born, and let you know what to expect during the first few years of your child's life. This is a terrific way to attract and hold someone's attention—there's nothing quite like getting an email that speaks directly to your needs, and answers the questions that are currently on your mind.

FIGURE 8.17

BABYCENTER NEWSLETTER

This weekly email newsletter follows the progress of pregnancy and child-rearing. Here's the newsletter that I received when my baby was two months old; it combines parenting tips, information about child development, and age-related product suggestions.

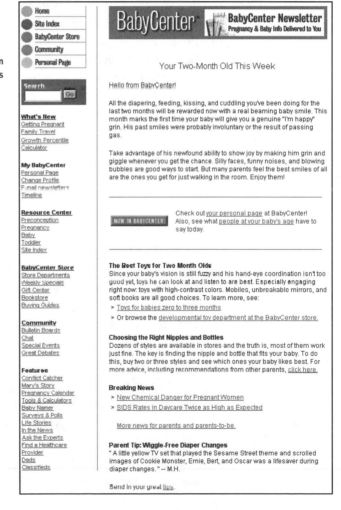

It's a good idea to help your members who are expecting connect with others who are at the same stage. For example, a highly popular feature on parenting sites (and all around the Net) are "birth month" groups or clubs where women (and some men) share stories and compare notes with other people whose babies are due at around the same time. It's also useful to provide a way for your members to get advice from someone at a later stage; for example, BabyCenter includes an evolving database of member-submitted parenting tips, which become part of the "just in time" content on the site and in the newsletter.

These examples are drawn from bearing and raising a child, but you can apply these ideas to any activity that unfolds in stages, such as planning a wedding or funeral, applying to college or grad school, or preparing for a bar mitzvah or confirmation. And because these activities require people to learn a lot quickly, and (often) purchase a variety of goods and services, you have an ideal opportunity to both deliver a needed service and package it with targeted e-commerce opportunities.

When Two Become One

Getting married is another life-changing transition, and while some Web sites focus solely on this issue (see, for example, www.theknot.com and www.weddingchannel.com), most online communities would want to include weddings as part of an overall events strategy. But not every community will want to showcase these very personal events. A professional networking community, for instance, might acknowledge but not emphasize weddings, while a religious or family-oriented community would definitely want to showcase weddings (and births and funerals), because they reinforce what that community is all about.

Weddings have a special place in online role-playing games like DragonRealms, Ultima Online, and EverQuest. In these games, weddings between *characters* take place within the fantasy environment (Figure 8.18), and they happen for a variety of reasons: to advance the story line, cement political alliances, or simply express the feelings and sense of commitment that have evolved between two players. Offline, the wedding participants might be married to other people or not even be the same gender as their characters. Community builders running this type of game can facilitate in-game weddings, perhaps by creating special places to hold the weddings, and encouraging support staff to officiate at these events. If you're really ambitious, you could even get into the wedding-planning business; for example, the Simutronics staff runs several weddings a month—complete with unique, hand-crafted outfits and a custom setting for the occasion—for which the players pay hundreds and even thousands of dollars.

FIGURE 8.18
AN ULTIMA ONLINE WEDDING
In-game weddings are popular in Ultima Online; players enjoy gathering their friends together and creating a festive setting for the ceremony. Here a Counselor officiates at the event. The UO staff acknowledges this role as an important part of a Counselor's duties.

In Loving Memory

Death is one of the most painful and challenging life passages we face, and when someone passes away who has touched our lives, we turn to our community for support and comfort. It's a common custom to create a lasting memorial such as a shrine or gravesite where mourners can go to honor and remember the person who has passed away. Such memorials are becoming increasingly common on the Web; there are even places like Virtual Memorials (www.virtual-memorials.com) that offer free, template-based online memorials that anyone can use.

When someone who has been active in a Web community dies, that person's online friends will often want to create a lasting memorial that's "blessed" (or at least acknowledged) by the community staff. You can strengthen your community and gain your members' goodwill by honoring and facilitating this process. For example, when a beloved GeoCities Community Leader named Bev Crowley passed away suddenly, her friends and fellow leaders created dozens of memorial Web pages and a special Web ring (**www.geocities.com/HotSprings/2432/ BevMemRing.html**) to express their grief and share stories about how Bev had touched their lives In response, the Geo-Cities staff posted an obituary in the Community Leaders news-letter and stopped by her memorial site to sign the guest book and pay their respects. David Bohnett, the founder of GeoCities, even sent a donation in Bev's name to her favorite charity. These gestures were meaningful and comforting to the mourners; in fact, several people that I interviewed said that this event made GeoCities feel like a "real" community.

A similar outpouring of emotion occurred on Ultima Online when an avid player named Sir Death (really, that was his fan-tasy name) was killed in a motorcycle accident. His bereaved guildmates asked the UO community staff to place a memorial in the game to honor their departed friend (only UO staff can create new and unique objects). So Lonestar, a gamemaster who'd had many dealings with Sir Death, created a customized, flower-bedecked gravestone in a field near his guild house (Figure 8.19). Lonestar also created a dolphin named Sir Death that would live forever and released it into the ocean near the gravesite. In the days and weeks following, hundreds of players visited the gravesite and left offerings of flowers, food, and money to the deceased. Since that time, several other memori-als to deceased players have been created, all of which are deeply appreciated by the community.

Another way to create a memorial is to dedicate particular areas or buildings within your community to members who have passed on. For example, the cancer area of the allHealth community is called Glenna's Garden (AOL keyword: Glenna) in memory of an active and beloved community leader (Figure 8.20). This area features a story about Glenna, along with a place for others who have lost a loved one to cancer to tell their stories. Whatever type of memorial you create, it's always a good idea to include a place where members can publically express their feelings and share their stories about loved ones that they've lost.

FIGURE 8.19 A
MEMORIAL FOR SIR DEATH
This memorial for Sir Death includes an inscription written by his guildmates, treasure chests for visitors to leave offerings, and an immortal dolphin named in his honor that swims near the grave site.

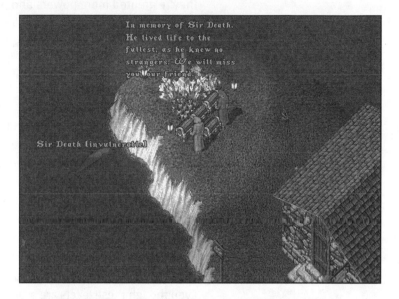

FIGURE 8.20
GLENNA'S GARDEN
After the death of a beloved community leader, Better Health renamed its cancer center Glenna's Garden in her honor. In Glenna's Grove, members can read stories about Glenna and tell their own stories about dealing with cancer. This area has recently been redesigned.

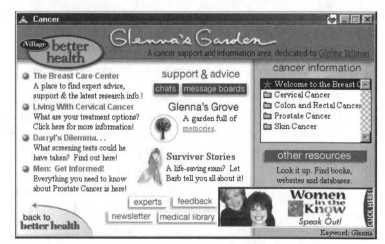

Acknowledge Achievements

Video and computer games have long used the lure of "the next level" to keep people motivated and involved. When players reach a new level, their experience changes in a tangible way; they're granted more powers and presented with more difficult challenges. As long as there are new skills to learn, powers to attain, and challenges to pursue, the players keep playing.

You can create a similar effect in your Web community by tracking and rewarding the accomplishments of your members and looking for opportunities to introduce levels into your reward system. The most appropriate achievement milestones to celebrate will (as usual) depend on the purpose and values of your community. For example, Ultima Online players gain increased powers as they develop their skills; and although these skills are based on an underlying continuous scale, they're divided into levels, which keeps the players motivated and gives them useful information about each other. Similarly, eBay's feedback system is basically a continuous scale that's divided up into levels of achievement, which are indicated by colored stars (as described in Chapter 3). Even though these levels are arbitrary points along a continuum, eBay members take great pride in achieving a new level. (You could further ritualize these milestone events by sending a congratulatory email or posting a daily or weekly list of the players who've achieved new ranking levels.)

Although achieving a new level can be its own reward, the key motivator is that the member gains something tangible by moving up. In a game, players often gain powers and access to new areas; in a trading community, members gain respect and success, although the gains are not as explicit. To translate these ideas to your community, think about how to reward members for achieving something that's valued within the community. For example, the Motley Fool rewards members who post frequently with star icons next to their names (Figure 8.21). This system would be even more effective if these levels of achievement also earned the members some tangible rewards, such as access to special features or a private message board, or even the opportunity to play a greater role on the site.

FIGURE 8.21
ACHIEVEMENT LEVELS AT THE MOTLEY FOOL
Members who post over 50 messages to the Fool boards get a star icon next to their names; by posting more messages, they can earn higher-ranking stars (lower image). TinkerShaw (upper image) has earned his three stars by posting over 500 messages.

MEMBER'S RATING

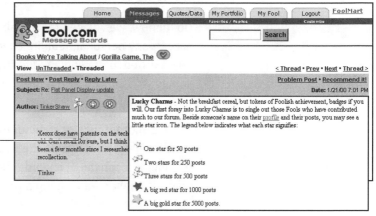

Becoming a Leader

As we saw in Chapter 5, becoming a leader can involve an extended initiation ritual that includes screening, training, and graduation (see Figure 5.11). During this ritual, unsuitable leaders are weeded out and the recruits who successfully complete the ritual are welcomed into the ranks and given a uniform. They're also given special powers and responsibilities and granted access to private, leaders-only areas.

Like all rites of passage, the purpose of this ritual is both personal and social; the process teaches would-be leaders how to play an unfamiliar role, while the graduation introduces new leaders into the leadership brotherhood. It's a bit like joining an exclusive club—and that clubby, behind-the-scenes feeling is part of why many people become community leaders in the first place. It's generally a good idea to encourage this sense of belonging among your leaders, because ultimately, what keeps people involved in your leadership program is their bonds with other leaders. You can start developing these relationships during your leadership ritual; for example, you could pair up trainees with mentors (as many programs do), or create special gathering places and events where recruits can get to know each other.

Welcome to the Group

Up 'til now, we've been talking about community rituals that accompany personal, real-life changes like acquiring a skill, getting married, or having a baby. These rituals transform how someone is viewed within the community and are thus structured around individual people.

There's another type of community ritual—one where someone joins a select group within the community. In the neighborhood, this might mean being invited to join a book club; in the workplace, it might mean joining a product team. Community leaders are one type of subgroup—and as we've seen, an initiation ritual can help leaders feel like they belong to the group.

If you're building a growth-oriented community, then fostering these internal subgroups is an important part of your job, because such groups allow community members to maintain a sense of intimacy within the larger social framework. And you'll discover that it's within these groups that people develop their strongest relationships.

Joining a Subgroup

A growing community will often host subgroups that are created and populated by members—such as GeoCities neighborhoods, WELL conferences, Ultima Online guilds. As with the leadership ritual, community subgroups can benefit from an initiation ritual that welcomes new members, and introduces them into the social hierarchy. In the next chapter, we'll take a closer look at subgroups, and at the rituals that bring these groups together and keep them going.

CHAPTER NINE

SUBGROUPS:
Clans, Clubs and Committees

One sure sign of a healthy, thriving community is the emergence of small, close-knit groups of members who make their home within the community setting. These groups attract members who share a common interest or purpose and allow them to maintain a feeling of intimacy as the community expands.

If your goal is to build a robust, large-scale community, then fostering member-run subgroups should be an integral part of your community strategy. Whether they're set up by the community staff or created by the members themselves, these small groups are where people will form their deepest relationships and strongest loyalties. That's why it's crucial to understand how these groups evolve and make sure that you cultivate a fertile environment within which they can take root and grow.

In this Chapter

Why Subgroups?

If a community is a place "where everyone knows your name," a place where members feel a sense of belonging, connection and camaraderie, then a community builder, it's your job to create an environment that fosters these feelings—a place where newcomers feel welcomed and old-timers feel comfortable and appreciated. In previous chapters, we've explored a variety of features and programs aimed at attracting new members and holding onto the members you've got.

What happens if your community takes off and becomes wildly popular and successful? How can you continue to deliver that small-town intimacy and sense of belonging when your community is growing fast and constantly changing? How do you maintain a trusting and friendly atmosphere when you're dealing with a perpetual influx of newcomers? And within a dynamic and evolving environment, how can you continue to help like-minded people find each other and develop those deeper relationships that keep them involved in your community?

Maintaining Intimacy, Managing Growth

If your goal is to build and maintain a small, focused group like a book club, support group, gaming clan, or family mailing list, these questions are moot, because such a group is usually small and stable enough to operate as a single unified community. As the leader, you'll still need to attract a "critical mass" of members, of course, and keep your group together, but when everyone knows everyone else, a sense of intimacy and belonging comes naturally.

However, if your goal is to build a large-scale, thriving, sustainable community organization, you'll need to find some way to sustain a sense of intimacy and familiarity within the larger setting. The first and most basic way to address this issue is to create meaningful subdivisions, as all large-scale communities do. Cities spawn neighborhoods, boarding schools form houses, universities include colleges and dorms, and companies create divisions and project teams.

Welcome to the Neighborhood

As we discussed in Chapter 2, a growing Web community needs subdivisions—which might be represented as towns, neighborhoods, topics, categories, conferences, or channels, depending on your metaphor. Like distinct neighborhoods within a big city, thematic subdivisions in a large Web community will bring together people who have something in common, and give them a smaller and more focused group to identify with. And just as neighbors might run into each other while walking the dog, shopping in the local stores, or playing games at the local hangout, Web "neighbors" will meet each other by hanging out in the local gathering places, attending meetings and events, or engaging in activities like playing games, trading collectibles, or building Web pages (see sidebar: Virtual Neighborhoods, Real Relationships).

Simply joining a large, general-purpose page-building community, like GeoCitites, for instance, doesn't give someone much sense of community identity—but when a lonely, isolated gay teenager creates his first Web page in the West Hollywood neighborhood (www.GeoCitites.com/WestHollywood) and receives a welcoming email from his local community leader, he's much more likely to feel that sense of belonging and camaraderie that makes the community feel "real." And when a new mom logs onto Parent Soup and searches for articles about co-sleeping, she's not really participating in the community, but if she enters the Parents of Babies area (www.parentsoup.com/community/babies.html) and posts her question on the Attachment Parenting message board, she'll connect with people who share her concerns and can offer her advice, support, and companionship. Now she'll start to feel that she's part of the scene.

Virtual Neighborhoods, Real Relationships

In the traditional sense, "community" refers to a group of people who live in proximity to each other—in the same tribe, village or town. The Internet makes it dramatically easier to meet and get to know people who may live far away, but with whom we share some special affinity; this means that our online "neighbors" can be people who share our interests, rather than our ZIP code. More and more, people are using the Web to recreate the network of relationships that once existed in a small town; they're meeting fellow hobbyists and fanatics, connecting with colleagues and clients, getting advice and support during life transitions, and staying in touch with family and friends.

Join the Club

As like-minded people come together in your community sub-divisions and gathering places, some of them will naturally begin to coalesce into more specialized groups that transcend the subdivisions you've created. This process happens in communities everywhere; neighbors form bridge clubs, churchgoers form bible study groups, parents form playgroups and PTA committees, and work colleagues create specialized mailing lists.

People form their strongest, most enduring relationships in small, focused groups.

Similarly, in a growing Web community it's natural for people with some initiative and creativity to want to form their own self-defined groups, without much involvement of the community leaders. You should welcome the emergence of these groups, because it means that you've created an environment where people feel a sense of belonging and ownership. You should also support and promote their efforts, because your members will form their strongest, most enduring relationships in small, focused groups, and these relationships are the glue that will ultimately keep people involved in your community. At GeoCitites, for example, the Heartland community leaders have formed many committees, including the Seasons committee that celebrates holidays and seasonal changes (Figure 9.1), and the FAITH committee that helps people who are grieving the loss of a loved one (**www.GeoCitites.com/Heartland/Hollow/ 6102**). A big, bustling place like GeoCitites can seem impersonal and disconnected, but self-defined groups like these can give participants the intimacy, personal attention and sense of purpose that makes them feel like they belong to something real (see sidebar: Groups are Communiuties, Too).

FIGURE 9.1
HEARTLAND HEADQUARTERS
www.geocitites.com/Heartland/7546
Heartland Headquarters (upper image), a Web site built and run by GeoCities community leaders, includes a listing of Heartland-based committees, including the Seasons committee (lower image) which celebrates major seasonal holidays.

Groups are Communities, Too

Fostering groups is much like building any community—it's basically about creating and maintaining a network of relationships. Everything you've learned in this book applies to groups, because they're communities in and of themselves. The nine key community design strategies provide a useful framework for setting up tools, features, and programs to foster subgroups. This restatement of the themes within the context of groups will get you thinking about building a group-friendly community.

○ **GROUPS ARE SUCCESSFUL WHEN THEY SERVE A CLEAR PURPOSE.** Whether they're staff-created or member-created, subgroups will thrive if they serve a clear purpose for the members. Make sure to provide ways for the group's leader to articulate and express that purpose. This serves as an invitation...

○ **GROUPS NEED GATHERING PLACES TO CONGREGATE AND COMMUNICATE.** When you're designing the tools and platform for subgroups, be sure to include one or more ways for group members to communicate with each other.Depending on your community needs, you might offer mailing lists, message boards, chat rooms, or buddy lists.

○ **GROUPS AFFILIATION SHOULD BE PART OF MEMBER PROFILES.** Groups thrive when they have "tribal markers" that show group affiliation, and are integrated into each member's ID and/or profile. Include a member roster or (searchable) group directory, so that other members of the community at large can see who the group's members are.

○ **GROUPS SHOULD ACCOMMODATE AND SUPPORT A RANGE OF ROLES.** Groups have their own membership life cycle. When someone joins a subgroup, that person becomes a newbie; the group founder is by definition an elder in the group. It's helpful to identify how long someone has been a member, along with any important roles that person plays within the group.

○ **GOUPS BENEFIT FROM STRONG LEADERSHIP.** A proactive and dedicated leader is often the catalyst that causes a group to coalesce, and makes the difference in keeping the group lively and relevant. Acknowledge those leaders and give them the tools they need to filter content and control group access.

○ **GROUPS DEVELOP THEIR OWN ETIQUETTE.** Groups sometimes need to define their own "local ordinances," which may include the membership requirements, a code of conduct, and privacy policies that are distinct from those of the community as a whole. Make sure that groups are able to create, publicize and enforce their own localized rules.

○ **GROUPS GET STRONGER WHEN THEY HOLD CYCLIC EVENTS.** Groups often enjoy holding community-building events like regular meetings, guest speakers, and competitions. You can foster this by offering your groups an events calendar, a public venue, and tools for promoting, running and transcribing their events..

○ **GROUPS ARE STRENGTHENED BY THE RITUALS OF COMMUNITY LIFE.** Like every community, groups benefit from rituals that strengthen their group identity and clarify internal roles. Be sure to provide subgroups with the mechanisms to implement rituals such as initiations, weddings, and memorial services, and also to include groups in community-wide celebrations

○ **AS THEY GROW, GROUPS MAY NEED TO FORM INTERNAL SUBGROUPS.** Something that community builders often forget is that subgroups, like every community, will need to subdivide themselves to accommodate growth. It's useful to provide mechanisms that allow subgroups to define an internal hierarchy and split into smaller, more focused groups.

Your Subgroup Program

Fostering self-defined groups is an important part of running any large-scale community, but deciding when and how to support these groups requires careful consideration. For a community aggregator like eGroups, Topica, or Yahoo Clubs that's focused on driving traffic and attracting existing groups, it makes sense to develop tools and features early on that will attract a wide variety of subgroups. But if you're building a more integrated and branded community that revolves around a shared activity like playing games, building Web pages, trading collectibles, or getting advice and support, it's often better to launch your subgroup program after you've had a chance to establish your community culture and let your members communicate their needs and desires.

Timing is Everything

"But wait," you might be thinking, "if member-created groups are so useful and important, why not implement a subgroup support program as early as possible?" While you should build some subgroup-friendly features into your basic community platform right from the start (see sidebar: Top-down vs. Bottom-up Groups), there are some good reasons to develop your official program later in your community's evolution. In the early, formative days, when your audience is small and you're in the midst of defining and articulating your purpose, you'll want your members to identify primarily with the community itself — and its key subdivisions — rather than with a particular subgroup. Once you've had a chance to establish your focus and develop a substantial following, member-created groups can then enhance your community and provide the intimacy that people felt when the community was new. Furthermore, your program will usually support your goals more effectively if you co-evolve your feature set and policies in partnership with your longtime members, rather than launching the program before you've had a chance to determine who's likely to stick around and contribute to the community.

In any community, there can be two types of member-run subgroups: top-down ones, which the staff sets up, and bottom-up ones, which your members create (as shown in Figure 0.3). At your local church or temple, for example, there may be a staff-created youth group and choir—and also some member-created study groups and charity committees. And in an online role-playing game, there might be some staff-created professional guilds (for warriors, magicians, merchants, and so on) and also some member-defined gaming guilds, like the ones discussed later in this chapter.

If you're building a focused, strongly branded community like Adobe, Nickelodeon, or BabyCenter, then you'll want to set the tone by initially creating and managing some top-down groups. When the staff controls (or at least filters) which groups get set up—as AncientSites does, for instance—it's easier to make sure they're run in a manner that's consistent with your brand identity. And because these groups are set up as part of the community infrastructure, it's more difficult for them to "migrate" to other communities the way that self-defined groups so easily can. Just understand the trade offs. Groups that are managed by the staff also have a built-in time lag—they'll never be able to address member's interests as quickly and accurately as bottom-up groups can.

By contrast, bottom-up groups have many advantages for a community aggregator like eGroups, Yahoo Clubs or Talk City. Because members set up and create their own groups, staff overhead is minimized and the groups are precisely and dynamically tailored to member interests. And although members tend to be more invested in groups they've created on their own—which makes group membership more "sticky"— this also means that members may be more loyal to the group (and the group leader) than to the community itself, which leaves you open to group migration.

Many online organizations, including Ultima Online, AncientSites, AOL, GeoCities, Third Age, and the WELL, are walking the line between being a branded community and a community aggregator. If you're buiding this "hybrid" type of organization, it makes sense to support both top-down and bottom-up subgroups, just as your local community supports both a town council and PTA committees. Ultimately, you'll need both types if you want to support a rapidly growing hybrid community organization.

This is demonstrated by the evolution of AncientSites, which launched with several cities. that were intended to attract members who shared an interest in a particular historical time and place (Figure 2.14). Early on, the community's social life revolved around these cities, which were small and intimate and provided a sense of shared context for the residents. As the community grew larger and more diverse, some of the residents began to ask for a more intimate setting where they could pursue their specialized interests. This prompted the AncientSites staff to create a program to support member-defined interest groups (Figure 9.2). This program is now one of the most popular aspects of their site, and its success is (at least partly) due to when and how the program was developed. If AncientSites had offered this program when the community was just getting started, they would not have had any real basis for deciding whose input to listen to, which features to offer, and which groups to support. Instead, they developed their features and policies in partnership with some of their most dedicated members, which allowed them to create a program that's uniquely tailored to their community.

A Mixed Blessing

Self-defined groups are undoubtedly one of the most powerful and effective ways to maintain intimacy while managing growth. But be aware that these groups can be a mixed blessing. Often their members form such strong internal bonds and tight friendships that, regardless of how carefully you manage your program, they'll become more loyal to the group and the group leader than to your community (see sidebar, "The Group that Got Away").

If a group is intent on leaving, you can't do much about it besides wish them well. What you *can* do is make your environment attractive for specific types of groups (as discussed throughout this chapter), and create "barriers to exit" that will encourage them to stick around. Here are some specific ideas that can help:

○ **BUILD GROUP IDENTITY INTO YOUR SYSTEM**

Many groups like to build and run their own Web site that expresses their identity and serves as their primary news center and gathering place (see, for example, www.sok.org/pms). These sites make it easier for the group to migrate between communities. You can combat this trend by offering rich and integrated group profiles that reflect a group's ongoing evolution and achievements.

FIGURE 9.2
AREOPAGUS, AN ANCIENTSITES GROUP
www.ancientsites.com/
groupsAreopagus

Areopagus is an AncientSites interest group devoted to respectful discussions about religion. The group's Entrance page (upper image) includes a tag line, a representative image, and links to major features, including a private chat room and message board. The Meeting Hall (middle image) includes a mission statement and a list of group leaders and members. Applicants who meet the membership criteria compose a statement that's reviewed by the group leaders, and viewable by all group members (lower image).

MEMBERS ONLINE

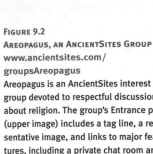
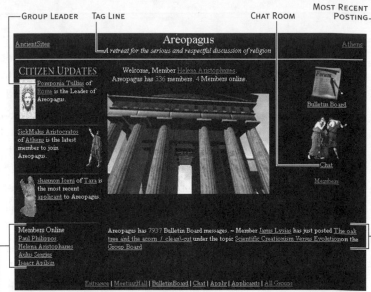

AncientSites   Athens

Areopagus
A retreat for the serious and respectful discussion of religion

CITIZEN UPDATES

Pomponia Tullius of Rome is the Leader of Areopagus.

SickMalus Aristocratos of Athens is the latest member to join Areopagus.

shannon Iceni of Tara is the most recent applicant to Areopagus.

Welcome, Member Helena Aristophanes.
Areopagus has 336 members. 4 Members online.

Forum
Bulletin Board

Chat

Members

Members Online
Paul Philippos
Helena Aristophanes
Aulus Sergius
Isaacr Apilsin

Areopagus has 7937 Bulletin Board messages. ~ Member Janus Lysias has just posted The oak tree and the acorn / clean\-cut under the topic Scientific Creationism Versus Evolution on the Group Board

Entrance | MeetingHall | BulletinBoard | Chat | Apply | Applicants | All Groups

---

The_Great_Library

LEADERSHIP ROLES

Positions
Curator   Ioudith Ramesses
Assistant Curator   Karamy Isetnofiet
Treasurer   Raseneb Amenemheb
Head Ass't   Memeith Hatshepsut
Librarian

MEMBER ROSTER

Members
Ioudith Ramesses
Karamy Isetnofiet
Memeith Hatshepsut
Hathor Ramesses
Raseneb Amenemheb
Nesnut Hatshepsut
Ashnan Etana
Senenanep Meritamen
Taunis Thutmose
Ricardez Cornelius
Shandel Nebuchadnezzar
Hapshetsut Nebet
Kallistos Alexandros

The_Great_Library Mission
To provide a comprehensive research tool for all members of AncientSites cities that includes of all the knowledge of the known world past, present and future.

MISSION STATEMENT

December, 1998   **January, 1999**   February, 1999
Current Applicants for Areopagus

CURRENT APPLICANTS

Date		Applicant	Decision
January 21		Annette Cylon of Athens Where I live people don't like other people because of their religion. I feel that listening to other beliefs will help me find my own sacred faith.	Undecided
January 21		Helena Aristophanes of Athens I'm interested in exploring the shared roots of *all* religions, and thus learning more about the essential humanity that binds us all together, in the spiritual sense. Edit	Undecided
January 21		Tecoahuaño Yupanqui of MachuPicchu I enjoy discussions dealing with religion. I'm interested in finding a balance between science and religion. I always try to cast respect before I do cynicism on religions. I feel the religious traditions of the world's past, are of more worth than being targets of modern cynicism. Thank you.	Undecided

○ **PROVIDE TOOLS, RECOGNITION AND SUPPORT FOR GROUP LEADERS**

Groups often coalesce around a strong, committed leader, and if that person decides to leave, the group will often follow. To combat this, be sure to provide group leaders with tools and features that help them run their group (as explained later in this chapter). You can also encourage good leaders to stick around by offering them recognition and rewards for their efforts and making a special effort to listen to their ideas and suggestions.

○ **CONTAIN THE HAVOC THAT BAD LEADERS CAN WREAK**

In addition to rewarding good leaders, it's equally important to have controls in place that minimize the damage a bad leader can do. If a a group is being run in a way that's inconsistent with your basic community values and policies, then you may want to relieve the leader of his or her duties or even encourage leaving the community if the problems are ongoing. At allHealth, a leader's disagreement with management was very serious—she was actively promoting a controversial "cure" to some very sick people, which directly violated the community leader agreement. The staff was glad to see her go; and many of the people who followed her ended up returning to Better Health, saying they'd missed the community.

Although subgroups involve their share of difficulties, they also offer many rewards; if your community is growing and thriving, subgroups *will* emerge, whether you actively support them or not. To get the most benefit from these groups and encourage them to stick around once they've formed, you'll want to create a fertile environment where they can take root and grow, and develop a powerful set of tools and features for supporting their activities.

The Group That Got Away

Shareese is the supreme leader of the Guardians, a tightly knit gaming guild that initially formed in the online role-playing game Meridian 59 (www.3do.com/meridian). She's a powerful and headstrong mage, with advanced healing skills and a small band of loyal followers. After several unpleasant encounters with the Meridian game masters, Shareese moved her "family" to Ultima Online, hoping to forge a better virtual life. When we last spoke, she had temporarily settled her family in Britannia, and was awaiting reports from trusted members who were playing EverQuest and Asheron's Call, so she could assess the merits of these brave new gaming worlds.

In real life, Shareese is a 34-year-old military wife and mother of three, whose husband gets transferred every few years, and whose online gaming friends are the one social constant in an itinerant life. Whenever the family moves, the first order of business is to make sure that the Internet account is up and working. "Even though I'm in a new city and may not know a soul," she says, "I know that when I log on, my gaming family will be there, waiting for me to lead them on a new adventure."

Shareese and the Guardians are an example of groups that I call "the wandering tribes of cyberspace." Such groups have their own identity that's apart from any one community or game, and they'll readily migrate to an environment that's more hospitable for the group. This phenomenon is particularly common among gaming clans and guilds, who migrate between games, and even play different games simultaneously.

Setting the Stage

As a way to foster member-run groups that will strengthen your community and support your purpose, encourage your members to put down some roots and participate in community activities before they create their own groups. As your members participate in these activities, they'll find people who share their interests, and naturally start to coalesce into smaller and more intimate groups.

Meeting Virtual Neighbors

One simple way for members to meet their virtual neighbors is to browse through the public profiles or home pages of people who share their interests. You can promote these connections by making it easy for your members to include communication features like email, guestbooks, and message boards on their profiles or pages, and by encouraging them to publicly announce their interests and affiliations (as discussed in Chapter 3).

One way to accomplish this is to have your members select the community subdivisions that appeal to them—the places where they like to hang out (which is the virtual equivalent of showing where your members "live").You can then use this information to categorize their pages or profiles. It takes a while for newcomers to get a sense of the community, so you may want to solicit this information after the member has moved beyond the novice phase (see sidebar: Putting Down Roots).

Some Web communities, like CoolConnect, take a more proactive approach and use collaborative filtering techniques to introduce members who share the same tastes. While this is one way for people with common interests to meet, it's unlikely that they'll forge a lasting relationship unless they share some other ongoing, mutually beneficial activity—just as you tend to become closer to your neighbors when you share childcare or dogwalking duties, attend the same church, or hang out at the same local gathering place.

Putting Down Roots

Communities that focus on page-building, including GeoCitites, Tripod and AncientSites, often ask each new member to select a place to "live" right up-front (Figure 9.3). This is a good way to get information about someone's interests, and categorize the pages that they produce, but it creates a barrier to entry for newcomers who don't quite know how to categorize their pages, and aren't ready to announce their affiliation to the world.

This can be a useful approach if you want to keep your community highly focused or increase your builder-to-lurker ratio. But if you want to attract a wide range of people, and make it easy to become a member, you'll want to let people choose their "home base" after they've participated in the community for awhile.

The Local Hangout

As we've seen, one of the most basic (yet effective) ways for like-minded people to connect is by visiting a public gathering place, and jumping into an ongoing conversation (see sidebar: The Great Good Place). In a purely conversational community like the WELL, the subdivisions *are* the gathering places, so expanding the taxonomy essentially means adding new "local hangouts." But if your neighborhoods are focused around content or commerce, you'll need to make sure to create new "great good places" as you add new subdivisions. For example, in the early days of eBay, a single general-purpose chat board functioned as a community-wide "great good place." As the auction site grew, the staff created new topical gathering places for each major collecting category, which helped each area develop its own distinct culture and personality, and provided a hangout where members with common interests could meet and get to know one another.

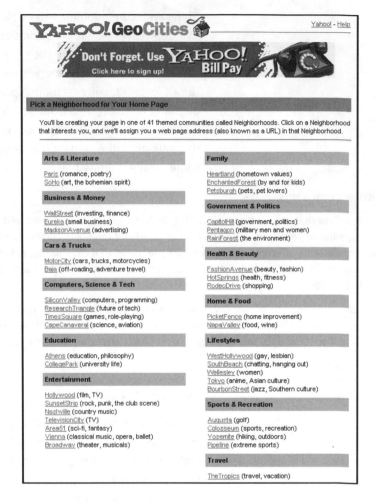

An avid Ultima Online player named Kazola earned enough in-game money to purchase a large house, which she and her friends developed into a thriving and successful tavern (see Figure 9.4). When Kozola's tavern was repeatedly ransacked by marauding hoodlums, the UO game masters came to her aid; they created special "immovable" furniture that couldn't be stolen or destroyed, and gave Kozola unique decorations to embellish the walls of her establishment. Since that time, player-run taverns have become a vital and important part of the UO social scene, and the support staff has created an official program to support and promote the most popular and well-run taverns.

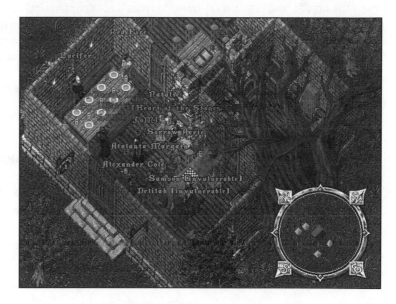

FIGURE 9.4

SOCIALIZING AT KAZOLA'S TAVERN
Kazola's Tavern is one of the oldest and most popular player-run taverns in Ultima Online. People come to Kazola's to eat and drink, play games, brag about their exploits, and shoot the breeze—much as they might gather in any neighborhood bar.

Scheduled Events

In any neighborhood, there will be people who enjoy dropping by the local hangout whenever the mood suits them, but others may prefer to get their community "fix" by attending regularly scheduled events or meetings (see Chapter 7). These gatherings are one of the most powerful ways to bring people together and deepen relationships, so if you want to stimulate subgroups, it's a good idea to start by hosting some of these events yourself, and then offer qualified groups the opportunity to plan, promote and run their own gatherings. For example, a group of members who met during weekly Better Health infertility chats decided to form their own support group called HOPE (www.hope-infertility.com)— this group now runs daily support chats on the allHealth site and also arranges occasional interviews with guest speakers. The allHealth staff supports these events by listing them in the schedule, promoting them on the home page, and giving them access to the allHealth meeting rooms (see Figure 7.8).

In his seminal book *The Great Good Place,* Ray Oldenberg illuminates the community-building power of a "third place," which he defines as a local, public establishment that's neither home (the "first place") nor work (the "second place"), but a friendly and neutral location where people gather together to relax, shoot the breeze, and take a break from everyday life. In our physical neighborhoods, a "great good place" might be a tavern, coffeeshop, barbershop, beauty salon, or even the local mall. In your Web community, any public gathering place, a mailing list, message board, chat room, or virtual world tavern (Figure 9.4), could function as "great good place;" all that's required is that the location is easy to find, and the purpose of the place is made clear to the participants. And as Oldenberg points out, it's always helpful to have a friendly and welcoming host for such a place, because their personality and dedication will draw people in, and keep them coming back.

Provide Leadership Opportunities

In any thriving community, there will be people who want to go further and contribute their time and energy toward improving the community. You should encourage these people by offering them leadership opportunities—they're the ones who'll have the time and energy to bring a group together in the first place, and the dedication to keep it together over time. By giving your most enthusiastic members an official role to play, you'll help them develop their leadership abilities and become more deeply involved in your community.

Hosting a Gathering Place

Community members often want to host a public gathering place like a topical message board, a virtual tavern, or an online store. As we discussed in Chapters 4 and 5, good hosts can help make your public hangouts lively and welcoming places. And developing a hosting program is a great way for enthusiastic members to gain status and recognition, and become more involved in running the community.

A well-run hosting program can also help you cultivate a subgroup-friendly environment by identifying and promoting natural leaders, and giving them the tools and recognition to develop their skills and attract a following. Most public WELL conferences, for example, are hosted by member volunteers who were active community participants before becoming hosts. Recruits are given special leadership training, along with access to a hosts-only "backstage" conference where they can share stories and compare notes with other hosts, and thus learn how to better perform their roles. By hosting a public conference (especially a popular one), these people experience what it's like to be a leader—many WELL hosts have gone on to form new conferences, both public and private.

Organizing a Committee

For some people, hosting a gathering place is a satisfying role, but others may want to flex their leadership muscles in different ways. You'll often see energetic and proactive volunteers contributing to their community by organizing a committee, perhaps to coordinate a bake sale, clean up the local park, or raise money for a charity drive. You can tap into this volunteer spirit by promoting the efforts of members who organize community-friendly committees. In the GeoCitites Heartland neighborhood, for example, members have formed committees to support a variety of topics (see Figure 9.1 for all the Heartland committees). The GeoCitites community staff promoted their efforts by highlighting these committees on the main Heartland page (although sadly, they're no longer doing this). Similarly, the AncientSites staff promotes self-defined member committees by highlighting their efforts prominently on the main city pages (Figure 9.5). By showcasing constructive groups like these in your own community you'll help the organizers recruit new members and also provide a model for other members to follow. For example, there are now member-run welcoming committees in most of the AncientSites cities, a development that was stimulated by having the first welcoming committee highlighted on the Egypt city page.

Running a Business

In any community, the most powerful type of involvement is ultimately financial. In a small town, the local businesses fuel the community's economy, and also provide the "great good places" that stimulate a community's social life (and remember, every tavern, barber shop or book store needs to be a sustainable business in order to stay open).

FIGURE 9.5
WELCOME TO EGYPT
www.ancientsites.com/xi/places/
home/index.rage?loc=Egypt

The Egypt welcoming committee (lower image) was created by AncientSites members who wanted to help newcomers enjoy their virtual city. In addition to providing Web space, AncientSites supported this self-defined group by promoting them on the Egypt home page (upper image)

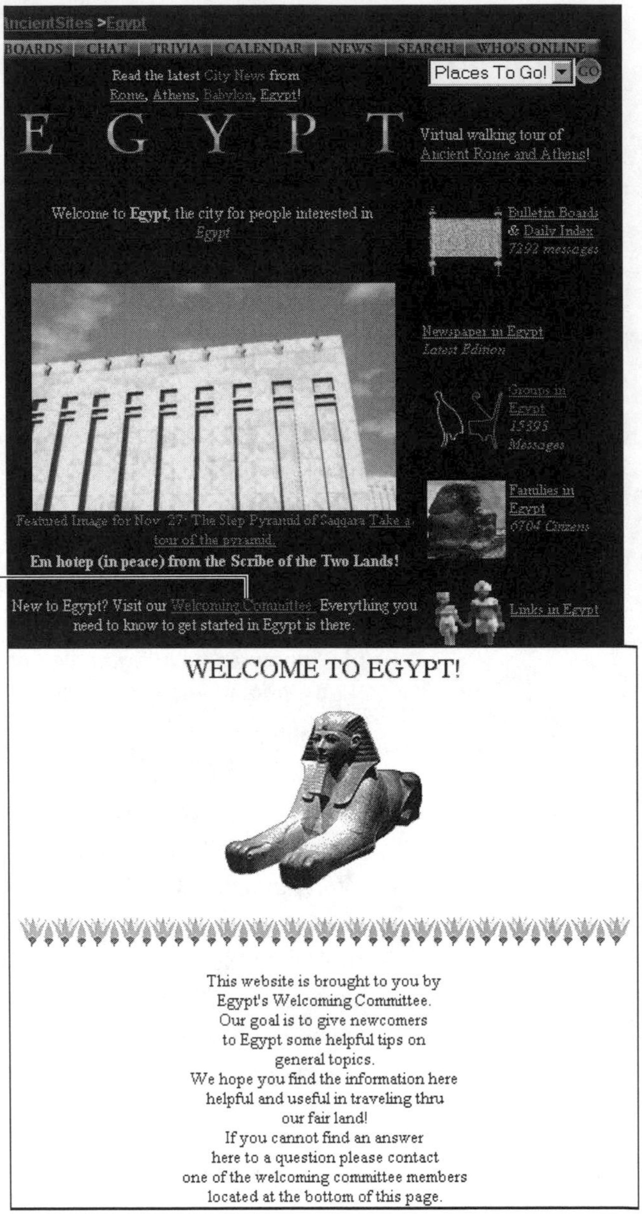

LINK TO THE WELCOMING COMMITTEE

That's why, if you're building a large, for-profit community, it's a good idea to help your members run some type of business within (or around) your community, using techniques like affiliate programs, classified ads, auctions, or even full-fledged online stores (see Chapter 4). If your members can earn some or all of their livelihood within your community, they'll be able to devote more time and energy to their efforts, and they'll be that much more likely to stick around. For example, many eBay merchants used to run brick-and-mortar stores, but have now moved their businesses online. They still get to know their customers, but now it's through email, message boards and chat, rather than in face-to-face encounters. eBay doesn't extend much in the way of tools and policies to foster these groups (a real missed opportunity), yet simply by offering an efficient global marketplace where buyers and merchants come together and get to know each other, eBay provides a fertile environment that spawns many meaningful and sustainable groups.

Cultivate Emerging Subgroups

As you can see, if you bring like-minded people together and get them talking and interacting with each other, they'll naturally begin to form self-defined groups with their own purposes and agendas; the member-created committees , support groups and small business networks described above are examples of this dynamic. When you see this happening in your community, it means that your culture is maturing and your members are starting to put down roots. At this point, your job is to cultivate these emerging groups by listening carefully to their needs and desires, and deciding the extent to which (and with what criteria) you'll support them and integrate their activities and achievements into your environment. At first, you'll be supporting groups individually, but the idea is to use your interaction with them as the springboard for launching your official program.

Every Group Needs a Clubhouse

One of the most basic ways to acknowledge and empower a self-defined group is to give it its own public gathering place to run—this can become an integral part of how you extend your taxonomy. For example, some years back a group of regulars on the Women.com Relationships board started calling themselves the Exotic Hags, and lobbied the community manager for a place to call their own. She responded by creating a new Relationships board called the Exotic Hags Treehouse, and listing it as a public discussion on the site. (Figure 9.6). The Hags were delighted to see their group acknowledged, and they settled in and made the board their home

FIGURE 9.6
THE EXOTIC HAGS TREEHOUSE
messages.women.com
The staff at Women.com first created the Exotic Hags Treehouse to give a group of regulars a message board to call their own. This board now hosts one of the most popular gathering places on the entire site.

EXOTIC HAGS IN THE TOP FIVE

Like the HOPE support group mentioned above, the Hags were formed by members who met in an existing discussion area and realized that they shared a more specialized interest. This dynamic of spinning off specialized subgroups from a more general-purpose gathering place is one of the ways communities evolve, and it offers you an easy and organic way to add gathering places to your community. For example, the broadly defined "Grateful Dead" conference has spawned a number of related conferences that were started by people who hooked up in the main conference and decided to host a more focused discussion elsewhere (Figure 9.7).

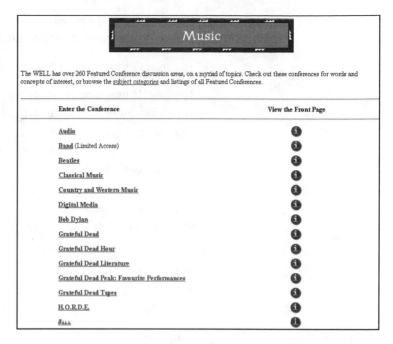

FIGURE 9.7
RECOMBINANT SUBGROUPS AT THE WELL
www.well.com/conf/music.html
People who hang out in a general-interest conference like Grateful Dead will often launch more specialized groups as the community grows, like Grateful Dead Hour, Grateful Dead Literature, Grateful Dead Tapes, and so on.

Member Freedom vs. Quality Control

Assuming you want to maintain certain standards in your gathering places, this situation raises the familiar dilemma of member freedom vs. quality control. At what point do you offer a self-defined group their own gathering place? And once it's created, how can you ensure that they'll run the place in a manner that's consistent with your community standards?

The WELL has been grappling with this dilemma for years, and over time has evolved a multi-tiered program that strikes a nice balance between clean, well-lit public gathering places and smaller, self-defined private (or semi-private) areas. *Featured* conferences are created and overseen (and sometimes hosted) by the community staff, who are ultimately responsible for content. *Independent* conferences are created by individual members who set the door policy and can run these gathering places in any way they choose. And finally, *Private* conferences are unlisted, invitation-only places that either members or staff can create and run. Any full-fledged WELL member can have an Independent or Private conference, to which the WELL staff takes a hands-off approach; they instead spend their time promoting and managing the Featured conferences.

The Option to Become Official

The WELL's program demonstrates one way that a community can empower emerging subgroups while still maintaining some level of quality control. This multilevel structure also provides a natural growth path; if a self-defined conference is popular and well-run, the WELL staff has the option to invite them to become a Featured conference. Some of the most popular Featured conferences have evolved this way, and conversely, some high-traffic conferences have been invited to become Featured, but prefer to remain independent.

The lesson here is that while it's great to encourage and promote self-defined subgroups, it's equally important to create an environment where becoming "official" is an option, not a requirement.

The Pros and Cons of Private Gathering Places

Probably the simplest way to deal with the tension between member freedom and quality control is to directly manage the people who run your public gathering places (whether they're staff, volunteers or contractors), and offer members their own private gathering places that they can run however they want. While this approach may meet the needs of some individual members, it doesn't encourage self-defined groups to contribute to the community at large, or help them recruit new members. Furthermore, this approach can actually harm your community by pulling people away from the public areas. On the WELL, for example, private conferences have been a godsend for some old-timers, because they offer a place to convene without the distractions of the public sphere. But many members feel that these private spaces have drained much of the life and vitality from the public areas of the site. Private gatherings can be a good place for subgroups to get started, but if you want your public areas to remain vibrant and interesting, try to provide incentives that encourage these groups to maintain some public presence as well.

Developing Your Official Program

It's great to foster self-defined groups on an individual basis, but if your goal is to develop a large-scale Web community, your job will be easier (and your community more manageable) if you develop an official program to recognize and support member-created groups. Cultivating emerging subgroups will have given you some valuable knowledge about the needs and desires of some of your most devoted and motivated members—you also may have run into groups whose activities you'd rather not encourage. Now it's time to put this knowledge into action, and create a program that will truly support and enhance your community.

Leverage Your Existing Platform

As we discussed above, every group needs a gathering place like a mailing list, message board or chat room to call their own. The easiest and most straightforward way to kick-start your official program is to leverage your existing platform by giving some unofficial groups their own gathering places, and then using their feedback to help you refine your program. For example, AncientSites launched its Groups program by cobbling together a private clubhouse using their existing chat and message board technology (see Figure 9.2), and inviting a group of old-timers called "The Rostra" to test it out (this was actually an effort to appease these disgruntled old-timers, who were threatening to leave because so many newcomers were intruding on "their" community). The Rostra loved their clubhouse, and soon another group asked for their own gathering place, and thus the official Groups program was born.

Similarly, the Yahoo Clubs program was originally created in response to requests from members who'd connected with each other in Yahoo's chat rooms and message boards and wanted a place to call their own. The staff created a program to give members their own personalized clubhouse that integrated existing Yahoo tools and features like chat, message boards, member profiles and personalized Start pages (Figure 9.8). This program was a huge success, and Yahoo has continued to develop their Clubs platform by adding new features like photo galleries and voice chat.

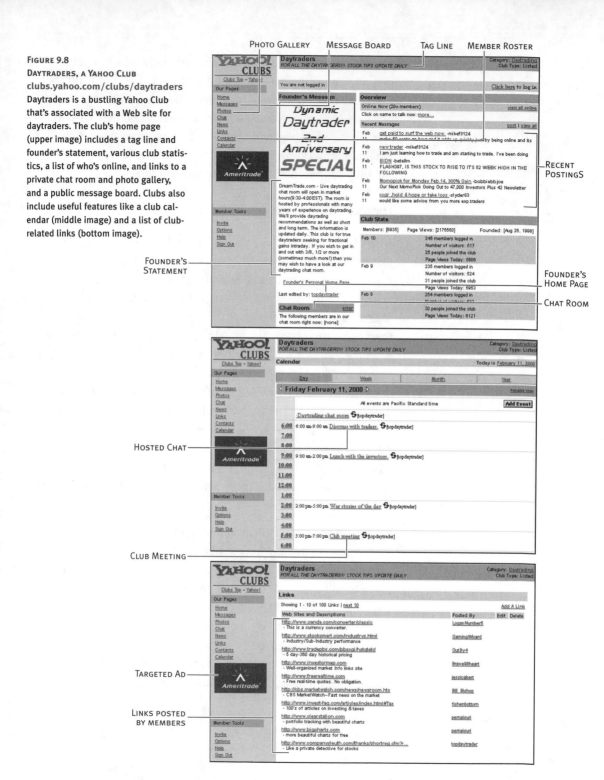

FIGURE 9.8

DAYTRADERS, A YAHOO CLUB

clubs.yahoo.com/clubs/daytraders

Daytraders is a bustling Yahoo Club that's associated with a Web site for daytraders. The club's home page (upper image) includes a tag line and founder's statement, various club statistics, a list of who's online, and links to a private chat room and photo gallery, and a public message board. Clubs also include useful features like a club calendar (middle image) and a list of club-related links (bottom image).

If your platform doesn't include gathering places, this approach may not work for you; you might want to license tools from a clubs provider like MyEvents (www.myevents.com) or PeopleLink (www.peoplelink.com)—this field is changing rapidly, see companion Web site for an current list of providers. If you do have some basic technology, don't be afraid to start with something simple; you can always add more features later on. For example, the Motley Fool leverages its in-house message board technology by offering investment clubs their own meeting place on the Motley Fool site (www.fool.com/InvestmentClub). While not as full-featured as some, this program makes good use of the Fool's existing technology and it's been very popular with the members.

You Are What You Do

Another way to leverage your current technology is to integrate each members' group affiliations into their online persona. For example, if your community platform includes member profiles (see Chapter 3) you could automatically list each person's group membership in their profile, as AncientSites does (Figure 9.9). This approach works well if members can join multiple groups, because the list can provide useful context about that person's interests and affiliations. It also reflects how deeply a member is participating in the site. (This feature would be even more useful if each member's profile included some indication of group participation, such as icons to show leadership, longevity or posting frequency; this is more complex, however, so think of it as a way to enhance your profiles later).

Yahoo also offers members the option to display the clubs they've joined in their profile (Figure 9.10). Should this feature be automatic or optional? That depends on what type of community you're running and what types of groups your members will be joining. AncientSites keeps fairly tight controls over its groups, which are all related to the site's theme (see below); Yahoo clubs can be built around any topic imaginable, so it makes sense that some members would want to hide their participation from prying eyes.

FIGURE 9.9

GROUPS IN AN ANCIENTSITES PROFILE
This is the profile of Zig ApilSin, the
"king" of Babylon. Notice the list of
groups that Zig belongs to; also the
best homes award he's won for developing his personal profile.

BEST HOMES WEB RING — BEST HOMES AWARD

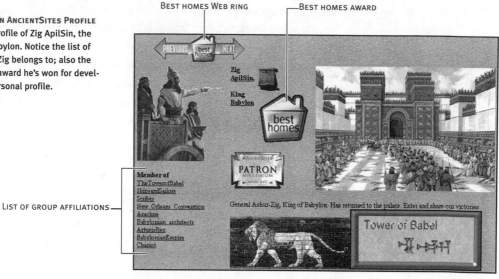

LIST OF GROUP AFFILIATIONS

FIGURE 9.10

CLUBS IN A YAHOO PROFILE
Yahoo profiles offer members the option
to display their clubs publically, as I've
done here for my clubs (links, picture,
bio, and favorite quote are optional).
Whenever I join or leave a club, my profile will be updated automatically.

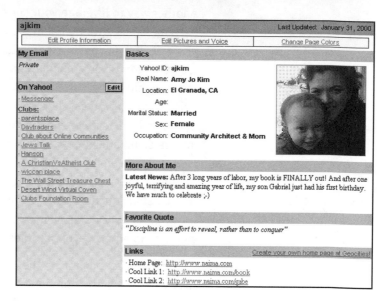

Are You One of Us?

In some communities, members can only join one group at a
time, and in these situations, group affiliation can (and should)
become a more prominent part of their identity. In EverQuest,
for example, each character can only belong to a single guild,
and that guild's name is appended to the character's name

(Figure 9.11). Similarly, when players join a guild in Ultima Online, they have the option to append their guild abbreviation (a shortened version of the guild name) to their character's name. UO also provides customizable clothing that can be "dyed" in various colors (see Chapter 3), so guild members can dress in matching outfits to show their solidarity and deepen their sense of camaraderie and group identity.

FIGURE 9.11

THE EVERQUEST WELL GUILD
Unlike Yahoo and AncientSites, an Ever-Quest player can only belong to one guild at a time. When someone joins a guild in EverQuest, that guild's name is automatically appended to their character's name— as shown here in a gathering of players from the WELL guild.

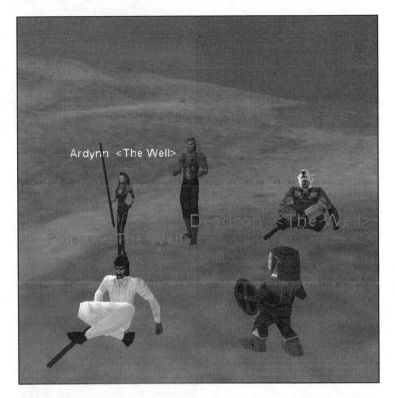

Group members enjoy announcing their group affiliation to the world, and if the system doesn't support this, they'll find alternative ways to make their allegiance known. Players who belong to a gaming clan will often integrate their clan abbreviation into their member name when they register on a site like Mplayer or the Zone (in fact, it was observing this behavior that caused the UO design team to integrate clan names into each character's identity). You can anticipate this dynamic in your own community by creating member profiles that can incorporate group affiliation right from the start, and also by providing "tribal markers" (such as icons, clothing or even reserved prefixes) that allow group members to express their primary affiliation in an immediate visual way.

Foster Group-Wide Communications

Gathering places are one way for groups to communicate, but you should also consider incorporating any other available communication-enhancing tools into your groups platform. Both Yahoo and AncientSites, for example, use existing technology to display a list of club members who are currently logged into the site (see Figures 9.2 and 9.8). This great feature functions like a group-oriented buddy list that makes it easy for someone to send an instant message to any other group member who's logged on, adding a sense of presence and dynamism to the group's clubhouse .

If you want to strengthen group identity, it's even more powerful to be able to "talk" to the entire group. EverQuest offers a custom-built feature called "group say" that gives each guild a private, real-time communications channel. This allows guild members to broadcast a message to all their guildmates who are currently online, no matter where they are in the virtual world. (If your platform doesn't currently support this functionality, talk to a third-party provider about adding this powerful feature to their upgrade list.)

Provide Tools for Group Leaders

As you're considering how to best leverage your existing platform, remember that the quality and focus of each individual group will largely be determined by the personality and dedication of the leader (or leaders). Consequently, you'll want to provide administrative tools and features that can help group leaders do their job effectively. For example, Yahoo Clubs includes a broadcast mailing list that makes it easy for founders to send reminders and updates to all the members. Yahoo also leverages their existing "My Yahoo" personalization technology to give founders the ability to create a shared Start page that everyone in the club can view (Figure 9.12). Founders can also create and display a mission statement, configure a shared calendar, and remove any links, photos or message board content that they feel is inappropriate or off-topic (see help.yahoo.com/help/clubs/cfound for details about tools for club founders). In short, founders are given access to many of the same administration and moderation tools that the Yahoo support staff use to maintain the community, which makes sense, since a club or group is essentially a microcosm of the community as a whole.

FIGURE 9.12

YAHOO CLUBS' NEWS PAGE
Every Yahoo Club can customize a group-wide news page that offers members some shared context. For people like daytraders, who thrive on timely information, this page helps members stay up to date on breaking news and market trends, and provides a common ground for the group.

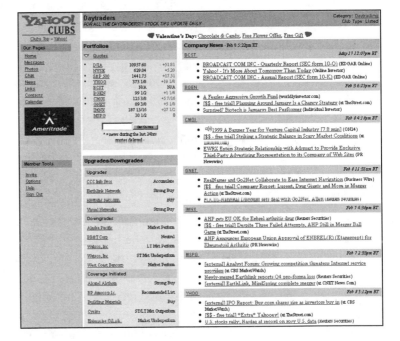

Create Group Management Policies

As we've seen, you can launch your program by creating a simple clubhouse that's based on your current technology, then adding more features over time as you continue to develop your site. But packaging your technology is only part of the program; you'll also need to decide what types of groups you want to cultivate, which ones you'll discourage, and what criteria you'll use for making these decisions.

Any community that supports member-created groups will need to develop policies that address these issues. My parents' synagogue, for example, has a program called "Havurah" that provides support for small, member-run study groups, social clubs and charity committees. But what would happen if a member wanted to use the synagogue's resources to create a for-profit investment club, or a multi-level marketing scam? If the program is to run smoothly, someone needs to articulate what types of groups the program is intended to support, and ensure that existing groups are run in a manner that's consistent with the organization's goals and values.

Manicured Garden or Wild Swamp?

You should develop group management policies that reflect your values and reinforce your brand. There's no single correct way to construct these policies; it depends on your purpose, goals and audience. For example, the programs at AncientSites and Yahoo offer similar collections of tools and features, but have very different policies for creating and managing groups.

Yahoo is a big, general-purpose portal with over 35 million registered members; their policies are designed to maximize traffic and lower the barriers to entry. To create a club, you fill out a form, accept the terms of use, click on a few buttons, and your club appears instantly (see **help.yahoo.com/help/us/clubs/cfound/cfound-09.html**). Joining a club is even easier—you visit a club you like, click on "Join," answer a few questions, and Voila, you're a member (see **help.yahoo.com/help/us/clubs/clubs-04.html**). As a result, group proliferation at Yahoo is "cheap, fast, and out-of-control." Scores of clubs are added daily, many of which have the same stated purpose, which means they're competing for the same audience. While some clubs host vibrant conversations in their gathering places, many others are unfocused and littered with spam, and some lie dormant and unused for weeks, even months. (At the time of writing, Yahoo has just begun to prune dormant subgroups.)

Contrast this with AncientSites, an integrated and focused community with about 80,000 registered members, mostly history buffs. AncientSites attracts a focused demographic, and actively promotes high-quality interactions, and their group policies support these goals. To create a new group, at least five members must band together and decide on the leadership roles that they'll play within the group (see **www.ancientsites.com/xi/group/builder**). The leader then submits an application, which is reviewed by the AncientSites staff for quality and thematic appropriateness; if their stated purpose is similar to another existing group, the staff will encourage them to join that group, rather than form a new one. When a group lies dormant, the AncientSites staff will contact the leaders to find out why, and may even remove or hide that group. Compared to Yahoo, group creation at AncientSites is as orderly and measured as a manicured garden; there are far fewer groups, but the ones that exist are generally lively, civil and focused.

As you're drafting your group policies, think about who your members are and what you're trying to accomplish. If you're running a general-purpose community site where the goal is to encourage a wide variety of different groups to use your platform, it makes sense to set the bar low and make it easy for people to create and join groups. But if you're running a more focused community, you'll want to create policies to support groups who reinforce your purpose and goals, and filter out those that don't. Your policies will evolve over time, as does every aspect of running a community, but it's worthwhile to think these issues through before creating your program so that you can set appropriate expectations right from the start.

Your Group Directory

In addition to drafting your group management policies, you'll also want to create a directory that lists the groups in your community. If self-organized groups already exist within (or around) your community, you could even launch your official subgroup program simply by creating a directory to promote these existing groups. For example, computer game players like to organize themselves into groups called clans, guilds or teams, so gaming sites like Mplayer, Heat and the Zone have created directories that allow these groups to announce their existence and recruit new members. A trading community like eBay could jump-start their official groups program by creating a directory for pre-existing collecting clubs, and a graphics-oriented community like Adobe could create a directory to promote pre-existing user groups. Although such a directory doesn't provide all the advantages of a full-blown subgroup support program, it's relatively simple to implement and can be a great way to get started when time and resources are limited.

Whether you offer a fully developed platform for group activities, or simply provide links to existing groups, you'll generally want to organize your group directory in a way that's consistent with your existing taxonomy. For example, the Yahoo Clubs directory is organized much like the well-established Yahoo hierarchy of categories (see Figure 2.16), while the AncientSites group directory is organized by cities (see Figure 2.14). The Heat clan directory is organized by game (Figure 9.13), which reflects the basic subdivisions within the site.

FIGURE 9.13
HEAT'S CLAN DIRECTORY
Heat profiles a list of clan and guild profiles, organized by game. This collection helps the Heat staff identify the "hotspots" of team activity, and develop competitive events to galvanize those players.

Highlighting Groups

If your program become popular, with lots of groups registering on your site, you'll find that browsing through your group directory will quickly become unwieldy. One way to keep this activity manageable is to develop automated methods for highlighting and promoting particular groups in each category. For example, Yahoo automatically highlights clubs with the most members (Figure 9.14), while Ultima Online highlights guilds that include the greatest number of *veteran members* (that is, experienced and skillful players) and that have the most enemies (Figure 9.15). Each approach reflects what the community staff considers valuable (and has the technology to track); Yahoo is focused purely on numbers, while Ultima Online factors in skill, longevity and inter-group rivalries, all of which are valued within the game.

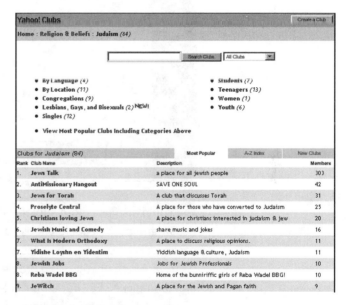

Bear in mind that your highlighting techniques can actually influence how groups develop; for example, when big groups are rewarded with attention and promotion, they'll attract more members and grow even bigger. It's fine to highlight large groups if that's what makes your community stronger, but be sure to think about highlighting behaviors that add value to your community. For example, you might choose to highlight your most recently active groups, or groups with the most activity on a given day, or groups that recently held well-attended events.

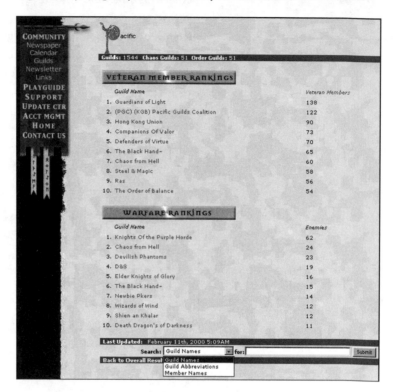

FIGURE 9.15
HIGHLIGHTING GUILDS IN ULTIMA ONLINE
town.uo.com/guilds/shard_2.html
Here we see the Guild directory on the Pacific shard (which is a self-contained Ultima Online game world). Guilds with the most veteran members and the most enemies are automatically highlighted, but the user can also search for a particular guild by guild name or by player.

You could also use more subjective measures to showcase particular groups. You could choose a particular group to highlight each week, as Lycos Clubs does (clubs.lycos.com/live/Directory/Welcome.asp), or you could profile several clubs each week that are hand-picked by your editorial team, like Yahoo Clubs (clubs.yahoo.com/clubhouse). Whatever methods you use, remember that these selections will be viewed as expressing what's valued in your community, so try to highlight groups that represent what your community is all about, (or at least what you'd like it to be about).

Searching the Group Directory

When a group directory is large, it's important to allow users to search for specific groups by typing in keywords. Many group directories provide a global search box, but whenever possible, try to provide more specific ways to narrow down the search. For example, if your directory has a hierarchical structure, it's a good idea to let users limit their search to a particular subsection as Yahoo does (see, for example, clubs.yahoo.com/games). It's also useful to let people specify the type of information they want to search for. For example, Topica allows users to search through either topic descriptions or message archives when looking for a particular mailing list (www.topica.com/search), and Ultima Online allows users to search on either guild names or member names when looking for a particular guild (see Figure 9.15).

Keep Your Listings Current

In addition to developing policies for creating and highlighting groups, you'll also want to develop some policies to keep your group listings up to date. This is especially important when you're setting the bar low, because without reasonable "pruning" policies, you'll end up with a group directory that's littered with dormant clubs and broken links. You can avoid this by figuring out what criteria you'll use to hide or remove dormant clubs and what mechanisms you'll use to implement these policies. For example, if there hasn't been any activity for several months, you may send an email to the group leader to find out what their plans are for the group; if there's no reply, that's a good sign that you should consider removing the club from the public directory and placing it in an "archive" area, or perhaps delete it altogether. Be sure to document your pruning policies on the site, tell people why you're removing the group, and give club leaders and members ample warning before you take any permanent action.

Many group directories include links to outside Web pages, which complicates matters further. Some community sites deal with this by listing a disclaimer next to any outside link to let users know that the community staff is not responsible for the content or validity of that link (for example, see zone.com/fighterace/links .asp). That's a good policy, but it's even better to check these links periodically (ideally by using an automated script), and then alert group leaders when their links are broken.

Use Events to Highlight Groups

In many communities, competitions and awards are focused on individual accomplishments, but if you want to encourage groups to flourish in your community, make a point to sponsor events and activities especially for them. Because team-based competition is a popular and accepted way for game players to interact, gaming communities are generally good about offering these events. For example, both Heat and the Zone hold regular tournaments in which teams of players compete for prizes and glory, and Ultima Online allows player-created guilds to declare war on each other, and then engage in a protracted and ongoing battles that add drama and zest to the community.

Events are a great way to stimulate groups, but team events don't have to be limited to gaming communities. When you plan a contest, for instance, think about how it might involve groups rather than individuals. A page-building community might hold a contest for the best group-oriented sites and turn the winning site into a template that other groups could use. Or a finance-oriented community could hold a monthly contest to highlight which investing club has the best returns. These contests and other events are another way to shine a spotlight on specific groups, which lets the rest of the community know about their existence, and helps them recruit new members.

Everyone loves to have their accomplishments acknowledged, so be sure to foster group pride by announcing the results of any group-oriented events in a public forum. For example, Heat announces the winners of group events on the News page of their site (www.heat.net/news), and Ultima Online often covers group events in their regular Spotlight column (www.uo.com).

A Group Can Focus a Community

Sometimes, an event can even serve to galvanize a group's identity, and put the community's values into sharper focus. For example, in late 1998 an active Heat member named Ralph2 asked the community staff to help him create and run a charity tournament. He donated his degrees (points that Heat members can use to purchase items at the Heat store) to the tournament, and asked other high-ranking Heat members to do the same. Heat matched their donations, and they wound up raising over eleven thousand dollars for charity. This event sparked the creation of the Baron's Club (Figure 9.16), which is dedicated to philanthropy, brotherhood, and teamwork. The Barons continue to sponsor regular events, which Heat promotes on their site, and has also served as a " role model" for several other similar clubs

FIGURE 9.16

THE HEAT BARON'S CLUB

The Baron's Club was formed within Heat to promote brotherhood and charity; the Heat staff promotes this group by highlighting their events in the Heat News section of the site.

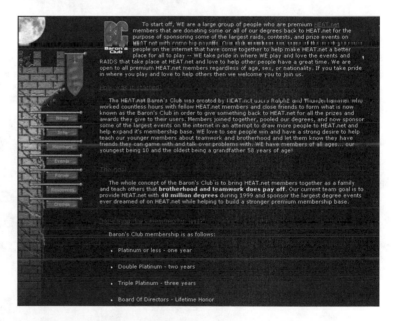

Send Staff Members to Special Events

If you want to lend some extra support and encouragement to a group that's running an important community-building event, send an "official" representative to the event. In Ultima Online, for example, the Golden Brew players put on a series of well-received plays in Britannia, and these hard-working players were especially thrilled when Lord British, the king of Britannia, dropped by to congratulate them (Figure 9.17).

FIGURE 9.17

THE PLAY'S THE THING

The Golden Brew players are a group of Ultima Online members who run a popular tavern and put on plays in various Britannian locales (upper image). After one particularly successful performance, Lord British (the king of Britannia) appeared, congratulated the performers, and encouraged them to continue their efforts (lower image).

You should also try to give extra support to groups who are celebrating transitional events like births, deaths, weddings and graduations (see Chapter 8). For example, when a HOPE member lost her longed-for baby a few weeks after giving birth, the staff helped to organize an online memorial service in a private auditorium. Their support and attendance at this event did a lot to strengthen the group's loyalty to the community, and increase their sense of belonging.

Create a Fertile Environment

Providing the social scaffolding to help subgroups coalesce and grow is very much like building any community—because, as mentioned earlier, groups are communities in and of themselves. So as you're absorbing these ideas, and thinking about which features and policies will foster groups in your community (see sidebar: Building a Group-Friendly Organization), remember that the single most important design guideline for building any community, large or small, is to make choices that reinforce your basic purpose.

Groups with a Purpose

Just like any community, a group willl thrive if it serves a clear purpose in the lives of its members. In this chapter, we've sketched out some features and policies to help groups find and fulfill their purpose—such as encouraging them to write a tag line and mission statement, and requiring that groups be formed by a synergistic team rather than by an Individual, as AncientSites does. We also talked about the importance of giving your groups (and especially group leaders) powerful communications tools, so that they can stay in touch—and stay on purpose.

But simply providing these features isn't enough by itself to cause a cohesive, sustainable group to form. As a community builder, you can't actually *create* close-knit groups—but you *can* provide an environment where purposeful groups can coalesce and flourish. Just like any community, a group will gel when there's a compelling reason for people to seek out each other's company. And so, the single most effective way to foster groups is to create an environment where groups (and especially group leaders) have a meangingful role to play. If someone can thrlve by being in a group, then groups *will* form—whether or not you acknowledge and support them.

Listen to Your Groups

You might be wondering, "If groups form on their own, why should the community bother to provide infrastructure for them?" That's a valid question, especially given the recent proliferation of community aggregators who offer free gathering places, communications tools and page-building platforms. The key reason to make your groups "official," whether you provide a directory, build group profiles, or offer a full-featured groups platform, is to create a feedback loop for staying in touch with them. The bigger your community gets, the more important these member-run subgroups will be in keeping your community running smoothly, and making it a pleasant and welcoming place.

You can't actually create close-knit groups—but you can provide an environment where purposeful groups can coalesce and flourish.

As we discussed in Chapter 2, there are two kinds feedback: behavioral (watch what they do) and conversational (listen to what they say). You'll want to use both to stay in touch with your groups. Depending on your statistical tracking tools (which you may want to build for yourself, since many packages don't include them), you can keep track of size, activity, participation, growth rate, building activity, or event attendance, and use the information to highlight groups. These statistics will also tell you which groups are thriving and what features they're using. You can also use email, message boards, scheduled chats, and good old word of mouth (especially input from your leaders) to listen to your groups and get a sense for what they want and need from you in the future.

Learn from Your Groups

As your groups evolve, their sense of purpose will evolve as well, and you may find that they come up with innovative ways to use your platform in order to address their changing requirements. Pay attention—self-defined groups will reflect your members' needs and desires more accurately than anything you create. For example, after watching members incorporate guild acronyms into their character names and dye their clothing in team colors, the Ultima Online design team developed an organizational structure called a Guildstone (Figure 9.18) that allows a group of players to become official and helps them run their organization. There are now more than 18,000 registered guilds in Ultima Online (see www.uo.com for an up to date count), and scores of player-run cities (such as www.networkautos.com/uo/rdcity.html) that use the Guildstone to organize their activities. The UO staff could never have foreseen the popularity of this phenomenon, but because they had the feedback loops in place to see it happening, they've been able to quickly add features and policies to help these cities grow and thrive.

FIGURE 9.18
GUILDSTONE IN ULTIMA ONLINE
Guildstones (on the left) are an in game mechanism for creating and running a group. The group leader purchases a stone, and can then setup and maintain a structure of leadership, membership and affiliation, and control the access to group meetings places (on the right).

So think of your groups, especially your group leaders, as one of your greatest assets. Not only will they help you scale your community; they'll also show you where to go next.

Building a Group-Friendly Organization

Here's a brainstorming exercise to help you think about how to build a group-friendly oranization. Using the chart below, ask yourself: which of the following features would be most useful to offer to groups in my community? Why are these features important? And how will these features be used throughout my environment?

You answers will depend on the role that subgroups play in your community, and even more so on your business model and existing technologies. You won't want to implement all the ideas you generate (at least not at first), but it'll get you thinking strategically about your groups program and platform.

STRATEGY	HOW MIGHT YOUR GROUPS PLATFORM USE...
PURPOSE	a short **tag line** that identifies the group's purpose
	a longer **mission statement** that explains what the group is all about
	a **distinct visual design** that sets a mood and sets the group apart from others
	a **backstory** that tells about the history of the group, and how it came to exist
	content, tools, and **links** that are relevant to the group's purpose
PLACES	**gathering places** (mailing list, message board, chat room, virtual building) group members can connect
	communication tools (group-wide buddy list, instant messaging, or email newsletter) that allow leaders or members to address the group, either synchronously or asynchronously
	a **news page** (Web log) where members can view (and post) group information
IDENTITY	a **member roster,** along with evolving and meaningful information about each member
	tribal markers (visual indicators) of group membership, integrated into each member's ID and/or profile
ROLES	a way to indicate **length of membership** and **leadership roles** in the member roster (or member ID)
	a way to indicate which features and activities are **accessible to visitors**
	a **welcome package** that's sent to new members
	advanced features that are only made available to regulars
LEADERSHIP	a list of **leadership roles** within the group, along with their powers and responsibilties
	a way to provide **training** and **instruction** for group leaders
	leader tools for filtering content, controlling access, and communicating with the group
ETIQUETTE	a place to announce the group's **membership requirements**
	a place to post the **code of conduct** and **privacy policy**
	reinforcement tools (ability to ban members, remove content, and so on)
EVENTS	a **group calendar** for planning and promoting events
	a **meeting place** for holding group events
	publishing tools for posting meeting notes, inteview transcripts, or contest results
	access to a **community calendar** for announcing group-sponsored community events
RITUALS	a way to create group-specific **welcome rituals**
	a way to place **seasonal and holiday decorations** in the group's clubhouse
	tools to support **rites of passage,** such as group and leader initiation rituals
	a way to track and send **birthday announcements** within the group
	a way to announce **important group events** (like the group's birthday) to the wider community
SUBGROUPS	mechanisms for creating **subdivisions** within the group

Epilogue

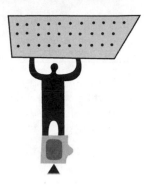

In this book, you've gotten an overview of what's happening in Web communities circa 2000. But the Internet is a dynamic and rapidly evolving environment—Web communities will look and operate quite differently in 2001, and even more so in 2010. In fact, I'll bet that by then people won't even speak of "Web communities" anymore—the ubiquity and bandwidth of online communications and the standardization of online protocols will make the Web as pervasive as the telephone or television. We'll come to view online communities less as isolated destinations and more as just another way to meet people, stay in touch with loved ones, and conduct the daily business of life. We won't distinguish them from other communities any more than we feel compelled to add "on the phone" when we say we spoke to our mother last night.

This process is already happening. Many towns, schools, families, and colleagues routinely use the Web to the stay in touch and share information; and numerous support groups, hobby clubs, social committees, and gaming clans first coalesce online and then hear each other's voices, share photos and videos, and make plans for face-to-face meetings.

So what does this evolution mean for you as an online community bulder? Not only will you need to continue to leverage the unique properties of the Web, but it will become more important than ever to understand the social and cultural aspects of your craft. This book begins to address these issues, but the field is very young and filled with unanswered questions. In the coming years, we'll see many more books, articles, stories, and examples for all of us to learn from—some of which will be created by you. I invite you to share your observations, lessons and stories by logging onto www.naima.com/community, so that we can all keep learning from each other.

To thrive as a 21st-century community builder, be on the lookout for opportunities to blur the boundary between the physical and the virtual, because that's where the Net is headed. This could mean bringing existing groups online, facilitating face-to-face meetings among your members, integrating commerce and communications systems, or creating specialized role-playing environments. Whatever you do, remember that the true power of communities—whether on or off the Web—lies in their power to affect people's physical, emotional, spiritual, and professional lives in a meaningful way. The more your community accomplishes this, the more successful you'll be.

Index

branching, and message
boards 36
brands 25–26, 123–125
brats 132
Britannia 149–150
British, Lord 149, 346
broadcast mailing lists 33
buddy lists 141–143, 190
Builder Buzz 79, 99
bulletin boards. *See* message
boards
businesses 325–327

C

calendars 245
Callaway, Melissa 159
candidates for leaders,
screening 180–181
card games 270
Case, Steve 148
case studies
Origin Systems, 12–13
Slashdot Moderator System,
178–179
Castle Infinity 137–138
categorical themes 52, 55
Caucus 34, 38
celebrations 277–308
celebrity events 257
censorship 210
ceremonies 149–150, 186–188
chain of command 196–197
champions 132
channels 56–57
character. *See* reputation
Charles Schwab 255
chat rooms 39–46
greeting rituals in, 286
handling problems in, 196
interviews in, 258–259
running focus groups, 17

scheduling events for novices,
137
scheduling meetings in, 251
scrolling in, 213
topical, 243–247
visitors to, 129
children, privacy of 215
choosing themes 54–55
clans 309–351
classes 253–256
classified ads 172
classifying information 55–56
Clater, Lynn 219
clubs 71, 143, 309–351, 343
Clubs program, Yahoo 331,
338–339
CNN 49, 129, 212, 219, 262
code of conduct 85, 191, 210
collaborative filtering 94,
283–284
colors, to express roles 111
command, chain of 196–197
commercial use of communities
214
committees 309–351
communication among groups
336
community aggregators 48–49,
207
Community Challenge, iVillage
274
Community Guidelines 210–216
Community Insider, Third Age
148
Community Manager 195–196
Community Standards Advisor.
See CSA
competitions. *See* events
complain feature 220
complaints 189–190
conduct, code of 185, 191, 210
conference calls 192
conferences. *See* message
boards

conflicts among members
218, 222
consequences. *See*
punishments
contests. *See* competitions
contractors 161, 164–165, 167
contributions of members 108,
291–293
controlled growth 70–73
conversational feedback 68
cookies 217
CoolConnect 284, 321
coordinators of events 145, 163
cops 145, 163, 196
Craig's List 30
crossover games 270–271
Crowley, Bev 304
CSA (Community Standards
Advisor) 196
CyberSites, communications
platform created by 50
Cybertown 47
cycle of etiquette 205–206

D

databases 38, 42, 86–94
deaths of members 303–305
Delphi Forums 37
demographic communities 5
design, community 61
developer diaries 152
diaries, developer 152
directories 340–343. *See also*
mapping communities
directors 163
discussions. *See* message
boards
dissidents 132
door policy 32, 219
Dunkin, Elonka 225
dynamic profiles 79

M

Macromedia 127, 283
macros 285–286
mail surveys 16
mailing lists 29–33, 39
Malda, Rob 178, 199
management policies 337–344
managers 163, 195 196
managing leaders 188–197
manuals for leadership training
    184–185
mapping communities 51–65.
    See also directories
market research 173
marriage announcements
    302–303
Maslow's Hierarchy of Needs
    3, 8–9
master lists of community
    goals 11
media themes 53, 56
meeting places. *See* gathering
    places
meetings. *See* events
member agreements 185,
    207–216
members of communities
    feedback from, 68–70, 72
    freedoms of, 329–330
    joining subgroups, 334–336
    as leaders, 155–199
    needs of, 3–13
    profiles of, 75–113
    rights of to create gathering
        places, 73
Membership Life Cycle 117–119
Membership Ritual 133–135
memorials 304–305
Mentor program, Simutronics
    159–160
merchants 145, 172–173
Meridian 59 319

message boards 32–39, 129,
    136, 286
metaphors. *See* themes
Microsoft SQL Server 86
Milo 31
mission statements 19–22, 25
models. *See* themes
moderated mailing lists 33
Moderator System 178–179
moderators 238, 260
Moms Online 23, 286
MoneyLife 125
Motley Fool
    Favorite boards, 282–283
    My Fool, 92
    profiles 91, 107, 108
    ratings of postings, 175–176
    reputations of members, 110
Mplayer 253
MUD players 132
multiple identities 97
Mute List. *See* Ignore Filter
MyEvents *333*
MySQL 86

N

navigation 55, 61
needs of community members
    3–13
neighborhoods, virtual 56, 62,
    311–312
neighbors, virtual 320–323
Net Gain 5
Net Perceptions 283–284
NetMeeting 250
NetNoir 6, 81–82, 288–289,
    295
New York Times 56
newsgroups. *See* message
    boards
newsletters 31, 56–57, 301

NFL.com 270
Nickelodeon, terms and
    conditions 209
non-proprietary buddy lists
    190
nondisclosure agreements 185
novices 118, 133–139

O

obituaries 303–305
obscenity filters 220
O'Donnell, Rosie 21
official leaders 177–188
Oldenberg, Ray 324
online identities 95–106
online stores 172
opinions, pooling 220
Oracle 86
organizing gathering places
    52–65
Origin Systems 12–13
owners of communities, goals
    of 9–13

P

Palace 45, 229
Parent Soup 25, 126, 293–295
parting rituals 281
passwords 86, 88
payments for leaders 194–195
PeopleLink 144, 333
performance of leaders
    189–190
performances. *See* events
performers 132
Perl 38
personal profiles 77, 91–106
personalities
    brand, 25–26, 123–125
    of communities, 60–63

virtual neighbors 320–323
virtual worlds 46–48
vision statements 18–26
visitors 118, 120–133
voice chat 45–46
volunteers 158, 161, 164–167,
194–195

W

warranties 209–210
Web Crossing 34, 49
Web-based text chat 41–44
WebMaster 42, 49
WebMD 127, 216
WebRiot 270
wedding announcements
302–303
welcome letters 133, 197
welcome rituals 280–286

WELL
Annual Writing Contest, 268
conferences on, 67, 329–330
custom software created by,
50
elders of, 147
launching of, 66
monitoring of leaders'
performance by, 191
quality control by, 330
social unrest in, 196–197
training for leaders, 183
Well Engaged 38, 219
Wilco, Roger 46
Williams, Gail 191, 230
Women.com 328
Wooley, David 38
word games 268–269
workgroup meetings 249–251
Worlds Away 46
worlds, virtual 46–48
writing contests 268

Y

Yahoo
classification scheme of, 55
Clubs program, 331, 338–339
games, 270
management policies,
338–339
private clubs, 143
support for leaders, 336–337
taxonomy of, 57, 59
Yahoo Clubs 37, 71, 337,
338–339
Yahooligans 215

Z

Zone, Microsoft Gaming 170,
189, 271